Praise for *Coaching Redefined*

"Sherry St. Clair offers a fresh approach to instructional coaching. Pulling on years of actual experience helping schools grow in this area, she offers practical strategies from which any educator can glean invaluable insight. The appendices alone will greatly expand anyone's coaching toolbox."—Eric Sheninger, Senior Fellow, International Center for Leadership in Education and Author, *Digital Leadership* and Co-Author, *Learning Transformed*

"*Coaching Redefined* will turn you from a good instructional coach into a great one with the application of new tools gleaned by St. Clair from the business world. And with coaching based on solid values and energized by new perspectives, you can guide the teachers under your care to greatness as well. This book is transformational in its scope and inspirational in its approach."—Daniel H. Pink, Author, *WHEN* and *DRIVE*

"Coaching can't be something we simply think about doing; it has to be something we are *always* doing. In *Coaching Redefined*, author Sherry St. Clair makes a compelling case for the "why" of instructional coaching, and also the "how." Delivering coaching is a skill; so too is receiving coaching. Whether you are the recipient of coaching, or the vessel through which it flows, you will find incredible value in the pages of St. Clair's book. I've had the privilege of coaching alongside her. She is the real deal. Start reading—and redefine what coaching can be."—Weston Kieschnick, Best-Selling Author of *Bold School* and Senior Fellow, International Center for Leadership in Education

"As in every professional function, executive and instructional coaching requires a unique set of skills. In this book, Sherry St. Clair captures and very effectively describes these skills. Drawing on her personal experiences as a highly effective coach for multiple school districts, she provides both the organizational leadership structure and specific instructional strategies needed for effective coaching."—Dr. Bill Daggett, Founder and Chairman, International Center for Leadership in Education

"A beautiful thing about effective coaching is that benefits accrue to both the coach and the coachee—often exceeding those anticipated. In *Coaching Redefined*, St. Clair combines the latest research across business and education with the wisdom of practice from years in the field to guide that journey and strengthen its impact."—Vicki Phillips, Executive Vice President and Chief Education Officer at National Geographic

"*Coaching Redefined* takes a refreshing 'systems' approach to working with educators, providing clear, actionable tools and protocols for anyone wanting not only to support individual teachers, but also to positively impact the way learning happens at all levels of a school."—Karin K. Hess, Author, *A Local Assessment Toolkit to Promote Deeper Learning: Transforming Research into Practice*

"*Coaching Redefined* by Sherry St. Clair is designed for all educators who aim to lead instructional change. It will provide you with what every teacher needs: a step-by-step process to enhance instruction in every classroom and impact learning in a positive way."—Jimmy Casas, Educator, Author, Speaker

"Sherry St. Clair has dedicated her career to guiding and supporting educators to achieve success with all their students. In *Coaching Redefined*, she sets out clear strategies that unlock the pathways to the fun and success we have always sought out in our profession."—Raymond J. McNulty, President, Successful Practices Network and the National Dropout Prevention Center

"Author Sherry St. Clair leaves no stone unturned in her mission to support educators to influence sustained change in schools. Drawing on extensive experience and research, she provides an all-encompassing, practical roadmap that will inspire you to rethink how we approach coaching to transform learning. *Coaching Redefined* is a phenomenal resource; I found myself rereading sections, applying them, then returning for more!"—Elisabeth Bostwick, Instructional Coach, Multi-Awarded Educator, Author of *Take the L.E.A.P.: Ignite a Culture of Innovation* and Co-Author of *Education Write Now: Top Strategies for Improving Relationships and Culture*

"In *Coaching Redefined*, Sherry St. Clair masterfully delivers how and why it is critical to create future ready schools and classrooms—and the pivotal role the instructional coach can play as a liaison among stakeholders. St. Clair guides us not only to create the instructional change needed to ensure that today's students thrive as tomorrow's adults, but also to tailor coaching to specific school needs and build a system of sustainable, hands-on professional learning that leads to teacher growth."—Thomas C. Murray, Director of Innovation, Future Ready Schools and Best-Selling Co-Author of *Learning Transformed: 8 Keys to Designing Tomorrow's Schools, Today*

COACHING
REDEFINED

A GUIDE TO LEADING MEANINGFUL
INSTRUCTIONAL GROWTH

Sherry St. Clair

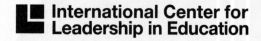

**International Center for
Leadership in Education**

Copyright © 2019 by International Center for Leadership in Education, Inc.,
a division of Houghton Mifflin Harcourt.

The Change Readiness Tool as well as other charts and graphs marked as such are
Copyright © 2019 by Reflective Learning, LLC.

Published by International Center for Leadership in Education, Inc.,
a division of Houghton Mifflin Harcourt.

Printed in the U.S.A.

ISBN: 978-1-328-02518-0

2 3 4 5 6 0304 23 22 21 20 19   4510006299 ABCD

International Center for Leadership in Education, Inc.
1587 Route 146
Rexford, New York 12148
(518) 399-2776
www.LeaderEd.com
info@LeaderEd.com

Dedication

While conducting classroom visits in an elementary school in Saipan, a young boy started quizzing me about who I was, where I was from, and if I liked his work. As I bent down to answer his barrage of questions, he said, "Why are you here?" I explained that I was helping his teachers, to which he replied, "Do you really think we are worth flying so far to help?"

Without hesitation, I looked into his beautiful brown eyes and said, "Yes, you are quite special." And I meant it. He smiled from ear to ear and hurried back to his work.

This book is for all children still figuring out their worth, their potential. May you come to know you are limitless.

This book is for the teachers dedicating their lives to something much bigger than a profession. May you know your value and importance in this world.

This book is for the coaches and administrators committed to ongoing instructional improvements. May you know we need your leadership more than ever.

It takes a team to create an exceptional learning environment for children. Oh, how I love to see children flourish when we all come together to serve them to the best of our abilities.

Contents

Acknowledgments

This part of the book has been the hardest for me to write. I am keenly aware of the number of people who have had a profound impact on my life and, in some way, contributed to my arrival at this moment of publishing my first book. I can never thank all of you here. But please know I am grateful to you.

To my parents, who taught me to work hard, give more than I receive, and respect all humans: thank you. To my husband, Eric: thank you for your endless support and encouragement that helped these ideas get published. Without you, this book simply would not have happened. To my children, Ava and Roman: I love you more than words can express, and it is a sheer joy to watch you learn and grow. You teach me every single day.

Thank you to the countless schools that have embraced my coaching through the years. Without the generosity of these teachers and instructional leaders, this book could not exist. Please know you all show up in these pages; it was working with you that helped create this process, which has in turn been able to help so many others. You, too, are part of changing so many teachers' and students' lives.

To the many dedicated instructional leaders who have shared their wisdom with me: Dr. Kathryn Akural, Karen Wild, Mic Huffman, Laura Pastirik Bankowski, Anna Clifton, Asap Ogumoro, and Judi Herm—to name far fewer than space here will allow—thank you for helping me develop my skills to the benefit of children everywhere.

To Kelly Griego: you have amazing talent that I can only hope to have one day. This book simply wouldn't have happened without you. I owe you a debt I will never be able to pay.

Thank you to all my caring and brilliant colleagues at the International Center for Leadership in Education. It's an honor to serve schools alongside you. A special thanks to Dr. Bill Daggett, Sue Gendron, Kristen Painter, Dr. Linda Lucey, and Kris Ross for believing in my work and helping me help schools. Your unconditional commitment to children is undeniable. Thank you for continuously supporting me and helping me become a better consultant.

To thought leaders whom I may never meet: Mark Batterson, Daniel Pink, Simon Sinek, Seth Godin, Karin Hess, John Maxwell, and Linda Darling-Hammond—thank you for generously sharing your knowledge with others. You have reached my life without even knowing it.

Finally, to educators everywhere, thank you for allowing me the opportunity to share life with you, to celebrate your students' successes with you, to cry with you when life is hard, and to walk with you as you grow into educators who show all your students the unlimited promise of their lives.

About the Author

Sherry St. Clair is the founder of Reflective Learning LLC, an educational consulting agency based in Kentucky. Her organization works with schools around the world, creating specialized training and coaching services for school administrators and educators. Additionally, Sherry serves as a Senior Consultant for the International Center for Leadership in Education and Houghton Mifflin Harcourt. She holds a master's degree in Instructional Leadership, as well as a Rank I in Instructional Supervision.

As an international consultant, Sherry draws from her rich experience at various levels of public education–teaching elementary school, being an administrator in a high school of 1,300 students, working as a state consultant, and creating and facilitating virtual courses. Sherry is a highly regarded national speaker and consultant, providing educational agencies with expertise in the areas of instructional leadership, effective classroom practices, classroom walkthroughs, effective use of data, and guidance on how to create structures for successful classroom coaching. Coaching schools to best meet the needs of all students is Sherry's passion.

Sherry is a contributing author to *Effective Instructional Strategies Volume 2*, published by the International Center for Leadership in Education. She has published numerous professional learning activity guides and facilitated webinar series focused on leadership and effective instructional practices. Additionally, Sherry developed virtual instructional workshops for the CTE Technical Assistance Center of New York. In partnership with the Successful Practices Network, Houghton Mifflin Harcourt, and AASA—The School Superintendent Association, Sherry has recently been a part of bringing innovative practices to scale.

CONNECT WITH SHERRY   Follow her on Twitter: @Sherrystclair
Visit her website: www.reflecttolearn.com to sign up for her newsletter and receive instructional ideas and support. Follow the hashtag: #CoachingRedefined

Testimonials

"Tasked with improving instruction, refining a curriculum to meet the needs of students, and improving the overall morale in a high school environment, Sherry's leadership skills immediately became very evident. I watched her earn the respect of a staff that was in need of an instructional strategies leader. She was able to communicate her ideas to a wide array of teachers and because of her thorough knowledge of successful instructional practices and a willingness to guide teachers individually, she very quickly earned the trust of our faculty. Once our staff recognized her honesty and sincerity in improving instruction, they often sought her out for guidance and advice. She has devoted her professional life to improving the delivery of instruction to students and helping teachers find sound practices they can use in their classrooms."

—Mic Huffman, Former School Principal

"I can say with every confidence that Sherry St. Clair is truly an exceptional educator. As our most sought-after consultant, she is an exemplary instructional and leadership coach who is also skilled at developing curriculum and assessments, restructuring initiatives, and other education improvement projects. Sherry is results oriented and holds herself to a very high standard. She subscribes to an 'under promise and over deliver' philosophy and is intrinsically motivated to meet the objectives of all the projects she undertakes."

—Tim Ott, CEO, Successful Practices Network

"Sherry St. Clair's coaching strategies rejuvenated me to provide instructional coaching to the elementary school administrators and teachers in our district. Her approach to instructional coaching was extremely beneficial to the principals of each building and to me during the transition to new state learning standards and a focus on Webb's Depth of Knowledge practices. Our principals and teachers still utilize the common language and approaches Sherry helped us to implement in 2014—and with great results."

—Dr. Debbra Martin, Assistant Superintendent, Streator
Elementary School District #44, Streator, IL

"Professional development is an integral component of school improvement efforts, requiring outreach to others to bring new ideas and practices to the forefront. In my experience, consultants are often knowledgeable yet unapproachable, and sometimes arrogant. Sherry St. Clair breaks this stereotype through excellent coaching, communication with understanding, and the ability to bring teachers and administrators on board without guilt or shame, but instead with genuine enthusiasm. Simply put, her exceptional relationship-building skill set is a proven, effective way of sharing her extensive knowledge and expertise."

—Dr. Mark Albertus, Superintendent, Carrollton City Schools, Carrollton, GA

"Sherry was able to build trusting, meaningful relationships with our staff, asking them to reflect on their teaching and instructional skills while challenging them to grow and better their practice. Sherry's wealth of experience, honesty, wisdom, and ability to ask thought-provoking, reflective questions pushed me and helped me to grow as an administrator. Sherry is a leader with character beyond reproach. Her passion is to help schools become the best possible learning environments for students."

—Laura Bankowski, Principal, Oswego East High School, Oswego, IL

"Sherry connects instantly with inexperienced and veteran educators and is masterful at cultivating productive relationships—with both teachers and school leaders. As a district-level administrator, I continue to benefit from her coaching, guidance, and feedback. While coaching on-site, you'll find her walking the hallways with administrators or rolling up her sleeves and working side-by-side with teachers to plan instruction and design performance tasks or assessments. Our teachers are always eager for her to visit their classrooms to provide coaching and feedback. Not only is Sherry an inspiring author and consultant, she's also a skilled practitioner."

—Dr. Todd Simpson, Assistant Superintendent for Curriculum and Instruction, Butts County School System, Jackson, GA

"Sherry is a gifted and insightful coach. Her work with our instructional teams was both inspiring and practical. Her coaching made teachers feel supported and equipped them with the tools that they needed to get them to the next level of instruction and collaboration with peers. Whether her focus was working with a new teacher reflecting on their classroom practices or with a departmental team reviewing assessment design, Sherry found a way to recognize each person's strengths while helping them to focus on their areas for growth in a positive way. Building respectful and trusting relationships is the hallmark of her work, and this allows her to push the 'thinking boundaries' of teachers and administrators."

—Ruth Steele, Director of Secondary Education, Vallejo City Unified School District, Vallejo, CA

About the International Center for Leadership in Education

The International Center for Leadership in Education (ICLE), a division of Houghton Mifflin Harcourt, challenges, inspires, and equips leaders and teachers to prepare their students for lifelong success. At the heart of all we do is the proven philosophy that the entire system must be aligned around instructional excellence—rooted in rigor, relevance, and relationships—to ensure every student is prepared for a successful future.

Founded in 1991 by Dr. Bill Daggett, ICLE, through its team of thought leaders and consultants, helps schools and districts bring innovative practices to scale through professional learning opportunities and coaching partnerships guided by the cornerstones of our work: the Daggett System for Effective Instruction® and the Rigor/Relevance Framework®. Additionally, ICLE shares successful practices that have a positive impact on student learning through keynote presentations; the Model Schools Conference, Leadership Academy, and other events; and a rich collection of publications. Learn more at LeaderEd.com.

Introduction

"At the most fundamental level, it is an honor to serve—at whatever type or size of organization you are privileged to lead, whether it is a for-profit or nonprofit. It is an honor to serve."

Alan Mulally, former CEO of Ford Motor Company

Through my work as a coach who guides administrators and educators to serve as instructional coaches, I've had the honor to engage with thousands in the field of education in locations near and far. To name just some, my work has taken me to urban centers in Detroit and Philadelphia; rural areas of West Virginia and Washington; suburban Illinois and Ohio; communities in Mississippi and Louisiana; all over Texas, California, and New York; and the islands of St. Thomas, St. John, St. Croix, Hawaii, Tinian, Rota, and Saipan. On these trips, I've worked in schools as small as one hundred students and as large as nearly two thousand. I've been in schools with large populations of English language learners and special education students. I've interacted with educators and students of numerous backgrounds, nationalities, and creeds. And I've guided improvement in a range of environments and circumstances—from schools with limited resources to those with excess.

As distinct as every learning environment is, there are three common truths among all. First, it doesn't matter where we are from or what we have; we are all human, and we all need the same things to grow. Second, all children deserve the learning that helps them find their boundless growth potential and create hopeful, successful futures. Third, getting all children to this point means supporting them and their educators in a way that meets their needs and is tailored to their specific circumstances.

No matter where I have had the honor to serve educators, I must serve *them* best. For me to do this, I must take the time to learn about them, their learning environment, the challenges they face, the resources they have, and the dreams they hold for themselves and their students. Only then can I respectfully lead them in a way that is meaningful, motivating, and impactful. To offer any school or educator an off-the-shelf improvement plan would be to lead them only to stalled growth and progress.

It was early in my coaching career that I realized coaches are so much more than our title would have us to believe. While coaching captures the nuts and bolts of what we do, leading captures its essence. We are not just asking people to teach; we are also asking them to trust us on a vulnerable process of change and growth. We cannot do this if we do not first get to know our educators and the students they serve so that we can serve their individual needs. And we also cannot do this if we do not also get to know the environment in which they educate.

To lead is to know. To know is to ask that people open up to you, share with you, be vulnerable with you, and trust you. That, simply put, is an honor.

It is also a responsibility, one I believe instructional coaches are uniquely capable of fulfilling. And one that I believe is taking on more weight in today's world.

The world that follows high school graduation is changing dramatically. Of the fall 2010 cohort of students enrolled part-time and full-time at all two-year and four-year institutions, the six-year completion rate was 54.8 percent. Meaning 45.2 percent of these students dropped out of college within six years of entering (Shapiro et al, 2017).

Class of 2017 college graduates hold an average of $39,400 in student loan debt, a six percent increase from the prior year (Student Loan Hero, 2019). In 2012, 1.3 million students graduated from college in debt, up from 1.1 million in 2008. Data released in 2017 from the Federal Reserve Bank of New York found that underemployment rate (the rate of college graduates working in lower-paying jobs that don't require a college degree) for recent college grads has bounced between 40 and 50 percent for the past 25 years; and 34 percent of all college grads have remained underemployed in that time.

The composite picture is of college students graduating (or not graduating) with more debt and fewer job opportunities commensurate to their college degrees that offer greater capacity to pay down college debt. The choices we guide our students to make after college matter. And the changing realities of these choices mean that we must change how we teach, what we teach, and why we teach.

For two key reasons, instructional coaches and instructional leaders are best positioned to lead the instructional change our students need and deserve. First, our teachers need our support and guidance as we ask them to deliver instruction at higher levels and in new ways to manage new realities. In this century, much of what we are asking educators to do they did not learn in school. It's unfair and doesn't show them due respect to change and raise expectations of them without providing guidance to meet those new expectations. Second, coaches have a singular vantage point in schools, as we get insights into how teachers and a school's system intersect to advance or obstruct student learning. To serve our students today, we must redefine coaching as existing on two levels of learning—the school level and the individual level.

This book is for instructional coaches—or anyone in charge of instructional improvement, be they principals, administrators, or consultants. With this book, it is my aim, first and foremost, to lead you through the process of becoming a coach *redefined*—one capable of unlocking the greatest instructional potential in both teachers and the school so that they may together create a virtuous cycle of limitless growth. A second aim is to recruit you and other future-focused coaches and educational leaders to join the movement of coaching *redefined*. The process I lay out in this book truly redefines how to change and improve student learning.

I have created, utilized, and refined this instructional coaching process throughout my decades in the field. It is the result of years of experience, which has been shaped and influenced by the great work of industry giants like Jim Knight, Robert Marzano, John Hattie, and Elena Aguilar. It's also been improved by the educators I've been privileged to serve. Their willingness to share and grow with me has fortified this work.

I have tested the steps and tools hundreds of times. Each time, I have reflected on the results, analyzed the process, culled it for new understanding, and then applied what I've learned to the next round. Based on my own ongoing learning, I have added new insights to it. At every turn, I have worked to strengthen this process so that the coach may be more effective, the teachers more intentional in their practice, and students more improved in their learning outcomes.

I have also imbued the entire process with everything I've learned from years of study in change leadership and management. To coach *redefined* is to ask educators to take a leap of faith with you and as a team. At the end of the day, your goal as a coach or instructional leader is to lead the school and its educators to lead their own ongoing learning such that their growth can far outlast their time with you. This is work that leans on leadership skills. To ignore them in my own practice and in this book would be a failure of my service to you. You will find examples of and references to best practices for leadership and management throughout the book. These are often drawn from the wisdom of renowned leadership and management thinkers, such as Gina Folk, Daniel Pink, Simon Sinek, Alan Mulally, Seth Godin, Chip and Dan Heath, and John Maxwell.

This book is designed to be as helpful as possible in preparing you to rise to the occasion of leading instructional change. It is divided into three parts. In part 1, we will discuss in detail why a new, redefined coaching paradigm is needed. I will then delineate the values every great coach must hold and follow to become as effective and valuable to educators as possible.

In part 2, I will walk you through the four steps of leading school-wide instructional improvement. The steps in these chapters will culminate in a school-wide plan for the year. By design, this part of the book is technical, process oriented, and heavy on planning. While at face value these chapters may look dense, please trust that they present a big process broken down into smaller, manageable parts. Each part serves to bring intention, purpose, focus, and clarity to the work ahead. In turn, you position yourself and your educators to achieve the greatest success possible.

In part 3, I will guide you through the mechanics and best practices of high-impact, one-on-one instructional coaching. We'll move through how to meet each individual teacher exactly where they are, so you can optimize growth potential from that point and provide the kind of coaching best suited to their needs. I'll explain in detail how to coach for high levels of rigor, relevance, and learner engagement as illustrated by real-world scenarios. And lastly, I'll show you how to build a sustainable coaching system in your school.

All told, what you will learn here will allow you to lead instructional change that optimizes the relationship between educators and school systems. This book will prepare you to do so much more than change instruction in the classroom. It will prepare you to change the school system to enhance instruction in every classroom, even those belonging to educators you aren't coaching. It will also teach you how to customize all of your plans to the specific environment, educators, and needs in front of you for greatest impact.

To simplify this work for yourself, I suggest reading the book in full so you can digest its content and reflect on it as a full-scale plan you repeat each new school year. Once you can step back and see how all the parts come together, you will gain perspective such that it begins to feel like the manageable process it is. As a best practice, I recommend revisiting the book or specific chapters as needed once you begin leading educators through the implementation of each part.

Marissa Mayer, former CEO of Yahoo!, who was hired at age 37 and while pregnant with her first child, is quoted as saying, "I always did something I was a little not ready to do. I think that's how you grow. When there's that moment of 'Wow, I'm not really sure I can do this,' and you push through those moments, that's when you have a breakthrough" (Toren, 2014). To those of you reading this book who are not yet accustomed to thinking of yourself as leaders of change at the school level, that is OK. It is OK if this feels uncomfortable to you now. Remember that you, too, have boundless growth potential. Trust that each time you apply the process, it will get easier and feel more comfortable and natural to follow. Experience will also hone your intuition. With time, you will find you do not need to complete all the component parts of each of the steps. You will grow more adept at synthesizing information and drawing informed conclusions automatically. Let the steps in this book serve as training wheels that, with practice and confidence, you can eventually remove.

Soon enough, you will be leading the meaningful, sustainable growth our schools deserve with ease, assuredness, and flexibility. Soon enough, you will be a great coach—*redefined*.

As a final note, I share stories from my own coaching experience throughout. While the point and heart of all stories are true, I have changed names, certain details, and identifying characteristics to protect privacy and identities.

I am truly honored that you are joining me in the important work of redefining coaching together and leading the growth and improvement our students deserve.

PART 1

Becoming a Coach
Redefined

"Failure is not fatal, but failure to change might be."

John Wooden, former head basketball coach,
University of California, Los Angeles

Chapter 1

A New Coaching Paradigm

A Tale of a Coach *Redefined*

Several years ago, I was enlisted to coach a woman named Lisa on how to coach teachers. She had recently been hired as the on-staff instructional coach at an urban high school. Previously, Lisa had been an instructional coach at a different high school where teachers, by and large, were motivated and well supported in a healthy culture. Together, she and her teachers had great success in improving instruction and student achievement across the board. As she started her job at this new school, she felt confident, emboldened by the instructional growth she'd been able to guide her former colleagues to achieve.

As they say, one of these things was not like the other. One of the aspects most exciting to Lisa about her new job was the abundance of low-hanging fruit for improvement. Student achievement was low by almost every indicator. Reading levels were low. Student engagement was low. Test scores were low. While she was aware she had her work cut out for her, she was also anxious to roll up her sleeves, get to work, and make several instructional changes and improvements with teachers.

What she was not aware of until after she'd started her job was how mistrustful the educators were of administrators—of which she was one. She wasn't aware that the recently exited district leaders had sown many seeds of discontent and resentment toward leaders. Such that the teachers at her school were demoralized, dispirited, fatigued, unmotivated, and almost totally disconnected from their jobs. In a district and a school where turnover was the norm, this school's teachers weren't exactly excited to see Lisa—just one more person who was going to force them to change everything they do to accommodate some supposed silver bullet, only to walk out on them soon enough, too.

But Lisa was different. She was a passionate educator who cared deeply for students and educators. She was sincere in her drive and desire to help educators be better. And she was hired to coach instructors to better instruction, so she knew that's what she had to do with integrity. Yet, as she would soon admit to me, she had no idea how to work through the morass and disdain that she confronted at this new school. She could feel all the confidence in her coaching ability that she'd gained in her last job steadily drain from her.

As her newly appointed coach and support, this was difficult for me to witness. I could tell that Lisa was a good instructional coach. She had a deep and broad toolkit of instructional strategies. She understood rigor, relevance, and learner engagement and had a full suite of tactics to increase them in the classroom. To me, it was no surprise that at her prior job she was able to guide multiple already-motivated teachers toward great personal and professional growth.

What Lisa didn't yet grasp is that how we coach changes depending on the environment in which we are being asked to coach. It was OK that she didn't yet know this. Because we often don't have to learn this as coaches until we find ourselves walking into an environment where we can just tell we are neither wanted nor welcomed.

My early coaching story isn't too different from Lisa's. I've been working in education since I graduated college, first as a teacher and then as an administrator, where one of my primary responsibilities was serving as the instructional coach. Like Lisa, I was in a school with a pretty healthy culture. My teacher colleagues and coachees were more motivated to learn and grow than not. We were well supported in efforts to improve our practice. The school was relatively open to change and therefore responded to most of my suggestions for change at both the school level and the individual level. And together, we had success improving student achievement.

I would eventually find myself hungry for new challenges and the ability to impact more people. So, I decided to break out on my own and work independently to coach educators to become instructional coaches to their teachers. Today, I get the great pleasure of guiding educators from all over the world to become great instructional coaches so that they can, in turn, coach educators to become great teachers. However, I will confess that the first time I walked into a school like Lisa's, it wasn't initially a pleasure.

Pretty early in my days as a consultant, I confronted a school not too different from Lisa's. Teachers had a low opinion of and a lack of trust in administrators and there was widespread resistance to change. Because I'd had a track record of getting results in the classroom, I'd assumed I would be able to replicate this in any school environment. But to be mistrusted and unwelcomed by these educators meant that I had to figure out a new coaching paradigm. I got a crash course not only in the most challenging kinds of instructional coaching, but also in learning to break through that resistance, the poor attitudes, the mistrust, and the lack of motivation.

By the time I was working with Lisa, I knew exactly what to do. Before we even began thinking about instruction at the classroom level, we had to repair trust between administrators and teachers at the school level. We had to begin building new and positive relationships. To do this, Lisa and I arranged several meetings with a range of people from all key stakeholder groups to ask them questions about the school. We talked to administrators, students, parents and guardians, and members of the community. Our goal was to understand what people with on-the-ground perspectives viewed as the problems standing in the way of change and student achievement. We wanted to know people's frustrations, fears, their dreams for the school, and their hopes for students. We wanted to listen and learn so that we could, in turn, figure out how to work to change perceptions, improve how the school operated, and restore faith in its educators.

Of course, we also talked to teachers. As many as we could, and all of the ones Lisa would be coaching. We wanted to know what had made them so demoralized, how they felt coming to work every day, and how they wished they could be supported to do their jobs better. We asked a lot of questions and listened carefully to what they shared, knowing that they were giving us a gift by talking to us at all. We listened to their assessment of the failures of past leaders and what they needed to be able to grow and be more effective in the classroom. We asked them what scared them about change and what would make them more comfortable with it. We listened as each of them told us how they wanted to be coached and supported.

Lisa and I also did a deep analysis of all student achievement data that we could get our hands on. We looked for clues and artifacts around the school about how much, or how little, academics were emphasized, praised, and valued. We tried to get a sense of what about the school was influencing culture, for better and worse.

Together we then digested, synthesized, analyzed, and processed all the qualitative and quantitative information we'd gathered. We were able to begin to see a picture of how we could slowly but surely coax the staff out of its resistance to change and into taking little steps to make improvements. We also began to see some potential early, and relatively easy, wins in boosting student achievement that wouldn't require dramatic upfront changes yet would help create a new, positive story—and even begin to redirect the culture. Eventually, we put together a school-wide improvement plan that met its educators exactly where they were as a collective. We didn't ask too much of them too soon because we refused to risk sowing even more resentment toward administrators. And we began to put together coaching plans that met every educator where he or she was, so that Lisa could coach them in a way that resonated with them, made them feel respected, and would drive their growth.

In starting her coaching process this way, Lisa was using far more skills than her prior job required of her. Yes, she was applying her excellent instructional strategy acumen. But she was also using leadership and management skills. She was thinking through how to frame and communicate her plans in terms that her educators cared about and valued so that her ideas would be heard and trusted. On an ongoing basis, she was listening to different concerns and collaborating to negotiate often conflicting needs to create new solutions. She was problem solving and troubleshooting in real time to help her educators and also to repeatedly show them that she was on their side. She was team and relationship building so that everyone would mobilize around shared goals to do better for students.

In other words, Lisa was using a range of skills she never expected would be so vital to instructional coaching. She was also expanding her definition of instructional coaching. As a result, Lisa transformed how she viewed her capacity and potential as a coach. She no longer viewed herself as myopically focused on classroom instruction. Rather, she viewed herself a conduit between individual instructional needs and the schoolwide systems and goals that had to be in place to support those needs. She understood that for individual change at the classroom level to take root, it must be able to grow from the fertile soil of a school ready for change and improvement. Thus, she began viewing herself as leading educators—of all different personalities, preferences, fears, and dreams—from being a loose collective of individuals into a team working toward schoolwide and personal growth. In newly seeing herself as both a leader and a partner in co-creating improvement plans, and collaborating to see all teachers through to success, Lisa became a *great* coach.

Today, my most challenging educators and schools are often my greatest joys. They taught me what great coaching is and what instructional coaching today must be—a process that requires deep thinking and thoughtful planning to consider the school and the individuals in it holistically. A process that includes driving change not just at the classroom level, but at the school level, too, so that the two can work together to unlock the greatest growth potential. It requires great coaches who know not just how to teach, but also how to lead and inspire.

These schools showed me just how much support coaches need to become great coaches *and* leaders. They showed me just how much the notion of coaching needs to be redefined to support the kind of change and improvement all of our schools today need to meet the ever-evolving demands on students for successful futures tomorrow.

Helping schools and educators all over the world redefine coaching has become my greatest professional joy. This book represents my desire to lead as many coaches as I possibly can to the greatness I know is there in each of them.

The Building Blocks of a Coach *Redefined*

Another confession: When I first started working as a coaching consultant and had that first experience of walking into a school where I could just *feel* that I was not wanted, I didn't just snap my fingers and know what to do. It took some years of trial and error and practice. And it took a bit of chance.

Prior to walking into this first challenging school, coaching always felt like a natural fit to my skills. As it turned out, certain skills that are so core to coaching—helping people discover their strengths, outlining with them steps to grow those strengths, and supporting them through the process of improvement—were skills I'd organically developed in my life and work. Using these skills also proved fulfilling to me, in part because I derive joy from watching people grow.

It felt serious to me, too. The work of instructional coaching is to support educators, yes. But it has a dual and ultimate purpose: to improve student learning and achievement specifically so that students may thrive in their futures. Each time I sit down with a new instructional leader I'm coaching, I introduce myself with the same promise to them. It usually goes something like this: "I'm here to serve you. I'm here to understand where you are, what you need, and walk beside you as you improve your ability to better guide your teachers, so their students will become better learners."

Early in my coaching career, when I was an administrator, it quickly became apparent that if I were to make good on this promise and continue to make good on it as circumstances around education changed, I had to keep learning. I had to stay on top of changing learning models and philosophies, the latest instructional strategies, new technologies, evolving content, newly understood science of learning, and any and all changes in standards. After all, how could I teach what I didn't know? I owed it to my teachers to keep my toolkit chock full of the latest and greatest in great instruction.

Fortunately, my commitment to my own ongoing learning paid off. While an administrator, my collaboration with teachers catapulted more and more of them to levels of growth that led to real change in their classrooms. As their successes grew, I was asked to coach the principal and other school leaders.

Thrilled by this new opportunity, I began diving into books about leadership and management. Again, how could I teach what I didn't know? How could I impart sage advice if I didn't have a well-stocked arsenal of it? This challenge exposed me to a world of books, websites, and podcasts about leadership. In most cases, each of these resources spoke to people in the business world, as so often it is in the business world where such concepts of leadership, management, motivation, and teamwork are discussed. It was slowly becoming clear to me that an exploration of business was going to help improve my work as a coach in a number of ways.

Let me try to build this point a different way: through LEGOs.

LEGO: A Mini Business Case Study

Who in the world doesn't know LEGO? Those primary colored, interlocking bricks were a feature in most all of our childhoods. For those of us who've had young kids of our own, we've watched them bring joy to yet another generation. One of the thrills of forming one's own creation for some world unfolding right in their very own imaginations. And then dismantling it to rebuild an entirely new one in some new imaginary world.

If you haven't seen any LEGOs in recent years, browsing their vast offering today might surprise you. There are bricks for all sizes of hands—from those of toddlers all the way to those of adults impassioned about models and building. There are traditional bricks of varied dimensions to be constructed into whatever a person could dream up. There are kits to build anything and everything from a diner to a Ford Mustang to the Taj Mahal. You can build entire cityscapes—on lands as we know them or distant planets as we imagine them. LEGO, today, truly is a universe of creativity and possibility.

And did I mention LEGOs now also come in pinks and purples?

The Lego Group, as it is known today, was born in Denmark in 1932. Ole Kirk Christiansen, a Danish carpenter, manufactured stepladders, ironing boards, stools—all kinds of practical objects. Then one day, he began carving wooden toys. He decided to refer to his budding little toy business as "LEGO," a derivation of the Danish phrase *leg godt*, which means "play well" (Lego 1930–1939, 2018).

In 1947, the shop began producing toys in plastic. Two years later, for the first time, they manufactured "Automatic Binding Bricks," a prototype of what we know as LEGO bricks today (Lego 1940–1949, 2018). Nearly a decade later, in 1958, the LEGO stud-and-tube coupling system (those raised circles and their corresponding divots that interlock) was patented, establishing the LEGOs we know today—and allowing them to stick to fellow bricks much more securely (Lego 1950–1959, 2018).

Not insignificantly, a market analysis department was formed a year later. For most of LEGO's history, the company has focused intensely on soliciting customer feedback and listening closely to it. They routinely engage customers for ideas and insights, which drive product changes and new product development at LEGO (Lego 1950–1959, 2018).

It was thanks to one of those recent solicitations of user information that LEGO discovered they had failed to connect with as many young girls as they had with young boys. LEGO believes constructive play nurtures lifelong skills, excites children's curiosity, sparks imagination and creativity, and taps into logic and reason. It was always LEGO's intention to make mini builders out of boys and girls (Lego Brand, 2018). But last decade, household studies of primary child LEGO users revealed they had not done enough to appeal to little girls. In the United States, they learned that of households with kids actively playing with LEGOs, girls were the primary users only nine percent of the time. They found similar patterns in several other countries (Tranbaek, 2012).

LEGO wasn't meeting one of its most important goals. To right this wrong, they sought the insights, desires, and requests of the very consumers they were targeting. Around 2008, the company set out on what would be a four-year listening tour with 3,500 girls and their moms to understand what about LEGOs hadn't been appealing to them and what would make them more enticing. LEGO was committed to seeing more young girls gain the benefits of constructive play. And of course, there was a business opportunity in growing an untapped market.

LEGO's listening tour was highly intentional. Per a news release on LEGO's website about the marketing undertaking: "The LEGO Group is globally known for its co-creation philosophy to ensure that we deliver the best possible products and experiences. We have achieved this distinction because we have a long history of listening very carefully to the opinions and requests of our consumers . . ." (Trangbaek, 2012).

LEGO is a business. They have to generate a profit to stay alive and continue to meet their business and consumer goals of enabling productive play. So they have to create value—real value, value people will pay for—for all of their customer segments. Only then will customers buy what they are selling. Historically, they have done this by seeking consumer feedback and opinions and then applying these insights to the development of their products—a process called co-creation. It's a process that ensures that what LEGO is selling to customer segments has meaning to them, meets needs and wants, and resonates with them. It's a process that never ends at LEGO. Asking consumers for feedback is ongoing because consumers change, markets change, and trends change.

As was the intention, this listening tour with girls and their moms taught LEGO what would make their toys more appealing and fun to girls. From that same paper on LEGO's website: "We heard very clear requests from moms and girls for more details and interior building, a brighter color palette, a more realistic figure, role play opportunities and a storyline that they would find interesting" (Trangbaek, 2012).

The result of the listening tour was LEGO Friends, which debuted in 2012. The LEGO Friends collection is based on five young girls who are all friends living in Heartlake City. Their mission, per the collection's landing page, is to "help make the world a better place." Each girl has a distinct personality and a different passion and, thus, a different way she contributes her gifts to her community. All can be built from LEGOs, of course, in a rainbow of bright colors, replete with pinks and purples (Lego Friends, 2018).

By *listening*, LEGO created a new product based precisely on what the segment of customers they were targeting wanted. A LEGO team showed up to their conversations with the moms and daughters with one agenda and one agenda only: to *listen* to what they had to say. They showed up with humility, ready to *learn*. Based on what they learned, they were able to *co-create* a new suite of LEGOs *with* their customers, not for them. This allowed LEGO to create real value for young girls—value for which parents would happily pay.

LEGO continued to listen even after LEGO Friends was flying off shelves. They listened to a chorus of people who'd taken offense at the implication that girls would only play with toys in the traditionally female colors of pinks, purples, and pastels. Feeling compelled to respond, LEGO stated:

We want to correct any misinterpretation that LEGO Friends is our only offering for girls. This is by no means the case. We know that many girls love to build and play with the wide variety of LEGO products already available. LEGO Friends joins this global collection of products as yet another theme option from which parents may choose the best building experience for their child's skill and interest. (Trangbaek, 2012)

LEGO did not manufacture pink and purple building blocks based on assumption; they manufactured them because that, among other features, is what little girls said mattered to them. LEGO understood they had to make a product that mattered to them to achieve the goal: get more young girls engaging in productive play. They knew LEGO Friends would work because LEGO met these little girls where they were and created the product from there.

Sound familiar?

Fortunately for me, when I first walked into that school that was making it known they were not excited to have an instructional coaching consultant around, I had some new tools in my toolkit. In fact, I had a new toolkit—one filled with leadership and management lessons and skills. Thanks to having begun a study into what are traditionally thought of as business skills, I had read a few things about leading change. I'd learned the importance of listening first to learn and then creating plans *with* educators that met their actual needs, not my perceptions of them. I'd read about how to present and communicate plans in terms that spoke to a person's values and aspirations. I'd read about how to convince people to embrace change by identifying the specific root cause of their resistance to it and targeting it with appropriate tactics and ideas. Thanks to my new crash course in business skills, I wasn't paralyzed by these highly resistant educators. I had ideas and began putting them to the test and adapting and improving them where they fell short.

I was beginning to put together what would become a full-scale program to guide coaches to listen to stakeholders in order to understand the issues and emotions across the school. And then how to devise a plan to break down resistance to change and begin to make small changes at the school level such that once individual instructional coaching began, teachers would be open to suggestion and their efforts to change were supported across the school. I was also beginning to establish my new paradigm of coaching—that it cannot happen only in the classroom; it must happen across the school, as well. One cannot exist without the other if either is to become sustainable.

I love the LEGO story. I love it because it so aptly captures what coaching is when it's at its fullest potential and its best: a co-creation. It's a true collaboration between coach and teacher and coach and school-wide educators built on listening, learning, adapting, changing, and growing together. It also shows how closely the skills needed to lead change in schools mirror the skills needed to lead change in businesses and that a study in business *is* a study in great coaching.

Put another way, the story shows one of the most important things I've learned about great instructional coaching: for it to have the impact we all know it can and hope it will, it takes far more than instructional strategies and skill alone.

Getting Out of the Education Lane

As I mentioned, this experience of meeting resistant educators dubious of me was in my early days as a coaching consultant. I had come to decide to function as an independent coaching consultant because of how much I love instructional coaching. Helping people grow fulfills me and gives me enormous joy. I wanted to be able to reach more people. Besides, the teachers and leaders at the school where I had been a full-time administrator and I were able to build a sustainable, system-wide instructional coaching program. I felt ready to confidently hand over the reins to those excited to lead the way.

All of a sudden, I found myself out on the road coaching teachers and leaders in districts across the country as a freelance consultant in charge of her own business. I didn't know the first thing about entrepreneurship. My head spun, but as a lifelong learner already familiar with a host of great business resources, I simply expanded my self-education into other areas of starting and running a successful business.

My education in business skills proved a benefit again. Something remarkable happened as I put myself through my little-to-no-cost, ad-hoc, mini MBA program of sorts. I was exposing myself to, learning about, and becoming immersed in the very skills I'm always coaching educators to teach their students—career skills. Of today. The relevant kind. The very skills we talk about all the time in education!

I was reading books about connecting with customers on a human level and creating real value—the kind they'll put their hard-earned money into. Listening to podcasts about surviving in a constantly changing industry environment. Consuming articles about setting the right goals and aligning entire teams and all decisions to them. About synthesizing and evaluating disparate information to make decisions amid ambiguity. About creating new solutions to old problems; collaborating with co-workers in different states, even countries; working nimbly and swiftly to iterate a product or service to respond to market forces; rebounding from mistakes; branding and rebranding and rebranding again; recovering from a public relations disaster; and leading in highly uncertain times.

How can we teach what we don't know?

In stepping outside of the education lane, I made myself a stronger educator and a stronger, more valuable coach to my colleagues and clients.

So often, we educators go to school to become educators. And then we become educators. And we stay educators. Through no fault of our own, all we know is education! Yet, how many students are we preparing to become educators? A scant few.

When the day is done, we are preparing students for careers. The overwhelming share of those will be in some kind of business or professional setting that draws on the skills discussed most frequently in the business world.

We can't teach what we don't know.

Why We Need Great Coaches & a New Coaching Paradigm

I am here to share with you all I've learned in my many years guiding others to become the greatest coaches, teachers, and education leaders they can be. I am here to help you avoid the mistakes I made. I am here to share the hard-fought wisdom I've gained. I am here to share my process to drive meaningful change at your school and with all your teachers so that all their students can achieve at the highest levels.

Let's now talk about why you're here—to become the greatest instructional coach you can be. To inspire teachers to be the greatest they can be so that they can inspire students to be the greatest they can be. Thank you for showing up. We need you more than ever. In my opinion, instructional coaching has always been important. But it's taken on even more importance in recent years.

At this point, it's almost cliché to say our educators are overwhelmed, overworked, overtired, overextended. But it's become cliché because it's true. It's true because we have eyes and ears and we can see that our world is different from the one in which most of us were educated and raised. We know that what our students today will be asked to do in their careers tomorrow is different. It's complicated, nuanced, technological, global, and often interdisciplinary. It rests heavily on social-emotional skills and the ability to deal with—no, *thrive*—amid constant change and ambiguity.

That's why I'm so glad you're here. Instructional coaches—or anyone responsible for, in some capacity, guiding educators to improve their practice—in my view and experience are the missing link between the old way of teaching and learning and the new, desperately needed way. Great instructional coaches can truly change the game for educators and, therefore, their students. They can help their educators focus their efforts and instruction, with intention, on those things that matter most to students and their futures. Coaches can help teachers cut through the confusion, the overwhelm, the distractions, and get to the heart of the matter. They can help them identify their strengths, set meaningful goals, and grow more effective and impactful in the classroom than they ever thought possible. And they can also help them see their growth as boundless, lifelong, fulfilling, and enjoyable. (Really!)

Great instructional coaches also have unique power because of their unique position: they serve as a link between instructors and the instructional system. Coaches, often more than most anyone else in a school, can see the gaps and systemic impediments that are thwarting teachers' capacity to build meaningful relationships with students and to deliver truly rigorous, relevant, and engaging instruction. Thus, coaches are uniquely positioned not only to push individual teachers toward improvement, but also to push the entire instructional system toward improvement so that individual improvement can sustain itself. Great coaches understand this. They see this vantage point as not just as an opportunity, but also as an obligation—to students, teachers, and the entire school. They grasp that without doing what is within their power to guide change at the school level such that it is built to support individual teacher growth, that growth will hit a ceiling. Great coaches, then, know that to unlock full educator potential, they must help unlock the full potential of the system to support educators' boundless growth.

Part of breaking out of the old way of thinking about instructional coaching and into the new is understanding what differentiates a good coach from a great coach. A good coach thinks instructional coaching only happens in the classroom. A great coach knows that an individual teacher can achieve only so much growth if the school she's in isn't also adapting and evolving processes and systems to provide fertile ground for her growth. A good coach guides individual teachers to improve their instructional practice. A great coach also guides the school through improvement so those individual practices can stick and be sustained.

A good coach will get straight to work coaching individual teachers in the classroom. A great coach will begin her coaching process first by listening to all stakeholders and working to comprehend the dynamics in and around the school. A great coach will have a leadership and management toolkit full of tools to determine a school's readiness for change, and then suggest changes only of a scope and pace that the school can withstand. A great coach knows that coaching on any level cannot happen without trust. A great coach understands that relationships build trust and set the stage for the most productive coaching possible. A great coach knows that in order to get buy-in for a school-wide improvement plan, it must be crafted and communicated in terms that speak to the school's and its educators' values and needs. A great coach grasps that she must continue to listen to learn, not listen to respond, and adapt plans—but not big-picture goals—to support her educators.

A good coach will have the instructional coaching cycle down pat. She will know how to design powerful instruction around rigor, relevance, and learner engagement and will have a full and growing toolkit of instructional strategies. She will know how to assess teaching and have suggestions for improvement. She will know how to apply data to individualize instruction. She will know what goes into building a sustainable coaching structure. In short, she will know all the nuts and bolts of instructional coaching.

A great coach knows that without bringing in the human element, the nuts and bolts almost don't matter. Great coaches understand that educators must teach the whole child if they are to set them up for successful lives. Therefore, they also understand that they must coach the whole teacher; they must break beyond talk of only instructional strategies and push into conversations about the educator's hopes, fears, frustrations, and dreams. A great coach will engage with their coaches as humans, not just as teachers. It is the humanity—the trust established between coach and educator, the relationship formed—that separates good coaches from great ones.

To be an instructional coach is to be an expert in powerful instruction. A good coach understands the mechanics of instruction and how and when to apply them effectively. A great instructional coach must know what great teaching is, how to spot it, and how to guide others toward it. A good coach is knowledgeable about academic skills and savvy about how to apply them to powerful effect in instruction. A great coach is also knowledgeable about career skills. She knows what they are, what they do and why, what they look like in practice, and how to include them to powerful effect in instruction.

To meet the demands placed on teachers and schools today, being a great instructional coach demands more than it did in years past. A great coach grasps that to be an instructional coach today requires having skills that go beyond instruction, or what we think of as typical teaching skills. It takes the learning and nurturing skills typically discussed in the business world. It takes marketing skills to share your suggestions for change in a way that resonates with educators; customer service skills to problem solve and serve teachers; and operations skills to strategically manage improvement plans and the coaching cycle, to name some. Ultimately, it takes strong leadership and management skills to inspire people to join your vision, make them feel like vital parts of a team, and keep them motivated as they work toward meeting goals.

To practice what I preach, I am peppering mini business case studies, such as the LEGO story, throughout this book when they show how leadership or more traditional business skills align to great instructional coaching. My hope is that these cases will begin to transform your capacity as a coach, expand your potential, and also stoke your desire to continue your own business- and leadership-skill learning outside of this book.

It is not my intention to make you feel overwhelmed with the suggestion of learning about other worlds of work. It is my intention to fortify your toolbox, even create new ones, to help you connect the dots in order to see the whole picture that is learning today. Thinking of instructional coaching strictly in terms of instructional strategies will keep your thinking stuck. It will keep *you* stuck. It will keep your educators stuck. And it will keep teaching stuck.

I assure you that by devoting just an hour per week to a new leadership podcast episode or a management book, your job will grow *easier*—not harder. You will be armed with new wisdom to apply directly to your interactions with educators and a deeper understanding of how students will one day use these skills in their careers. Trust me: this will only help you. It's a surefire way to grow your skill sets, to help yourself reach a new level of potential, and to find new tools for new challenges in a new world. It will grow your capacity so that you can break free from being merely a good coach and evolve into the great coach you are.

After all, we are not only leading the teachers with whom we work; we are also leading a significant shift in how educators need to think about and approach instruction. We are leading them toward career- and college-ready instruction—in that order. We are leading them to be of greater value to their students in their rapidly changing world.

We are also leading a new paradigm of great instructional coaching. To lead this change confidently and competently as the great coaches we are, we have to step out of our education lane and explore other ones. We have to fearlessly redefine coaching.

Supporting Great Educators Through Great Coaching

To continue moving our education system to a place that meets the needs of today's learners, who will all need careers in a changing world, we are going to have to change. We are going to have to change how we lead schools. We are all going to have to think differently and deeply about instruction. We are going to have to better understand the skills our students will need in careers. And we are going to have to provide for all of our students as many learning opportunities as we can to get them thinking deeply and applying real-world career skills to their school work.

We cannot ask our teachers to move through changes of this scale successfully without support. It's not fair to teachers, and it's certainly not fair to their students. All educators deserve the ongoing help they need to do right by all of their students.

To any principals, superintendents, or administrators reading this book—and I hope you are—your teachers need you to advocate on their behalf. I urge you to discuss with your teams how you can bring great instructional support to ALL of your educators. We are asking them to teach in ways that will be new to most of them. If we ask them to do this without a trusted, competent guide, many will fail. Then our students will fail. Effective instructional coaches make the difference between an education system that remains static and stuck and one that breaks out of its myopic, educational lane to fully meet the needs of all of today's students.

To that end, I ask you also to read this book in its entirety. It will equip you with the know-how to discern a good coach from a great coach. It will provide a roadmap for you to support your clients to become great coaches capable of making the fullest impact of great coaching. And it will help you know how to provide them with what they need to lead school-wide instructional change and build a sustainable coaching structure to allow ongoing, limitless growth across the school.

It will, I hope, also get you to see coaches as the trusted advisors they can be. As the link between instructor and instructional system, coaches can be a powerful informational resource as you work to move the entire system toward better supporting rigorous, relevant, and engaging learning. In chapters 3, 4, 5, and 6, in particular, we will discuss the process that great coaches follow to build a school-wide instructional improvement plan. This process can also serve as a blueprint for you to partner with the coach to transform instruction on two levels: the school and the individual.

Our Co-Creation: A Guide to Great Coaching

To the instructional coach reading this book, it is my hope and intention that it will equip you to be a great coach—the kind leaders clamor to hire and teachers enthusiastically request. It will make you wholly prepared to lead the way through transformation.

Coaches, you are the conduit for change at the school level, which can in turn better support individual teachers. You are the conduit to change for individual teachers, who can in turn be the conduit to change for their students. We need you.

By the time you finish this book, you will be ready to be a great coach *redefined* and an expert in the new coaching paradigm. You *can* do this, and you *will* do this. Together, we will co-create your path toward remarkable growth. Trust that what follows works and is here to serve you, so that you may serve any and all educators, from the enthusiastic and motivated to the demoralized and dispirited. Trust that once you get through this book, you will be ready to transform their lives and their students' lives. Commit to the craft and to ongoing learning, and believe in your boundless potential. I will be here by your side the entire time, always available for you to return to for support, ideas, encouragement, and those nuts and bolts. I will show up fully here for you, sharing all the lessons I've learned in my many years of instructional coaching, all the mistakes I've made so that you can avoid them, and all the wisdom I've gathered.

My ask of you is that you in turn show up fully as well. Without you, we can't co-create. And ultimately, coaching *redefined* has to be a co-creation.

PONDER & POST

To grow as an instructional leader, I will get out of the "education lane" and _____ .

#coachingredefined

Chapter 2

The Instructional Coach's *Real* Values

"I've never met an effective leader who wasn't aware of his talents and working to sharpen them."

General Wesley Clark, retired four-star
general of the United States Army

Real Values for the Real World

In 1994, Jim Collins and Jerry Porras—both Stanford Graduate School of Business professors—published *Built to Last*. The book, which detailed research findings about what sets apart those companies that thrive for decades and outlast competition, held a spot on *BusinessWeek*'s bestseller list for six years. In it, Collins and Porras mainstreamed several practices that, at the time, were seen in a relatively small number of companies— those that were, according to the authors, built to last.

One of the best practices Collins and Porras brought to the masses was the idea of corporate core values. According to the authors, core values are guiding principles or beliefs that are deemed non-negotiable to a company. They are cultural touch points, in that they function as a backbone of sorts to how all employees are meant to conduct themselves, behave, and interact with colleagues and customers. Core values should be achievable and doable today—not aspirational for tomorrow—so that they can truly guide considerations, decisions, and behaviors.

Core values need to be embodied, particularly by those leading others, to be taken seriously, respected, and emulated by all. When they aren't, they are hollow and can lead to cynicism and mistrust of the company and those in it. Core values are also there to remain there; they aren't meant to be compromised to make something easier or to get around a challenge. One need look no further than the infamous Enron—whose core values were "communication, respect, integrity, excellence"—to see how off the rails things can get when core values are nothing more than lip service.

Enron's is an extreme case. But meaningless core values are relatively common. Fortunately, there are several examples of companies that do core values the right way. At these companies, core values are taken seriously. Southwest Airlines and clothing company Patagonia are known for clear core values that drive all decisions and culture. Their leaders, and those out there like them, took time to unearth the tenets integral to the success and sustainability of their companies. They are principles that are achievable today, guide tomorrow, and make known to all employees the behaviors and interactions everyone is expected to embody every day. Amid changing dynamics, core values are a constant to keep everything and everyone grounded in shared beliefs.

Netflix—famous for introducing the world to "binge-watching" television—is in particular known in the business world for revamping and reality-checking corporate core values. In 2009, Netflix CEO Reed Hastings shared publicly an internal slide deck that articulated "the *actual* company values, as opposed to the *nice-sounding* values," pointing to Enron as a case where values were nothing more than the latter. Leadership had used the 126-slide "Netflix Culture" deck to make clear what was vital for success and what employees could expect from colleagues. In uploading it to SlideShare (an online, public platform to share and review slide decks) for all the world to see, Netflix universalized the idea of *actual* values that were *actually* embodied by leaders and employees and were *actual* drivers of culture.

The original Netflix Culture deck is no longer in use at the company. It remains the most viewed deck on SlideShare, still studied and emulated in the business world. Today, Netflix has adapted the deck into a page on their website for all the world to see and review. Netflix defines its "real values" by who gets rewarded or let go and as "the specific behaviors and skills we care about most." These real values are: Judgment, Communication, Curiosity, Courage, Passion, Selflessness, Innovation, Inclusion,

Integrity, and Impact. Each has a handful of bullet points that elucidate how these values are supposed to be practiced by every employee. Here's an example:

Curiosity

- You learn rapidly and eagerly
- You contribute effectively outside of your specialty
- You make connections that others miss
- You seek to understand our members around the world, and how we entertain them
- You seek alternate perspectives (Netflix, 2019)

Reading Netflix's real values is a great way to get a sense of what today's career skills look like in action. Visit https://jobs.netflix.com/culture to learn what one influential company expects the ideal job candidate to be able to do.

The thoughtfulness of and employees' respect for Netflix's real values have made for a unique culture that attracts a certain kind of person committed to the company's values and success. They set the stage for the co-creation process. When all in the company are united in the same foundational beliefs, the process of creating together a product of meaningful value to customers can much more readily unfold.

Instructional Coaches' *Real* Values

Instructional coaches also need real values—those ideas and beliefs that serve as a foundation for all our work. As our educators grow, the educators we work with change, resources and contexts change, and all the many circumstances around education and our jobs fluctuate and evolve; our real values are our constant. They keep us grounded in a system of beliefs so that we remain guided by principles. Everything around our work can change, but thanks to our real values, we still know what we believe and how we must proceed. Most importantly, it is in adhering to the instructional coach's real values that we ensure we bring humanity to our work.

Nine real values of coaches *redefined* follow. This list is authentic, in that it is what I've observed again and again as being essential to the success of instructional coaching. In the absence of these values, trust is not built or it gets eroded, jeopardizing the relationships that must take root between coach and educators if co-creation is to unfold and change is to happen.

Please be aware that in calling the values "real," I do not mean to imply that the values you are already bringing to this work aren't real. In fact, I expect you will see yourself in most, if not all, of these values. They are simply called "real" to remind us that they are serious, lasting, and here to lead us through all of our work and decisions as coaches.

As you read this list, also note that this is my guide to the work of instructional coaching. It is not meant to be preachy about how one lives one's life. Instead, it is meant to provide a foundation to your work as a coach. These real values will always be there for you, waiting for you to embody them, waiting to guide you as you navigate the always changing landscape of work with different educators in different environments. They are your companion in this work.

Note which real values you already practice today and which ones you will commit to cultivating as you aim to embody them fully tomorrow. A key part of our real values is lifelong learning—it is not perfection. Commit to these real values and always working to grow in the areas that show the need for improvement. It is in the commitment to your growth in all of these values that you unlock your ability to become a coach *redefined*.

Real Value #1: Listening to Learn

For coaching to work, it must meet the precise needs of a school and its educators. The coach can only learn and respond to these needs by listening often and actively to what educators are—and are not—saying.

Exemplifying Listening to Learn as a value means:

- You are aware that how you listen to your educators is essential to building trust with them.
- You listen to learn, not to respond.
- You listen actively: You give cues to the educator that you are fully present in the conversation and respecting him with your undivided attention. The smartphone/laptop/tablet is far from view. Eye contact is strong. And body language signals total focus.

- You take notes, as needed and where appropriate, as you listen to signal you are capturing your educator's thoughts and will reflect on them again later.
- You respond to what the educator is saying, not to what you think he should be saying, to indicate that you are there to respond to and serve his needs.
- You understand that a possible result of listening is a situation where you might put certain goals temporarily aside to pursue the educator's more urgent goals for himself. You also understand it is up to you to trust your expertise and make sure you do not lose sight of the ultimate end goal as you keep your educator on track, despite brief and temporary deviations.

Real Value #2: Leadership & Lifelong Learning

President Harry Truman once said, "Not all readers are leaders, but all leaders are readers." Inspired by this notion, I share my own take on his quote with my educators: "Not all learners are leaders, but all leaders are learners."

Exemplifying Leadership & Lifelong Learning as a value means:
- You recognize that to be an instructional coach is to be a leader. You are leading the school and its educators through the vulnerable, challenging, and highly rewarding process of change.
- You understand that to get any educator to see you as a leader, you must establish trust and build relationships. You know that to achieve this, you listen to learn about them; you establish a coaching plan tailored to the strengths, weaknesses, and goals of both the school and your individual coachees; you treat everyone with respect and as the whole humans they are.
- You understand that leaders are only leaders if they are always learning and growing.
- You understand that your capacity to be effective is contingent upon your commitment to maintaining your instructional skills and keeping your fingers on the pulse of the latest technologies, newest instructional strategies, and changing content.

- You understand that to lead educators toward the powerful change today's instruction requires, you must routinely travel outside of your education lane and expose yourself to the business world and its skills. Doing so will equip you with both the change-leadership and management skills you need and the career- and real-world-relevant skills you are asking educators to teach students. You commit to learning about the business world for at least an hour every week in the mode that makes the most sense for you. In Appendix 1, you will find a list titled "Resources for Ongoing Learning: Business and Leadership" to help guide you.
- You know that you will eventually be overwhelmed with work if you continue your lifelong learning alone. Personal learning networks (PLNs) are powerful tools for great coaches. Whether it's Twitter or professional organizations such as Association for Supervision and Curriculum Development, National Science Teachers Association, or National Council of Teachers of Mathematics, you know that you must find a group of like-minded people or a network that will keep you motivated, champion your wins, and push you to keep growing. In Appendix 2, you will find a list titled "Resources for Ongoing Learning: Valuable Educational Organizations."

Real Value #3: Deep Thinking

Instructional coaching can be distilled to one thing: you are trying to get your educators to think deeply so that they do the same with their students. To do this, you must be able to recognize the levels of thinking (which, by definition, is an exercise in deep thinking).

Exemplifying Deep Thinking as a value means:
- You understand that your educators deserve and expect your deepest thinking in the coaching process, particularly as you observe their instruction and approach to eliciting deeper thinking from students.
- You know the hallmarks of deeper thinking: analyzing, synthesizing, evaluating, and creating. You consciously apply them to your

work, look for them in your educators' work, and ensure they are incorporated into all instructional plans.

- You seek to see the whole picture and synthesize all relevant information at hand so that analysis and evaluation are pertinent.
- You are reflective, allowing time and thought to take place in order to preclude knee-jerk reactions or opinions.
- You consider and reflect on your educators' current development, goals, and progress relative to *their* needs, not your own.

Real Value #4: Communication

Without communication, there can be no coaching. At its core, coaching is an ongoing dialogue. The success of this dialogue depends on the coach's ability to communicate respectfully, clearly, and frequently.

Exemplifying Communication as a value means:

- You communicate openly and often with your educators. You frequently and clearly communicate with them your expectations of the coaching relationship and process.
- You offer routine and unambiguous feedback respectfully and with sensitivity to an educator's pride, so that it will be heard with openness and without defense. You choose your words with care and speak in a calm, respectful tone.
- You frame your suggestions and plans in the terms and values that are important in the school and to your educators so that the ideas will be most likely to resonate.
- You set clearly articulated and personalized goals, including milestone expectations, with each educator.
- You offer praise and encouragement to educators so that they are confident you see and celebrate their strengths and growth.

Real Value #5: Honesty & Courage

Great coaching draws upon honesty and courage in a number of ways. It takes courage to keep a school moving toward instructional goals when there is a dip in motivation. It takes honesty to consider if you need to coach a teacher differently and then to change course.

Honesty and courage are also vitally needed when you must have those inevitable difficult conversations with educators. It might never be in your nature to be comfortable with such conversations, and that is OK. You don't have to change who you are, but simply move through these conversations with honesty and courage.

Exemplifying Honesty & Courage as a value means:

- You critically evaluate your own approaches to coaching and your coaching past and admit when you need to change course or improve.
- You persevere through inevitable setbacks, dips in motivation, and challenges to continue pushing toward the instructional improvements you know the school must make on behalf of students' futures.
- You say what you mean and mean what you say because it's the educator's right to get the truth with respect, and you know they are smart and capable of picking up on dishonesty.
- You do not let fear stand between you and a difficult conversation with an educator where it will be an ultimate benefit to that educator—and his students. You recognize that *what you permit, you promote*, and all educators deserve your honesty.
- You honor your own expertise and tactfully explain to a teacher his blind spots or behavioral patterns that might be standing in the way of his growth or improvement.
- You recognize that difficult conversations might never get easier, but they are almost always powerful when delivered with candor, diplomacy, and respect. You let what is ultimately in the best interests of students provide you the courage to tolerate the discomfort of difficult conversations.

Real Value #6: Realistic Optimism

A coach must believe that her work can work. She must believe that when all the pieces come together—when trust is established, relationships are taking root, and educators open up to the process—coaching can change lives. It is your job—and a profoundly inspiring one at that—to help each educator become better. This means helping the strongest teachers become even stronger and helping the struggling teachers get in touch with their capacity for limitless growth and improvement.

Exemplifying Realistic Optimism as a value means:

- You believe *all* teachers are gifted, can learn at the highest levels, and are capable of growth and improvement. You have faith in the potential of every last educator—no matter the circumstances of her . . . or his . . . life and work. This belief provides the motivation for your entire coaching process.
- You believe *all* children are gifted, can learn at the highest levels, and are capable of growth and improvement. You have faith in the potential of every last student—no matter the circumstances of his or her life. This belief provides the motivation for your entire coaching process.
- You understand that, just as students can sense when we lose hope in them, educators can sense when we lose hope in *them*.
- You understand that people only rise to the level of expectations we set for them or believe they are capable of.
- You also understand that you cannot help those who do not want to be helped. In these cases, you remind the educator of his potential. You reiterate your faith in him. You ask how you can be of greater service. And, ultimately, you know it is up to the educator to change.
- You believe every school is capable of change once the educators in it have been heard, respected, valued, and reassured that change will only go at a pace, and be of a scope, they can withstand.

Real Value #7: Compassion

The coaching process will have its frustrations. A teacher or the school staff at large might get discouraged or exhausted at some point in the process. This is normal and OK. What matters is how the coach responds and redirects the process.

Exemplifying Compassion as a value means:
- You expect, allow, and understand that educators will get frustrated or discouraged now and then.
- You patiently offer compassion and empathy when your educators struggle. You communicate that you understand their frustrations. Where appropriate, you share moments from your own life when you have gotten discouraged and believed you weren't capable of something.
- You always redirect the conversation to what is working and where the teacher or school is growing. You focus on every little win and strive to restore hope and optimism in the process.

Real Value #8: Professionalism

While the work of a great coach is to bring humanity to the process, the process is still a professional one. Professional boundaries must be present and honored at all times.

Exemplifying Professionalism as a value means:
- You use discretion in all your professional relationships. You choose language that is not personal but constructive and appropriately business-like.
- You know gossip has no place in the process, and you also know not to have sensitive or professional conversations in open spaces.
- The coaching process often requires reporting to educators' leaders and administrators. You take care to speak diplomatically to these colleagues. You only say things to them that you have said directly to the educator and have received permission to share.
- You start each teacher-coach relationship with a clean slate, despite any past encounters with the educator.
- If you shift role from teacher to coach and begin coaching teachers who were once your direct peers, you adapt relationships with them accordingly so that professionalism is maintained, while taking care to treat teachers as partners in a co-creation, as opposed to acting like their superior.
- You don't hold grudges and can start anew after difficult conversations.

- You remain objective and focused on guiding the school and its educators toward their goals so that their students may grow into better learners.

Real Value #9: Commitment to Instructional Skill Building

Bringing humanity to the coaching process is essential for good coaches to become great coaches. From there, great coaches must keep their coaching skills sharp and updated. After all, we can't teach what we don't know. We also can't coach fully if we haven't honed all the skills that go into the coaching process, from having solid skills around instructional planning to building a sustainable learning system that can grow all educators into leaders of their own learning, no longer dependent on you.

Exemplifying Commitment to Skill Building as a value means:
- You understand that part of your coaching practice needs to include time carved out to routinely refresh your coaching skills and knowledge.
- You understand that the six skill sets that follow in this chapter are integral to becoming a great coach and you commit to grasping, practicing, and honing them all.
- You seek out the methods that work for you to maintain an ongoing study, whether it's with a PLN, in a course, or as an independent study.

In this final real value, we will deviate somewhat from the prior eight. There are six categories of skills, or skill sets, that every coach who seeks to be a coach *redefined* must commit to learning and refining. As you read through these skill sets, you might find that you are new to some or still working to develop many. That is OK. What matters here is your commitment to growing and expanding them. Take heart that in the later chapters of the book, we will dig deeper into the hows and whys of all of these skill sets and equip you with many of the tools you'll need to build these skills. Once you are done with all chapters, you will feel ready to put all of these skill sets to work and develop an expertise in them.

The 6 Instructional Skill Sets of Great Coaches

1. Instructional planning skills

- You learn the nuts and bolts of designing powerful instruction that elicits the deepest thinking and most relevant work from students.
- You know how to infuse learning tasks with high-level cognition and how to make them relevant to the world beyond classroom walls.
- You know what it takes to make a lesson engaging and exciting to students.
- You know the component checklist that goes into rigorous, relevant, and engaging instruction: goals for the lesson; ideas to enable student agency; strategies to increase rigor; higher-order questions for deep thinking; work that is relevant and the responsibility of the student; moments for formative and summative assessment to guide instruction, to name some.
- You know that your work extends beyond looking for these hallmarks of rigorous, relevant, and engaging instruction; you are also able to identify the mechanics of each, so that you can guide the educator through instructional planning, explaining the thinking and intent behind every strategy, tool, and step.

2. Research-validated instructional skills

- You know research-validated instructional practices that can be used across a curriculum and how to apply them to instruction.
- You are familiar with John Hattie's work and have a sense of which high-effect-size instructional strategies are most effective for different scenarios and content areas.
- You are familiar with the Rigor/Relevance Framework™ and know how and when to move instruction through the various quadrants.
- You are familiar with The Hess Cognitive Rigor Matrices to understand Depth of Knowledge.
- You are familiar with Marzano's Nine High-Yield Instructional Strategies.

- You know that your awareness of effective instructional practices must be broad and cover several content areas. When you coach teachers in content areas where you have less familiarity, you do research to learn the most impactful instructional practices for that area, so that you may be of greatest value to them.
- You know how and when to use technology as a tool that enhances the teacher's effectiveness and the students' learning. You also know when technology will be nothing more than a distraction to teachers or students. (For guidance on this topic, I suggest reading *Bold School* by blended learning expert Weston Kieschnick. In it, he explains and showcases how to use technology to drive improved instruction and learning outcomes, including how to apply several blended learning instructional strategies.)
- You have a database of formative and summative assessments and know which work best for yielding different kinds of information.

3. Data skills

- You know that data—not opinions—must guide the school-wide improvements and coaching processes.
- You understand the power of both quantitative data (such as test scores, formative and summative assessments, class attendance, etc.) and qualitative data (student reactions, degree of engagement in learning, etc.) to reveal issues and demonstrate progress in correcting them. You are adept at using both kinds of data to advance the school-wide improvements and coaching processes.
- You understand that data help bring more trust and transparency to the coaching relationship by validating claims, ideas, and suggestions.

4. Vision-casting skills

In his book *The 21 Irrefutable Laws of Leadership*, leadership coach John Maxwell writes: "The truth is that nearly anyone can steer the ship, but it takes a leader to chart the course . . . they see the whole trip in their minds before they leave the dock. They have a vision for their destination . . ."

This quote gets at the heart of vision casting, a tool common in the business world to help teams move together toward a clear vision for the future (2007).

When it comes to instructional coaching, the point of vision casting is to help the school at large and individual educators set a vision for themselves in the future. The vision is meant to be inspiring, motivating, and give purpose, for all parties, to the effort that goes into coaching. Vision casting goes beyond simply explaining the vision. It is meant to be vivid, to come alive, to feel tangible to educators. It's also simple to do.

- Taking what you have learned about your school or an individual educator (through active listening, through ongoing relationship building, in conversations about what they hope to achieve, through the coaching cycle—tools and tactics we will delve deeper into throughout the book), you cast with them a clear picture of what their instruction will look like in the future, once identified goals have been achieved. The vision is detailed and specific, including the skills and strategies that will be present and utilized in the realized vision.
- You include details relevant to any goal. If a school-wide goal is increasing learner engagement, the vision will include specific details of what high student engagement will look like in your educators' classrooms (e.g., students are encouraged to persevere through productive struggle; students take ownership of their learning and set goals toward future learning; students demonstrate respect for the thoughts of their peers; etc.). If a goal is to help an individual make regular and skilled use of data in instruction, then the vision will include details of what instructional planning looks like when the educator is routinely applying data with competence and confidence (e.g., the educator constantly monitors student progress and shares data with students, to increase their ownership, and with the students' parents/guardians, to increase their engagement; data informs interventions; etc.).
- As you vision cast, you fold into the vision the talents and potential you see in your educators, even though they might not yet see them. In doing so, you help your educators unearth hidden gifts

and get in touch with the vastness of their potential. If you have an educator who is discouraged by a goal that feels too lofty or too out of reach (because it is based on the potential you see in him), you remind him that this is exactly what he does with his students all the time—help them reach the potential he knows they have, even if they don't yet know it.

- Once your school or an educator has embodied the vision you and they laid out together, you cast with them a new vision toward new goals they will work to embody next on the path of ongoing learning and growth.

5. Differentiated coaching skills

We expect teachers to differentiate in the classroom. As coaches, we have to differentiate our support for the teachers we are serving. There is no one-size-fits-all approach to coaching.

- You understand that coaching is personal and requires that you tailor guidance to the specific circumstances of the school or needs of an educator. You must, therefore, remain flexible and be willing to adapt plans and thinking based on the school's progress or an educator's progress and growth.
- You recognize that the best coaches differentiate on two levels—content and coaching modality (explained in chapter 7).
- You know to alter the content and information you discuss with educators based on their current level of aptitude with any topic at hand.
- You use the full range of coaching modalities as needed to maximize your effort and your educators' learning. You know how to differentiate the modality of your coaching based on an educator's needs (not on what feels easiest to you in a given moment) or on the circumstances at hand.

6. System-building skills

Bestselling author and leadership guru Tom Peters said, "Leaders don't create followers, they create more leaders." A great coach will create more leaders of their own learning. This is because great coaches know that eventually the work will grow beyond what any single human can handle. Therefore, the best coaches grow ongoing learning capacity at the organizational level, which usually means working toward a full learning system—an endeavor that relies on the following:

- You know that the ultimate goal of coaching is to grow the school's coaching capacity by evolving the school into a learning organization—a school that systematically supports the ongoing learning of all educators within it. When a coach helps a school become a learning organization, she weens educators off of her one-on-one coaching support so that they can lead their own learning and the coach can begin coaching new teachers. (In chapter 11, I will guide you through the process of building a learning organization.)
- Early in your work coaching a new team, you begin to identify the near- and long-term professional learning needs for them, which will be informative as you build out a learning system.
- You also survey the strengths of educators to determine who might be able to help you in your work of building a sustainable learning system. This might include hosting professional learning sessions on identified needs, taking on leadership roles on their professional learning teams, or becoming a point person for a particular topic. Using this information, you begin to think about how you can scale your efforts to reach more teachers by matching needs to strengths.
- You keep your eye out for educators who prove capable of bringing new ideas and perspectives to the ongoing learning system.
- You know that you must speak up well before you reach your personal coaching capacity limit and advocate for resources and support to build out a learning system that can grow beyond you.

Assess Your *Real* Values & Vision Cast Your Coaching Future

When I first begin working with future instructional coaches or those who want to take their craft to the next level, I advise them to read these real core values a couple of times. From there, I ask them to note which elements of all nine core values they feel they embody right now and which they know will take some commitment to improvement. From there, together, we vision cast based on those areas needing improvement.

Visit www.leadered.com/ coachingredefined to download these Vision Casting Guiding Questions as a worksheet.

I suggest you take a few moments to do the same now. Not only will you paint for yourself a clear vision of your future as you grow your instructional coaching strengths and capacity, you will also practice the process of vision casting and, I hope and expect, become a believer in it as you begin to see yourself fully embodying your vision in the not-so-distant future.

Vision Casting Guiding Questions

Use the following questions to guide your vision cast. Write out your vision in detail so that you can return to it often to keep motivated, remind yourself of your vision, track your progress, and recognize when you have fully embodied it.

1. Which real core values can be considered strengths I embody today?
2. On which real core values, or components of them, do I need to work in order to grow and improve?
3. Building from my strengths and aiming to turn weaknesses into strengths as I cultivate my coaching practice, what are the near-term goals I hope to achieve?
4. What will my coaching practice look like once I have achieved these goals? Describe this in specific detail. The following questions serve as an example of the kinds of questions that might be relevant at this point. Select the ones that are pertinent to your goals and/or come up with others as you see fit.
   - What will my relationships with educators be like?
   - What will our interactions look like?
   - What will my instructional process entail or look like?
   - What will my educators think about me? How will they feel about our work together?
   - How will they describe our process to their colleagues?

- What will be the outcomes of our work together?
- What will my educators' instruction look like as we progress on our co-creation process together?
- What will the school look like after I have helped lead it through the level of change it can withstand?
- What will my attitude about instructional coaching be?
- How will I consistently seek feedback to improve my practice?

As you achieve your goals and embody your vision, return to this process to set new goals and propel yourself to even higher levels of growth—as many times as needed to maintain growth and be a true life-long learner.

Once you have assessed your strengths, identified your areas of growth, and cast your first vision for yourself as an instructional coach, you are ready to get begin your coaching process as every great coach does: conducting a listening tour, à la LEGO, to initiate the school-wide change planning and implementation process.

PONDER & POST

My vision for my instructional coaching growth is to _____.

#coachingredefined

PART 2

Leading School-Wide Instructional Change

"Don't be intimidated by what you don't know. That can be your greatest strength and ensure that you do things differently from everyone else."

Sara Blakely, founder and former CEO of Spanx

The promise of this book is to turn you into a coach *redefined*—one capable of driving true, meaningful, and sustainable change that holds the hope of changing students' lives. For this to be possible, you will need to coach on the two levels of great coaching and coaching *redefined*: the school and individual levels. In the next four chapters, we will focus entirely on the work that goes into setting yourself up to lead school-wide change successfully.

Two primary factors go into leading school-wide change: 1) the school's improvement needs, and 2) how ready for change the educators in the school are and your capacity to influence change.

The ultimate goal of planning and leading school-wide change is to improve student learning. Everything that happens in a school impacts student learning. There are direct inputs on student learning, such as instruction, what happens in the classroom, and student work; and indirect inputs, such as community engagement, equity, technology, and teacher empowerment. To build the best, most promising improvement plan for your school, you will need to appraise all the inputs, direct and indirect, on student learning at your school.

You will also need to get a handle on the attitudes about change among the school's educators, including their attitudes about you attempting to lead it. This will help you determine how much change you can suggest and how fast.

In the next four chapters, I will walk you through all the steps that go into understanding the two primary factors of leading school-wide change so that you can build a tailored and productive school-wide improvement plan, win educator support, and set yourself and your educators up for great success.

The Four Steps of Leading School-Wide Change

The process of school-wide change can be broken down into four steps:

Step 1: Conducting a Listening Tour (Chapter 3)—As your first step in leading school-wide improvement, you will conduct a listening tour with all key stakeholders to get a sense of the school culture, the perceptions of the school, the quality of the instruction and learning, and the attitudes of the educators. From this tour, you will begin to see opportunities for school-wide improvement, particularly those that pertain to indirect inputs on learning, such as community engagement or teacher empowerment. You will also get a sense of how ready for, or resistant to, change the educators are. All of this great, rich information will begin to help you determine how much change you can push for initially and what some of those changes need to be specifically.

Step 2: Assessing Your School's Change Profile (Chapter 4)—Next, taking insights from the listening tour, you will evaluate how ready for or resistant to change the educators in your school are. In chapter 4, I provide two frameworks for making an educated judgment on this front. I will also guide you through the process of analyzing your own capacity to influence change. The result will be a profile of the scope, ambition, and pace of change your school can withstand at the outset of change initiatives.

Step 3: Identifying and Prioritizing Improvement Needs (Chapter 5)—The need for improvement of indirect inputs on student learning will, by and large, be revealed on your listening tour. To get an informed and data-driven sense of the instructional improvement needs that pertain to direct inputs on student learning, you will need to get into classrooms and observe teachers in action. In chapter 5, I will outline how to conduct initial classroom observations with a rubric to assess the general levels of rigor, relevance, and engagement taking place at the school. Merging your observation assessment with improvement needs culled from the listening tour will give you a complete picture of all improvement needs, which you will then turn into improvement goals that will be prioritized.

Step 4: Building and Implementing the School-Wide Improvement Plan (Chapter 6)—In the final step, I will then walk you through the nuts and bolts of building the school-wide improvement plan. Once you're done with the work laid out in chapter 6, you'll have a plan ready to go. Because of how you've come to identify and establish all the components of the improvement plan, it will be a true co-creation between you and educators, students, parents/guardians, and community members. In addition, you will be winning their support and buy-in throughout. Lastly, I will guide you through the process of communicating the plan's purpose, winning stakeholder buy-in, and beginning to implement it.

Revisiting All Four Steps Every Year

The plan you will produce in chapter 6 will be for one school year. As a best practice, I suggest repeating all steps of this process of leading school-wide improvement at the start of every year. Based on the improvements made in the prior school year, you will need to set new, clear, and focused goals. You will also happily find that with time and as a result of leading educators through change and achieving early successes, your educators will begin to trust you more. This will allow you to set bigger goals and move with a bit more speed—but still only as much as you determine the school can withstand each year.

Merging Your Plans with an Existing School-Wide Improvement Plan

Many states and districts mandate that schools develop a multi-year improvement plan. If you're in a school that already has an improvement plan in place, for any reason, that is OK. In almost every case, these plans get revisited and updated every year. The goal as a coach *redefined* is that you drive so much impact that you will then be seen as instrumental in revising the plan for the next year.

Until you are in this position, proceed with your school-wide instructional improvement plans. Simply work within the existing plan's protocols. The most important thing here is to know what you do and do not have control over. Don't get hung up on what you cannot change. Instead, think about what you can change. Specifically, think about how you can infuse meaningful instructional improvement into existing protocols.

If the existing plan calls for more group work, then find ways to increase rigor, relevance, and/or learner engagement through group work. If the existing plan calls for more interdisciplinary learning opportunities, add into your plan changes that will ensure all interdisciplinary work makes learning connections of high rigor and relevance and keeps students engaged.

Of course, work as closely with others on the leadership team as needed to make it clear you are on the same team. Your objective is not to usurp existing plans; it's to make sure that they truly do improve student outcomes through increased rigor, relevance, and engagement.

Calibrating the Four Steps to Your Circumstances

The next four chapters speak to the most common coaching circumstances, where a coach is responsible for coaching a range of educators and a large number of them. I do understand that there are cases where a coach is charged only with coaching a few educators in one department. If you are only coaching within a department, please use common sense and your best judgment to calibrate the steps in the following chapters to your needs.

As an example: on your listening tour, you would still want to talk to members of all stakeholder groups. However, you would only need to talk to teachers in the department to which you've been assigned. When it comes time to do classroom observations, you would only need to conduct them in the classrooms of teachers in the department. Instead of building a school-wide improvement plan, you would only need to build a department-wide improvement plan.

The overall steps and process would be the same, simply adjusted to the scope of your responsibility. Please do still read this book, especially the following chapters, in full. After all, even if you're coaching one department, you still want to be a great coach *redefined* and coach systematically and holistically.

A Note Before You Read Part 2

The four chapters of part 2 are necessarily dense and technical. After all, they are setting you and your educators up for successful school-wide change over the course of a year. I have tried to be as clear and detailed as possible. I have also tried to break each step down into smaller and manageable sub-steps. Please know, my intention in creating sub-steps is not to create work but rather to frontload it so that you are as prepared as possible for smooth and successful plan implementation. The sub-steps are designed to make your thinking and planning on the front end exhaustive, intentional, and methodical. This will empower you to avoid misunderstandings of the school's readiness for change and its needs; going after the wrong goals; and miscommunication and confusion. Through the sub-steps, your plan will be custom tailored to both the school and its educators.

And, of course, my intention is to support your growth into a great coach who functions as a high-impact change agent and a model of coaching *redefined*.

I suggest you read all four chapters in full simply to digest them and see how they all come together. Only on a second read do I suggest actually doing the steps and completing all the charts for your school.

Chapter 3

Conducting a Listening Tour

"Most people do not listen with the intent to understand; they listen with the intent to reply."

Dr. Stephen R. Covey, educator, author, and businessman

I n chapter 1, we discussed how LEGO uses listening tours to build trust and rapport with their customers. It's a way to solicit information from the very people they hope will open their wallets to buy LEGO products. Thus, it's a way to build products based specifically on what customers tell them they want. In doing so, they reduce the risk of designing products based on what they *think* customers want. The listening tour brings clarity, purpose, confidence, and validity to LEGO's product design process. By definition, it also greatly impedes the egos of individuals at LEGO from leading to products irrelevant and unappealing to potential customers.

In re-reading the *real* values of instructional coaching in chapter 2, you'll notice two things: 1) Listening to Learn is, by no coincidence, the first real value; 2) The ego doesn't show up in any of the real values, as it has no place in instructional coaching—at least instructional coaching that is effective. Great instructional coaches are true servant leaders—they are there to serve the specific needs of educators and a school. While their expertise always has a place in the process, their egos don't. Great instructional coaches understand that listening, specifically to learn about their school and the educators in it, is a powerful tool for keeping egos at bay.

Listening is also practical and the first step you will take as a coach. The listening tour will provide you the information you need to begin to grasp how the school needs to change and what it needs to change. It will shed light on how resistant to change its educators are, how to identify their brand of resistance, and how to lead them out of it—all of which we'll walk through in chapter 4. What you learn on the tour will also lay the groundwork for the improvement needs we identify in chapter 5 and, ultimately, the school-wide improvement plan we will build and implement in chapter 6. Even if you've been working in your school for years, you will still be surprised by how much you learn by talking to so many people with so many different perspectives.

Perhaps most importantly, at least in starting your coaching process on the right foot, the listening tour will begin establishing trust. Without listening, there can be no trust. Without trust, there can be no relationships. Without relationships, there can be no openness to change and growth. Put another way, without listening, there can be no instructional coaching that gets anyone anywhere but frustrated.

The First Step of Leading School-Wide Change: Learning Through Listening

In the first chapter, we talked about how coaching *redefined* takes place on two levels—at the school level and the individual educator level. We also touched on the interplay between these two levels. If the instructional system can only support so much change and development to improve teaching, eventually individual teacher improvement will plateau or begin to hit roadblocks. To unlock total potential for individual teachers, the system has to evolve to support their ongoing growth and lifelong learning.

Great coaching, then, requires understanding all the dynamics at play that impact the two levels of coaching *redefined*. Getting to this understanding is a process of listening to learn. The first step of leading school-wide change—and the first step of great instructional coaching in general—is learning all you can about the people with whom you will be working and the culture and environment in which you will be working.

Learning About the School Culture and Instructional Environment

While instructional coaching happens with a teacher, it also happens within a school culture. For our recommendations to be usable to teachers, they have to work with, not against, the school's culture. The instructional system needs to evolve to a point where it supports our recommendations to individual teachers, so that they can persist in and sustain their own growth, and so that the school as a whole can change and grow.

All educators teach in a school with a unique culture. They teach in an environment with unique strengths, challenges, potential, and resource constraints. They also work in an environment that boosts or obstructs their instructional process and improvement. Put another way, it is within a school environment that you can find so many of those indirect inputs on student learning (e.g., the approach to and success of community engagement, professional learning, innovation, technology, etc.) and how they are used, or not, to fortify student learning.

Coaching in a way that can get you a foothold in your school to steadily drive change—at the systemic and individual levels—requires knowing the realities of the teaching environment. The culture has a big impact on what you can do as an instructional coach, how you can do it, and how fast you can get it done. To learn about a school's culture requires listening to people beyond the teachers with whom you're working. It means listening, as well, to students, parents/guardians, and key stakeholders in the community. It also means observing the school environment through various qualitative clues and data.

Learning About Individual Educators

A doctor would not walk into her office to meet a patient and suggest a treatment for a condition the patient did not have. She would first ask the patient why he's there, what is ailing him, and what health issue he wants to improve. Only then can any responsible doctor make a sound assessment and discuss a plan specific to that patient's needs.

The same is true of coaching. There is no one-size-fits-all approach to instructional coaching. Every time we sit down with an educator to discuss her practice, we must make a point to discuss *her* practice. Our coaching must be adapted to her needs, her goals, her progress, and her circumstances. Otherwise, it won't do her any good and she will quickly lose trust in us.

We know this by imagining being coached ourselves. If a coach spends a session guiding us on something they think is important even though we know we are already skilled at it, our time feels wasted. If we offer up to a coach that we want to work on something, yet the coach decides we are going to work on something else with no explanation, we feel unheard. If a coach begins working on something with us at a level that is too advanced, we feel frustrated and discouraged. If a coach has only gotten to know our faults and not our strengths, we feel demoralized. We will not trust this coach, and we will likely get very little from our time with them.

Conducting Your Listening Tour

To get to know all your educators and the school and cultural environment in which they work, you will conduct your very own listening tour—in the spirit of LEGO. The point of the listening tour is to set yourself up to coach on the two levels of coaching *redefined*. In listening to learn from key stakeholders, you will lay the foundation to take full advantage of your unique vantage point as a coach—that front-line access to the interplay between the instructional system and instruction in the classroom. The listening tour is the first step you take in getting to understand all the dynamics of this interplay in your school.

In talking to key stakeholder groups, certain things about the school culture and environment will reveal themselves. You will begin to understand the instructional system in place and how it supports or thwarts teacher growth. It will tell you where the teachers are well resourced and where they are not, which will impact the instructional strategies you recommend. It will tell you how well rigor, relevance, and engagement are understood and where improvement is needed so that all three become daily features of instruction. It will let you know if relationships are valued in the school and if students feel cared for and that their wellbeing is important to teachers. The listening tour will help you unearth school-wide beliefs or attitudes that might be standing in the way of growth. It will help you identify gaps that school leaders might not see in their instructional programs and systems. It will also make it possible to diagnose systemic pitfalls that might be impeding school leaders' ability to support truly rigorous, relevant, and engaging instruction at the school and individual levels.

Through the listening tour, opportunities and areas of need will reveal themselves. The tour will naturally begin to reveal what needs to change at the school level to support instructional improvement. It will point you to what personalized and contextualized co-creation plan to suggest to each of your educators. It will also show you the strengths of the school at large and of individual teachers, which can serve as positive entry points to school-wide change initiatives. Importantly, you will begin to get a sense of the school's relationship with change—if it fears it, embraces it, opposes it, wants it, has not tried it, or is already doing it.

All of this will amount to a gold mine of information that will shape how you can push for growth in the school and with the teachers you coach. After all, teaching doesn't happen in a vacuum. It happens in a school. The teachers and the school must be aligned in improvement if improvement is to stick.

What follows are questions to ask each of the key constituent groups that make up the learning environment: the teachers, the students, their parents/guardians, and the community. If you are not a member of the administrative team, the tour will also require listening to an administrator. Your process can be formal and informal and through in-person one-on-ones, groups sessions, or even surveys. The specifics should suit your style and the norms of the school. What matters is that you do this listening and learning work.

A Practical Note Before You Get Started

A note as you set out to listen: When I first discuss the listening tour with coaches, they almost always feel a little overwhelmed. They feel daunted by how much time it will take, how difficult it might be to set up some meetings, or how many people they need to converse with to get sufficient information.

Of course, how much of your time the listening tour will take will be a function of the school's size. As a rule of thumb, I like to talk to enough people that I begin hearing the same comments repeated. Rest assured, to get to this point I've never had to spend more than two dedicated weeks on a listening tour. Less time will be needed in a smaller school.

I am always asked how many people a coach should talk to in each stakeholder group and how much time they should spend with them. Typically, fifteen minutes is plenty with any individual person. In larger schools, I will meet people in stakeholder groups of no more than five people to make the process more efficient, and 30 minutes is typically sufficient with groups.

Pinpointing the number of people you should speak to in each stakeholder group is a challenge. This is a situation where the more people you talk to, the better. But you are human, and eventually you will need to get to the work of leading change and coaching. The more comfortable you get with the listening tour, the more you will begin to sense how many people you will need to meet to get to that point where you are hearing the same comments repeated. But as a general rule, you can begin by aiming to meet with 30 percent of people within the teacher and student stakeholder groups. In a larger school, this might only be possible if you group staff members and group students for discussions, which is fine. Where you simply cannot reach that 30 percent mark with teachers, ask them to bring feedback from other colleagues and speak on their behalf.

When it comes to meeting parents/guardians and members of the community, you will probably meet with a much smaller percentage. Nonetheless, aim to meet with a diverse cohort of parents that represent a variety of students. Solicit help from school staff to connect you with members in these groups. If you cannot connect with many people in either of these groups and the school cannot help for any reason, move on. Do what you can, then accept this might be beyond your control.

A note as you set out to learn: as you begin talking to people, listen not only to what they have to say but also to what they are *not* saying. Listening to what is *not* said can be as powerful, if not more powerful, as listening to what is spoken. Notice what people seem unwilling to share with you or what topics might make them uncomfortable enough to stop or change a conversation. Jot down what was not said so you can reflect later on what the silence might be telling you.

Lastly, as you listen, take care to embody components of the "Listening to Learn" real value listed in the prior chapter. Review them as needed to keep them fresh in your mind. Give those with whom you're speaking your full attention. Keep your ego out of it, and keep in mind that you are here to serve. Take notes as you listen to show you are truly listening and indicate that what the person is saying is important enough to be written down. Take notes also so you can remember what is shared with you, as you will use it to build your school-wide improvement plan. And put your smartphone far out of reach.

Listen to Administrators

For those of you who are not administrators or are new administrators at the school, you will want to begin your listening tour with by sitting down and learning from an administrator. I suggest always going first to the principal as a matter of respect. If he or she doesn't have the time to engage, ask for a recommendation of an administrator who does.

The goal of this conversation is to get a sense of what she sees as important in terms of instruction and student learning. You'll want to learn where she believes the school and the teachers need in order to grow. You will also want to gauge how much respect she has for teachers and their privacy. Finally, it will be so important that you learn her understanding and definition of coaching, specifically whether she views it as separate from evaluation. Before you get into the coaching work with your teachers, take the time to make sure you and the administrator have reached a common understanding and definition of coaching—one that does not have to do with evaluation. Tying instructional coaching to evaluation is a classic and surefire way to set up the instructional coach to fail and the educators she works with to be suspicious of and disengaged from the process.

If you are not an administrator or don't already have access to school data, ask the administrator you speak with for any and all data relevant to instruction, student learning, and student achievement. Ask the administrator to share her perceptions and interpretations of the data, specifically what she thinks is working in instruction and learning and what she thinks is in need of most improvement.

Listening to Teachers

The first people you will want to listen to, once you've connected with the top administrator, are the teachers with whom you'll be working. It is truly a privilege to serve as a coach to teachers, and it's important always to show the highest level of respect toward them. Listening to their voices *first* shows that you respect them. Then, and only then, can you begin to establish the trust that will be so vital throughout your entire relationship with them. If you start with another constituency group, you risk letting your teachers think you are trying to learn about them from others or that this is a *gotcha* process.

Other key things to keep in mind to establish trust: ask open-ended questions that will not make a teacher feel judged; make sure your tone remains calm and friendly; remind her she's in a safe space and is free to speak candidly, as nothing she says will be used against her in any way; as needed, reassure her that the point of this listening tour is to get to know her, so that you can better serve her growth and goals.

Core to serving a teacher's growth is getting a sense of her willingness to change and whether she has a growth mindset. If a teacher is eager to learn, you will likely be able to dive into the nuts and bolts of instructional work quickly. If a teacher is showing resistance to change, you might have to spend more time establishing trust, trying to understand if an experience has left her so discouraged that she has shut down, and determining what she might need to shore up her courage and confidence.

Suggested questions to ask your teachers follow. They seek to uncover things about the teacher and her perceptions and beliefs about the school culture. Asking questions and listening to answers is a dynamic process. It is helpful to go into your conversation with a set of questions in mind. However, have the confidence to continue a line of questioning you believe is valuable and important to learning the teachers' attitudes toward teaching and their roles, intentions with you, strengths and weaknesses, goals, and what they believe is achievable in their school.

Questions to ask teachers about themselves:

- What are your strengths as a teacher?
- In what ways would you like to grow professionally? What, if anything, has stood in the way of your professional growth and ability to meet goals?
- How can we improve learning for your students?
- How do you hear the voices of your students in your classroom?
- How do you know students are learning in your classroom?
- What has been the most meaningful professional learning experience you've had? Why was it so meaningful to you? How did it help you change instruction?
- Have you been involved in coaching before, and how did you come to get involved in it? What did you think of the experience? How do you feel about having a coach now? (This series of questions will require extra reassurance that the more honest teachers are in their answers, the more they will get out of their experience with you.)
- Is there anything else you feel I should know to help me serve you best as your coach?

Questions to ask teachers about school culture:

- What do you feel is the greatest strength of the school?
- Do you feel your school is growing, evolving, and improving?
- What aspect of the school needs to grow the most and why?
- How do you hear the voices of students in the school?
- How do you hear the voices of parents and the community in the school?
- Is equity important in your school? If so, how is it addressed?
- How do you feel the school prepares students for careers and college?
- How do you feel supported in your professional growth and development? Who or what is most supportive?

> - How do you feel about the demands currently placed on you and your colleagues? Are they reasonable or do they feel impossible to meet? Please explain.
> - Would you describe the school as one that sticks with a few initiatives or one that cycles through many initiatives? Please explain.
> - What resources are you most grateful to have? What resources do you wish you had?

Listening to Students

At the end of the day, every instructional coach is there to serve student growth. If we cannot see the school we are in through the eyes of its students, we will not be able to help them grow. As you talk to students, you will want to get a sense of their perceptions of the school and their learning in it. You will want to get their take on what the school values and promotes—learning, sports, rigorous academics, real-world instruction, high engagement, teachers, etc.

Students can offer powerful, frank insights into a school's culture and values. They tend to have fewer filters than adults—a fact we should embrace, but not abuse. They might be more likely to offer insight into, for instance, how inclusive their school is compared to how administrators might view this. But this means we must also take care to avoid questions that could lead to answers that feel gossipy—and reflect poorly on us—if and when shared with leadership. Avoid asking students about specific teachers. Keep in mind that the point is not to get opinions about people but perspectives on the learning environment.

This can only be truly achieved if those perspectives are broadly representative. Work with teachers and administrators who know the students well to connect with a group of students that will offer the most diverse perspectives of the school: students of different racial and religious backgrounds; of different economic circumstances; of a range of achievement levels; of a range of social circumstances (e.g., the most and least popular); and of a range of engagement (e.g., students involved and not in extracurriculars and/or student leadership opportunities).

Before you set out to meet students, ask leadership how they prefer you to go about this. In asking, you will be sure to respect cultural norms, and perhaps even rules, about engaging with students. Especially when we are dealing with sensitivities around children, it is vital we respect school customs.

Suggested questions for students follow. Of course, each question will need to be altered for each age group. Based on what you have learned from your teachers, adapt questions or add to them as you see fit.

Questions to ask students about their learning:

- Do your classes feel hard to you? If they are hard, what makes them hard? If they are easy, what makes them easy?
- Do you know why you're learning what you're learning?
- Do you think what you are learning will be helpful to you in your future, while you're still in school, and after you've graduated?
- Do you feel that your school values and rewards academics or sports or both? Or something else?
- Are your learning successes celebrated? If so, how?
- When you are in a class where you are having fun, being challenged, and learning a lot, what about the class makes it so engaging?
- When you are bored in school, why are you bored?

Questions to ask students about school culture:

- What makes you most proud to be a student at this school?
- If you could change something about the school, what would it be?
- Do you think that the school tries to give the same opportunities to all different kinds of students? Why?
- When students have ideas, do you feel that the adults in your school are open to hearing and considering them?

I assure you, you will always find this process of learning about students eye-opening, rewarding, and incredibly valuable to your coaching work and to the school. Students often provide some of the most insightful perspectives into what is really happening in classrooms and in the halls, and to what effect on students. They are the ultimate keepers of knowledge of a school, and what they share can be used to elevate your instructional coaching—and thus transform instruction and the school at large.

A few years ago, I was working with a woman who had recently taken an instructional leadership role at a school in Georgia. She and I were doing a series of classroom visits. We entered the classroom of a teacher who was a rock star. He led some of the most engaging and rigorous high school classes I'd seen. As this new leader observed him in action, she was blown away by the level of energy and enthusiasm in the classroom. So blown away that at a natural break in the instruction, she held an impromptu conversation with the students. She wanted to know what about this class made them so excited to engage and learn.

The instructional leader expressed her excitement to the students that they were answering such rigorous questions with enthusiasm. She asked them what made them so ready and willing to make this kind effort in this class. A student shot her arm up and answered that they are happy to work hard because they know the teacher believes in them. "I can tell he really cares for us," this student said.

Another student chimed in to explain that the teacher's tasks are also always rigorous, but because he takes time to scaffold them, they don't feel as hard. Lastly, another student said, "Did you see how he teaches? He never tells us the answer. He always answers our questions with another question, so we have to think."

Listening to Parents/Guardians

As part of a study on the nation's most innovative schools and districts from the Successful Practices Network and AASA, the School Superintendents Association, I was sent to observe a district in Kentucky. Following step one of the instructional coaching process, I talked to all key stakeholders, including a cohort of parents. One of this district's schools was a newly established, STEM-based high school designed to serve a broad set of unique student needs. As a smaller and project-based learning school, it wanted to better reach students often overlooked in a large, traditional high school. It had become known as a place where students with specific challenges and needs could thrive. At least, that is what school leadership told me. I was inclined to believe them, but it was my job to validate what the school said with stakeholder voices. In talking with a number of parents, it was clear that this was, in fact, a special place for students who needed more one-on-one attention and personalized care.

Here are the words of a parent of a student with autism:

(The school) has been the absolute answer to our prayers for (our son). He is a very smart and unique young man. He has always "gotten lost" in the school system. (In past schools, he) followed the rules, he did what was expected, and just sorta got through his day. (This) school has given him confidence, and he is blooming. He has been pushed outside of his comfort zone, and he is learning a lot about himself.

Students' parents/guardians are gatekeepers to valuable information about a school's culture. In most cases, their lens on a school is one of concern for their child's wellbeing, academic achievement, and sense of belonging in the school. Therefore, they hold perspectives that can shed light on how well a school practices what it preaches, how much it cares for its students as whole human beings, and the effort it puts into all activities to engage students and families in student learning.

When evaluating what the cohort of parents/guardians you meet and interact with says, look for trends and themes in their answers. Look for alignment—and misalignment—between what parents say and what school leaders say, as this will reveal much about school culture.

Suggested questions to ask parents/guardians follow. The demographics of the school you're working in or with will also factor greatly into the questions you ask. Take care to connect with parents who represent the school's diversity in all senses of the student population.

Questions to ask parents/guardians about their child's learning:

- Is your child's learning rigorous, where rigor can be defined as requiring complex and deep modes of thinking (e.g. analyzing, synthesizing, and/or evaluating information; creating new ideas, concepts, solutions, etc.)? If yes, what makes it rigorous?
- How relevant is your child's learning to her future? Please explain.
- How is your child academically supported at school?
- Is your child engaged in school?
- Is your child learning interpersonal/social-emotional skills and today's career skills? If yes, how are these skills taught, and which ones are taught?

Questions to ask parents/guardians about school culture:

- Do you feel that your voice and input are wanted, solicited, valued, and heard at the school, and how?
- Can you think of a time something at the school was changed because of parent feedback?
- Would you describe the school as one that is eager and open to changing instruction and programs as college, career, and technology demands change?
- How does the school communicate with you, and how often? What are they communicating? Are there ways they could communicate more effectively with you?
- Does the school give equal opportunity to all students? Does the school seem to value equity? If not, what makes you say this?
- Does the school show it cares about your child's emotional well-being? If yes, how do they show this?
- Do you feel the school values and rewards academics? Sports? Something else? How, and how often?
- What makes you most proud to send your child to this school?
- If you could improve one thing about the school, what would it be?
- Is there anything else you feel is important for me to know?

Keep in mind that the level of parent/guardian involvement in school necessarily declines and changes as their children grow older. We can expect to see different kinds of parent/guardian engagement at the high school level; at that point, the school and parents/guardians are trying to help children become more responsible for their own learning and more proactive in voicing their needs. While these parents/guardians are less involved during school hours, they are often involved in other ways, e.g., volunteering at sports events or cultural days, speaking at career days, talking with their children at home about how to be advocates for their own learning, etc. That said, regardless of the grade level, parent/guardian engagement is always vital to any school. As you review this feedback, simply remember that the nature and frequency of parent/guardian involvement is dependent on the age of their children.

Listening to the Community

People in the community hire those who go to its schools. They care about career readiness and professionalism. They also will, one day, hand their community over to the generation of students currently being educated in it. They want these students to grow into productive, positive guardians of a community they care deeply about and have put energy into protecting. They care about the students' interpersonal skills, honesty, and integrity. They care about the students' level of respect for the community and whether they are learning about social responsibility.

As you engage members of the community, you will be trying to learn how well the community feels the school is grooming students to be conscientious, productive members of society. You will be looking to see if the community and the school share the same values about what a positive community looks like, and if the school's perception of itself matches the community's view of it.

Seeking community input poses a unique challenge, in that leadership at the school might intentionally or unintentionally steer you to or away from certain people. It's useful to find multiple inroads to key community stakeholders to make sure you get a range of objective perspectives from it. If you are a member of the community, you will likely have a good sense of where to go for these perspectives. If you don't or if you are not a member of the community, ask school leaders, teachers, administrators, and parents for suggested contacts. In going to multiple sources for community contacts, you will be more likely to get a broad range of perspectives.

As with all other stakeholder groups, you'll want the people you talk with to represent diverse viewpoints. Talk to white-collar and blue-collar members of the community, civil servants and private citizens, people who hire the school's graduates, and people who interact with them at local establishments.

Suggested questions for members of the community follow. The local community and its population will shape these questions. Some of these questions will not apply to certain community members. Adapt these questions or add to them as you see necessary to connect with the group you'll be meeting.

Questions to ask community members about the school:

- In your experience, are school graduates prepared for careers?
- Do graduates show the necessary academic and technical skills for success in careers? If yes, how?
- Do graduates possess the interpersonal/social-emotional and professional skills for success in careers? If not, what are they lacking?
- Are current and past students polite and well behaved in the community? Do they show a sense of social responsibility?
- In general, do you feel confident handing over your community to the school's next generation of graduates? If so, why? If not, why not?
- In your experience, does school leadership show a sincere concern for the achievement and wellbeing of its students and their capacity to be productive members of your community?

> • If you have ever tried to engage with school leadership to bring forth improvement and change, do you generally find them open to ideas and collaboration?

Learning Through Observing: "Listening" to the Environment

As you learn about your teachers, the school's students, their parents, and the community, you will be able to identify the school's values. You will also begin to grasp if those working at the school practice what they preach.

On this front, what you observe can be equally revealing. Walk the school's halls. Are there trophies or banners that celebrate achievements? What kind of achievements? Does the school seem to celebrate academics? Or is the emphasis on sports? Does the school make announcements? What are they about?

Ask an administrator if he can share with you samples of student newspapers, newsletters that go to parents, and information about ceremonies and assemblies. What is the content of these communications and events? Who is mentioned in them? Who is not? What do they say about school culture and values?

Ask to flip through a couple of yearbooks. Do clubs include students from a range of backgrounds? If there are bulletin boards around campus, note their content. What are they showcasing? Whose names are included, and who is in the photos? Are different ethnic groups proportionally represented in pictures?

It can be very informative to watch interactions. Observe how leaders talk to teachers, how teachers talk to their colleagues, how teachers talk to students, how students talk to teachers, and how students talk to their peers. Are these interactions respectful? Does everyone have a voice and the chance to use it? Is any group condescending or dismissive to another? How do interactions match what people say about the importance of interpersonal/social-emotional skills in the school?

The school's walls and materials, and how people interact on campus, can speak volumes about values. Consider all of these things as powerful resources at your disposal to help you get to know school culture. Pay close attention to how much it matches up with what people tell you about the school.

Suggested Learning Tools as You Gather Information

Don't hesitate to incorporate tools or technologies into your listening tour should they bring greater efficiency or success to it. To that end, two of my favorites that I often utilize follow.

WE™ Surveys

WE™ Surveys are a great tool to reach more people and perspectives more quickly. Developed by The Successful Practices Network, a non-profit organization founded by Dr. Bill Daggett, and with which I often partner to develop content and coaching material, in conjunction with ICLE and the Quaglia Institute, WE™ Surveys are digital and anony-mous questionnaires that ask students, staff, and community members to share insights, opinions, and perceptions about the learning environment, instruction, and leadership in a school or district. The detailed results reveal overall perceptions about the quality of instruction, leadership, and culture. They also compare how different groups feel about the same questions, which exposes mismatches in perceptions of things such as rig-orous instruction, community outreach, how supported a group feels, and so on. Insights culled from this are powerful door openers to conversa-tions that have yet to be had that can drive significant, meaningful change.

Visit http://wesurveys.org for more information.

The Five Whys

To solve any problem, you first have to know what the problem is. Wher-ever appropriate and possible, as you ask questions of any person or group, you will want to get to the root cause of a problem. The Five Whys is a perfect tool to keep on hand for just that—unearthing a root cause. This lightweight and powerful tool allows you to probe a problem by ask-ing "why" five times. As you answer each "why," you begin to peel back the layers, or symptoms, of that problem until you discover its source.

I was in my first days coaching an instructional leader at a middle school. The instructional leader and I were observing an English class. One-third of the students were on their phones. They were on Snapchat and Facebook, exchanging text messages, playing games. One was recording the student in front of her. The teacher continued to lecture as though this wasn't happening at all.

After the class, I asked the teacher why so many students were ignoring his lecture and on their phones. He responded that it was their choice not to care about the class and he'd given up on trying to get them engaged. When I probed further, he said he'd asked these students why they choose to play on their phones instead of pay attention and learn. He shared that most of these students' claimed it was because they did not care about school. He took this as a lost cause and gave up.

My hunch was that there was more to this story. Students who play on their phones in class are typically bored and disengaged from the work at hand. This is an issue of engagement, not of lack of caring. It was a perfect case for the Five Whys to get to the root cause of the students' lack of engagement.

The conversation I had with the teacher went something like this:

Me (why #1): Why are so many students on their phones while you are lecturing?

Teacher (answer #1): They are easily distracted.

Me (why #2): Why are they distracted?

Teacher (answer #2): Students simply don't care about school and automatically tune me out when I start lecturing.

Me (why #3): Why don't they care about school?

Teacher (answer #3): They don't see the content as important.

Me (why #4): Why do you think they don't see the importance of the content?

Teacher (answer #4): I don't think they see themselves using this content in their future.

Me (why #5): Why are they having difficulty connecting the class content to the skills they will use in the future?

Teacher (answer #5): Maybe I'm not telling them enough times that they will use these skills in the future.

At this point, the Five Whys had done its job. Through this simple exercise, the teacher got unstuck from his opinion that his students were just easily distracted and that this was the beginning and the end of the story. By question five, he'd begun to consider his own role in their distraction, which then put him in a place of empowerment, a place where he had choices and could take action. He and I discussed the larger issue further, and together we came up with some learning tasks he could try to deepen relevance and improve engagement.

Processing What You Learned on the Listening Tour

You now have an incredible amount of valuable information about the school, and from a wide range of sources, at your fingertips. You will refer back to your notes and what you learned on your listening tour throughout your entire coaching process. Most immediately, though, you will use these insights to help ascertain how ready the school is for change and, thus, how much change you can ask of its educators in the next year. You will also use the insights to determine where the school needs to make improvements—particularly pertinent to those indirect inputs on student learning—and identify goals you will lead the school to achieve in the next year. We will tackle both of these immediate uses of the listening tour in the next two chapters.

First, though, while the information you gathered is fresh in your mind, read through all your notes and reflect on what you learned, what people said, what people did not say, and what you observed. Refer back to the Deep Thinking core value in chapter 2 to frame how you should reflect on this information—synthesize, evaluate, and analyze it to look for patterns, themes, and outliers. Consider how all this information relates to the school instructional and student achievement data you've reviewed and analyzed. Look for patterns and trends in the data and think about what they say about where the school is today relative to where it needs to grow tomorrow to work toward becoming an exemplary school.

As you review your notes and reflect on the listening tour, write down some specific details now, as they will be needed in the next chapter:

• Write down major positive and negative patterns and themes you see in what you learned.

- Write down your overall sense of the school's attitude toward change.
- Write down where you see obvious needs for improvement pertinent to any inputs, direct or indirect, on student learning. Examples could be: community engagement; school communication; attitudes; relationships between and among staff; culture of learning; beliefs about professional learning; rigorous, relevant, and/ or engaging learning; relationships among students; assessments; teacher empowerment; access to technologies, etc. (Note: in chapter 5, you will do a first wave of classroom observations to pinpoint instructional improvement needs, which are the direct inputs in student learning.)
- Write down what the school is doing well today, no matter how small. Be sure to include at least one point that speaks to instruction and/or student achievement. You will come back to this in chapters 5 and 6.
- Write down the names of individual staff members who demonstrated enthusiasm for change and an interest in getting involved in school initiatives, as they might be able to help you implement change and, in due time, build out a sustainable learning system.
- Write down the names of staff members who seem particularly resistant to change, as they will likely benefit from additional one-on-one time with you.
- Finally, write down anything that stood out, in a positive and/or negative way, in your mind.

Managing Outlier Information and Data Points

On your listening tour, you will likely get some information that doesn't seem to fit in with the majority—outliers, or opinions that come from one or two people. When this happens, do a little more digging to see if you can determine if this information is worth influencing change and your coaching or if it doesn't warrant much attention. Evaluate it against the patterns and themes you observed and wrote down.

One time, when I was gathering perspectives from the community at a high school with which I was working, a manager of a local fast food restaurant was in attendance. This person had hired many of the school's students. He shared his belief that the school was not sufficiently preparing students for jobs that require math, noting that many of the school's students whom he had hired struggled to count money.

No educator ever likes hearing that a student who graduated from their school left without basic math skills. That said, those of us from the school hearing this feedback knew that the trends at the school overwhelmingly told a different story. This school happened to have high math test scores. We responded by saying that we were grateful for this feedback and that it is important to us that every student graduate with fundamental skills. We promised to take action with this feedback. And we did—on a small scale to target instructional coaching with one teacher and a specific group of students.

Since this feedback was an outlier, it did not warrant taking up space in the school-wide improvement plan or impacting the instructional coaching program at large. Had the instructional coach spent time reviewing how to teach basic math skills with all math teachers, or had all math teachers devoted instructional time to teaching basic math skills, it would have wasted almost everyone's time.

Not every piece of information you get in this learning process should drive change, nor could it. If it did, you would be overwhelmed and unfocused—going after a bunch of goals while meeting very few. Certain small problems brought to light might call for a small, targeted solution. But it will be the majority messages that drive school-wide change and set the stage for instructional coaching that connects with teachers while still respecting their needs, goals, realities, and the school culture at large.

With all this great information learned on your listening tour in hand, you are ready to tackle the next big goal of a coach *redefined*—determining how ready for change the school is and how much you can influence change in the school.

PONDER & POST

On my school listening tour, I hope to _____.

#coachingredefined

Chapter 4

Assessing Your School's Change-Readiness Profile

"Growth and comfort do not coexist."

Ginni Rometty, chair, president, and CEO of IBM

C ongratulations on completing your first listening tour. From it, you have culled a gold mine of information that will help you begin to determine the school's improvement needs. Of equal importance, the tour allowed you to show key stakeholders how invested you are in the improvement process and how thorough you want to be throughout it. It provided a means for you to cultivate trust and build relationships with several people in and outside of the school. This is how coaches *redefined* start their coaching efforts on the right foot. It will only serve you well as you begin processing everything you learned on the tour to, eventually, craft the yearlong, school-wide improvement plan.

Before you can do that, though, you'll need to complete step two of leading school-wide change; that is, you'll need to do some thinking about how ready the school is for change, and about your capacity to influence change within the specific dynamics of the school. Change leadership, as it's called in the business world, is a delicate process that requires meeting all those affected by change where they are and recognizing where you stand in relation to them. It demands ascertaining how resistant to change a team is so that they can be led out of that particular resistance and into a place of openness to it. The business world is full of stories about forcing too much change on people before they're ready or not changing enough before it's too late to adapt to market forces. The result is either, at best, stymied change efforts or, at worst, loss of trust and failed plans.

However, there is a secret to circumventing failure and loss of trust as you lead change in your school. And it so happens to be the very thing that, when the day is done, separates good coaches from great coaches—the ever-present awareness that we are coaching humans. We are not coaching teachers or cogs in a wheel that need to be managed. We are coaching *humans*. It is in always remembering to bring humanity to our coaching that we allow the process to be most fertile for success.

The Lessons of New Coke

On July 10, 1985, ABC's news anchor Peter Jennings interrupted the day-time soap opera, *General Hospital*, with some breaking news. Believe it or not, the news was that Coca-Cola would be putting its 100-year-old, obsessively protected original Coke recipe back on the market. It's hard to imagine in today's world that this would get the "breaking news" treatment. But many of us here might not remember when Coke changed its recipe and thrust "New Coke" upon the world—and the controversy that ensued (Cobb, 2015).

Nearly two and a half months earlier, Coca-Cola's CEO announced the introduction of a new Coke recipe, one that was "bolder" with a more "harmonious" flavor (Cobb, 2015). It was also, as customers would soon learn, significantly sweeter.

In 1886, Atlanta-based pharmacist, John S. Pemberton, invented a sugary syrup to add to soda water—the very same concoction that we know as Coke today. He eventually sold the recipe to another Atlantan, Asa G. Candler, who envisioned Coke as the favorite drink of all Americans. By 1895, the Coca-Cola Company was selling its soft drink in every state in the union. For decades, Coke was more or less the only game in town. It lined the shelves of small mom and pop grocers in Middle America's predominantly rural, farming communities, and it streamed from soda fountains at community watering holes (Cobb, 2015).

For most of its history, Coke's prominence was largely unchallenged—that is until America underwent massive economic and structural shifts after World War II. In the 1950s, Americans began abandoning farming communities for the modern convenience of suburban living. Rural and small-town grocers fell like dominos as larger supermarkets took over the suburbs. Gone were the days of small markets with limited shelf space. Instead, with their long aisles and many rows of shelves, supermarkets opened up the possibility of scores of new food and beverage entrants into the sphere.

All of a sudden, Coke sat alongside all kinds of new soft drinks, including Pepsi, which had steadily encroached on its market share. In 1948, Coca-Cola held a towering 60 percent of the market share. During what became known as the "cola wars" of the 1980s, its share fell to 21.8 percent, and Pepsi's had reached a threatening 18.8 percent (Cobb, 2015).

Pepsi was known as a sweeter alternative to Coke. Coca-Cola's leadership interpreted this as changing consumer preferences for sweeter soft drinks. This prompted the decision to throw out the hundred-year-old recipe in favor of a new and sweeter one.

That April 1985 announcement from Coca-Cola's CEO was met with a torrent of anger the company never saw coming. After all, they had market tested New Coke. In fact, in taste tests with over 200,000 participants, over half preferred the taste of New Coke. However, it was a blind taste test and participants didn't understand that their preference could translate into the wholesale removal of original Coke (Edwards, 2015).

On that data alone, Coca-Cola introduced New Coke. Hundreds of thousands of Coke drinkers sent angry letters to corporate headquarters and flooded its phone lines, demanding the return of original Coke. Gay Mullins, a resident of Seattle, founded the Old Cola Drinkers of America organization devoted to demanding Coca-Cola return original Coke to the masses. He put his money where his mouth was, spending $30,000 of his own money to support the campaign. He was quoted in a June 24, 1985 *People* magazine article saying:

> How can they (Coca-Cola) do this? They were guarding a sacred trust! Coca-Cola has tied this drink to the very fabric of America—apple pie, baseball, the Statue of Liberty. And now they replace it with

a new formula, and they tell us just to forget it. They have taken away my freedom of choice. It's un-American! (Sackett, 1985)

How did Coca-Cola make such a disastrous blunder? It's a question that business scholars have asked for decades. Most agree on a key error, one that is well captured in Mullins's *People* magazine quote. Coca-Cola investigated New Coke on taste alone. They never inquired about people's emotional connection to Coke as a brand and what it represented in their lives. They failed to recognize that people make decisions for a range of reasons, many emotional and personal, and practicality is often not a priority.

To many Coke drinkers, Coke represented a choice—and one that took on even more significance as the cola wars heated up. Choosing Coke over Pepsi was a way to draw a line in the sand. It was identity. It was also nostalgia and a relationship to the brand.

The ferocity of the backlash and the media's ongoing coverage of it meant that Americans were paying attention when Coca-Cola announced it would pull New Coke from shelves and put Coke Classic back in its place. A day after Peter Jennings announced the company's impending plans, Coca-Cola President Donald Keough held a television press conference, in which he said: "The simple fact is that all of the time and money and skill poured into consumer research on a new Coca-Cola could not measure or reveal the depth and abiding emotional attachment to original Coca-Cola felt by so many people" (Haoues, 2015).

In 2015, thirty years after the New Coke debacle, CBS reached out to Coca-Cola for thoughts on the affair. A Coca-Cola spokesperson gave to CBS the following comment:

Thirty years ago, we introduced New Coke with no shortage of hype and fanfare. And it did succeed in shaking up the market. But not in the way it was intended. When we look back, this was the pivotal moment when we learned that fiercely loyal consumers—not the Company—own Coca-Cola and all of our brands. It is a lesson that we take seriously and one that becomes clearer and more obvious with each passing anniversary. (Haoues, 2015)

Change is emotional. Change is personal. Change is human.

Determining Your School's Change-Readiness Profile: A Two-Part Change Analysis Process

In this section, I will walk you through two parts of helping you refine your assessment of how much school-wide change you can suggest and how fast. The first part is to assess your capacity to influence school-level change given your role. Your role does not tell *if* you can or cannot influence change (because you can); it tells you *how* you can influence change. The second part is to assess your school's readiness for change. This will tell you how ambitious you can be in crafting your school-wide plan. It will also help you understand why people are resistant to change and how you can encourage them to embrace it.

The result of completing these two parts of the change analysis will be your school's Change-Readiness Profile, a chart that provides a composite picture of your school's capacity to withstand change today. In the next two chapters, you will apply the insights of this profile to steps three and four of the school-wide change process, identifying and prioritizing improvement needs and building the one-year, school-wide improvement plan.

Each of these steps serves a point beyond gathering and synthesizing information for the ultimate plan. In addition to learning that change is emotional, Coca-Cola also learned that their customers are the true owners of the brand. That's why it felt so personal when the company replaced Coke with New Coke—people felt like something that was rightfully theirs had been taken from them without being asked, without clear communication as to why, and without justification. When it comes to school-wide change, bear in mind that you will be leading people who feel like the rightful owners of the school. This makes their attachment to the school, and many of the programs in it, that much more personal and emotional.

In following the two parts of this change-analysis process, you will be signaling your respect to the school's staff. In honestly acknowledging your capacity to influence change, you will preclude yourself from over-asserting power where it might not be welcome. In changing at the pace the school is ready for, you will acknowledge and respect the ownership educators feel over the school.

You will also be taking the necessary steps to avoid failure. Management consulting company McKinsey & Company has studied change management for decades. Per their findings, 70 percent of change programs never achieve their goals—with employee resistance as a leading cause of failure (2015). Know that as you go through the steps and considerations of this chapter, you are doing yourself and your school a great service by removing one of the most common pitfalls of change initiatives and change leadership.

Part 1: Assessing Your Capacity to Influence Change

Great coaching happens on two levels because change happens on two levels—it happens through individual teachers and at the school-wide level. By working through both channels simultaneously, you optimize that interplay between educators and the school environment. This is how true change can be achieved. And with time and concerted effort, your plan can begin to change the culture.

No matter your relationship to the school, you will be able to set the wheels in motion for change at the school level. How you go about doing this will depend on your role, and it's important to think about your capacity to drive change in your role today.

If you are an administrator, by definition your ability to influence change at the school level may be deeper and broader. This is because it is, generally speaking, known that administrators have some degree of decision-making power at the school level. If this is the case for you, you will be more likely able to begin making changes that are larger in scope from the get-go.

If you're not an administrator and your capacity to influence change is by definition smaller, that is completely OK. It means you will likely first tackle changes that are smaller in scope to preclude the appearance of prematurely overstepping your perceived bounds. It also means that, initially, the relationships you establish with the individuals you coach will serve as the biggest and most immediate drivers of change. As your smaller, school-wide efforts begin to meet success, you will earn that much more trust. With time, you will likely find you are able to take on larger changes across the school.

How long you have worked in a school or with its educators will also impact your capacity to drive change initially. The longer you've worked with these educators, the more time you've had to cultivate relationships and trust, which, in theory, could allow you to take on changes broader in scope at first. In reality, this will depend on your reputation and the health of your relationships to date with colleagues. Simply put, having a positive reputation means you initially have more capacity to influence change; having a less than positive reputation means you have less capacity.

No one likes learning their reputation is anything less than perfect. But it is powerful and worthwhile to find out how you are perceived in your school. The process of seeking feedback into how you are viewed by its very nature will boost your reputation on two fronts. First, in asking colleagues to open up about you shows both your vulnerability and your respect for and trust in them. It also shows your seriousness about being a great coach. The courage it takes to ask for this kind of feedback will cause peers to gain respect for you, whether that's more respect or newfound respect. Just take care not to appear defensive if someone tells you something that is difficult to hear. Instead of fighting back, ask this person to share specific examples of his opinion, and then ask him how he thinks you could improve. Second, these insights will better inform your actual capacity to influence change. And when you are more accurate in this assessment, you will more appropriately suggest initial changes that show your full awareness of your colleagues' comfort with change and your respect for them.

While this is rare, I will sometimes work with a coach who was not known as a great teacher. This can impact the coach's credibility and also impact her capacity to influence change. If you find yourself in this circumstance, once you get into implementing the school-wide improvement plan and one-on-one coaching, I advise you to avoid referencing your own teaching; instead only reference exemplars. (It should be noted: I always advise coaches only to reference exemplars, not their own work; it merely takes on more importance in these scenarios.) Please do not get discouraged, though. Remain aware that teaching skills and coaching skills are a Venn diagram; while there is overlap, coaching takes other skills, and you still have the full potential to be a great coach. Part of that is recognizing your limits to influence change and proceeding accordingly to show respect for your colleagues and earn more of theirs in return.

If you are relatively or brand new in the school, you might find it advantageous to begin school-wide change initiatives after you've had more time to establish trust and build those relationships—both with the teachers you coach and others you identify as contenders to help you implement change.

In the book *Tribes: We Need You to Lead Us*, author Seth Godin argues that lasting and substantive change can be best effected by a "tribe," or a group of people connected to each other, to a leader, and to an idea. On that point and regardless of your role, think about whom in the school demonstrates enthusiasm for change, leadership potential, and/or awareness that getting involved in change efforts can boost their personal growth. This tribe will help get your message out there and support change initiatives in a host of ways, depending on your plan. If you are not an administrator, you will likely lean on your tribe more (2008).

Visit www.leadered.com/coachingredefined to access and download the full Change-Readiness Profile chart. Complete this chart to create a composite picture of the scope and ambition of change you should initially suggest.

RECAP: **Scope of change** is defined as the size—how big or small—of changes you can make. It depends on your capacity to influence change, which is a function of your current level of decision-making power at the school, your reputation, and how long you've been working in the school.

Your School's Change-Readiness Profile— Part 1

As mentioned, the result of the two-part change analysis will be your school's Change-Readiness Profile. At the end of the chapter, you'll see and complete this chart in full, which also includes sections that speak to your school's readiness for change, which we'll tackle next. For now, put an "X" in the row that aligns to your capacity to influence change to see the recommended corresponding scope of initial changes.

Based on the aforementioned considerations of your capacity to influence change, determine if your capacity to influence is large, medium, or small. Put an "X" in the row that aligns to your capacity to influence change. The corresponding adjacent cell in the next column will tell you the appropriate scope of changes you would be wise to suggest in the school-wide improvement plan.

CHANGE-READINESS PROFILE		
Scope of Changes		
Your Capacity to Influence Change		Recommended Corresponding Scope
Large		Changes that are **larger** in scope
Medium		Changes that are **moderate** in scope
Small		Changes that are **smaller** in scope

Step 2: Assessing Your School's Readiness for Change

Just as how you go about change at the school level is a function of your role, it's also a function of how ready for change the educators are in your school. In simplest terms, a school can be ready for change, not at all ready for change, or somewhere in between. In my experience, most schools are somewhere in between. A school's overall readiness for change will dictate how ambitious the plan for school-wide instructional improvement can be, especially in the first year. When a school is ready for change, you can take on challenging goals at a relatively faster pace from the get-go. If a school is highly resistant to change, you will want goals to be simpler and slower.

From your listening tour, your school's readiness for change might be unambiguously clear. If, however, you can't quite gauge the overall readiness, I will walk you through two analytical processes to help you pinpoint it. Ultimately, you will be making a judgment call. But these two analytical processes will help you make an informed and educated judgment call.

Visit www.leadered.com/coachingredefined to download the Readiness for Change Assessment tool.

Analytical Process #1: Readiness for Change Assessment Tool

The first analytical process is the Readiness for Change Assessment Tool. It asks you to rate how strongly you agree with thirteen statement pairs in order, ultimately, to calculate where your school sits on a sliding readiness-for-change scale. A school can fall into one of three categories: 1) low resistance to change, 2) medium resistance to change, 3) high resistance to change.

Directions:

1. Read the following pairs of statements. Based on what you learned on the listening tour, and what you might already know about the school, select the number between 1 and 10 to rate how strongly you agree with a statement. The more you agree with the statement on the left, the lower the number you select will be. The more you agree with the statement on the right, the higher the number you select will be.

Readiness for Change Assessment Tool

A majority of respondents stated that problems are dealt with effectively and efficiently.	O–O–O–O–O–O–O–O–O–O 1 2 3 4 5 6 7 8 9 10	A majority of respondents spoke of persistent problems that have not gotten attention.
A majority of respondents shared that all groups of students were making significant achievement gains.	O–O–O–O–O–O–O–O–O–O 1 2 3 4 5 6 7 8 9 10	A majority of respondents mentioned a deficient degree of student achievement gains or mentioned achievement levels that have remained stuck.
School staff acknowledged changes are in process to boost or continue to boost student achievement gains.	O–O–O–O–O–O–O–O–O–O 1 2 3 4 5 6 7 8 9 10	School staff appeared defensive about a lack of school-wide student achievement gains.

The school has participated in instructional coaching for a number of years.	O-O-O-O-O-O-O-O-O-O 1 2 3 4 5 6 7 8 9 10	There is little to no history of instructional coaching at the school.
The majority of respondents expressed excitement regarding the leadership's willingness to hear and/or take seriously staff/community ideas for improvement or change.	O-O-O-O-O-O-O-O-O-O 1 2 3 4 5 6 7 8 9 10	The majority of respondents expressed frustrations with leadership's willingness to hear and/or take seriously staff/community ideas for improvement or change.
A majority of respondents expressed a genuine desire to improve in whatever ways are necessary to help each child succeed.	O-O-O-O-O-O-O-O-O-O 1 2 3 4 5 6 7 8 9 10	A majority of respondents expressed a degree of hopelessness that the school can improve or change.
A majority of respondents were pleased with the level of support for instructional improvement initiatives.	O-O-O-O-O-O-O-O-O-O 1 2 3 4 5 6 7 8 9 10	A majority of respondents voiced concern over a lack of support for instructional improvement initiatives.
When asked what needs to change at the school, the majority of respondents could identify primarily and/or only smaller changes, e.g., specific changes that pertain to individual instructional practices.	O-O-O-O-O-O-O-O-O-O 1 2 3 4 5 6 7 8 9 10	When asked what needs to change at the school, the majority of respondents suggested big-picture, sweeping changes were needed (e.g., curriculum is outdated; equity is not taken seriously; lack of blended learning), as opposed to smaller changes (e.g., incorporating strategies for student discourse, integrating rigor in assessments).
There is a strong sense that most staff members love their jobs.	O-O-O-O-O-O-O-O-O-O 1 2 3 4 5 6 7 8 9 10	There is a sense that most staff members are not happy working at the school.
The majority of respondents expresses enthusiasm for their school and what is taking place within it.	O-O-O-O-O-O-O-O-O-O 1 2 3 4 5 6 7 8 9 10	The majority of respondents expresses a sense of fatigue, overwhelm, or disillusionment.

There is a general perception that leadership cares about other people's ideas and takes them into consideration when making instructional decisions.	O—O—O—O—O—O—O—O—O—O 1 2 3 4 5 6 7 8 9 10	There is a general perception that leadership is complacent and not open to new ideas or suggested changes.
There is a general perception that teachers care about their students and are willing to do whatever it takes to help them succeed.	O—O—O—O—O—O—O—O—O—O 1 2 3 4 5 6 7 8 9 10	There is a general perception that teachers are complacent and not open to new ideas or suggested changes.
The school has a good or outstanding reputation and has done a great deal of work to improve its standing in the community.	O—O—O—O—O—O—O—O—O—O 1 2 3 4 5 6 7 8 9 10	The school has a poor reputation and has done little to improve its standing in the community.

2. Add up the numbers you selected for all statements to determine your school's score. Refer to the following scale to determine where on the readiness-for-change scale your school falls. Where your school falls can shed light on how strongly they may resist change. For instance, if your score came to 45, this can be interpreted as a lower intensity of medium resistance to change than if it came to 95.

Change-Readiness Scale

1–10	11–20	21–30	31–40	41–50	51–60	61–70	71–80	81–90	91–100	101–110	111–120	121–130

Low Resistance to Change   Medium Resistance to Change   High Resistance to Change

Analytical Process #2: Resistance to Change Root-Cause Assessment

In this section, we will explore the most common reasons why people resist change. Note that this root-cause assessment serves two purposes: 1) As discussed, it can help you further pinpoint the degree of resistance to change in your school; 2) It will also guide you to identify why your educators are resistant to change, so that you can determine how to lead them out of resistance. On that front, refer back to this section as needed for tactics and communication tools to break through specific kinds of resistance.

Why People Are Resistant to Change

In their 2010 book *Switch*, brothers and business writers Chip Heath and Dan Heath explore why it can be so challenging to make meaningful changes in our lives, communities, and organizations. The Heath brothers identify the most common reasons people resist change. Borrowing from their great work, I will summarize the reasons that pertain to educators and adapt their suggestions to break through each reason for resistance to fit schools and educators.

First, it's important to mention the common misperceptions the Heath brothers note about those who are resistant to change. At the core, resistance can come down to two factors. One, people resist when they are unclear about what's being asked of them or how to achieve it. Two, while those who resist can often be perceived as lazy, they are usually just exhausted. For us—coaches *redefined*—these misinterpretations are reminders to keep humanity in the process. Beneath a person's excuse is a person. An excuse often signals an inability to identify or admit the real reason behind it. And that real reason is usually something understandable, like fear, confusion, or just plain exhaustion. Keep this insight from the Heath brothers in mind, as it will help you avoid making a snap judgment and to see the resistant person before you as a human, trying to survive in an overwhelming job.

Using Resistance Reasons as a Readiness Assessment

To help turn the following nine reasons for resistance into a readiness-for-change assessment tool, I've given each resistance reason a label of "medium resistance to change" or "high resistance to change." Some reasons for resistance are easier to break through than others, and I have labeled those as "medium resistance to change." In these instances, you might find you have a little more room to suggest moderately more ambitious goals and/or move at a moderately faster pace. That said, trust yourself. My labels next to each reason are not scientific. They are from decades of experience. But you, not I, are on the ground in your school, and you just spent all that time connecting with key stakeholder groups to strengthen your understanding of the school environment. Let my labels be a guide to bring more precision to your readiness-for-change analytical process, but trust your own judgment and don't be afraid to disagree with mine.

As you read the nine resistance reasons, write down which ones appear to be active in your school and note if it's a medium or high resistance level. In comparing your notes from this section to those from the readiness-assessment tool in the prior section, you will be ready to make the most educated and informed judgment about the intensity of resistance your school exhibits.

Resistance Reason 1: People just lack the motivation to change

High resistance to change

People might not be motivated because they are exhausted and overwhelmed. This exhaustion and overwhelmed feeling can impact how people see themselves. Meaning, they might no longer see themselves as people capable of climbing over that exhaustion to somehow change. This, then, is a matter of identity and energy levels. When I confront this resistance, I like using vision casting (which we discussed in chapter 2) to help people see themselves as capable of different behaviors and growth, however incremental and small. To that point, the Heath brothers recommend taking goals and breaking them into the smaller and more manageable steps. Keep your focus solely on one step at a time before moving people to the next one to preclude yet more overwhelm.

The Heath brothers also suggest using positive social pressure to nudge people to take action toward change. One way to do this is to put the end result of change, or the several smaller-step destinations along the way, in positive and inspiring terms. Let's say a school struggles with learner engagement. A positive peer-pressure tactic could be to let teachers know you'll be asking each to share an engagement strategy they used with success in the past week in their next professional learning session or team meeting. This makes it clear that they are expected to try an engagement strategy in the next week. Because they must also speak about it in front of peers, they are positively pressured to seek validation and confidence as they share their experience in the next learning meeting.

When it comes to breaking through a lack of motivation, it can be necessary to have private conversations with those who still resist change even after your otherwise successful efforts to motivate people. This will signal your genuine concern to these individuals. Make sure they know they are safe speaking their fears to you. Let them know that by opening up to you, it will allow you to help them overcome their fears. As you continue to push forward with change at the school level, break change efforts down into even smaller steps, as necessary, for these people. That you are taking time to reach out and help them can itself be a very powerful motivator, especially in environments where people are not typically given such personal attention. What matters is that you don't allow them to slow down the momentum of the school at large or let their resistance become an endpoint for school-wide growth. As the coach, you must maintain control and not let go of the goal.

Resistance Reason 2: People don't believe there's a need for change

High resistance to change

Not seeing a need for change is a problem of logic—to those in this group, they see no logic behind suggestions for change. Therefore, it cannot be broken down through logical persuasion. The Heath brothers say the way to break through this reason is to strike an emotional chord. This reason for resistance is exacerbated when the problem is defined only through data. Data is not human and can feel too clinical. But data can represent a human experience, and that is where the Heath brothers advise focusing.

For example, if the problem is that math scores have been low for years and this alone does not convince people to change, then extrapolate this fact into an actual human experience. Low math scores don't only impact students' ability to excel in math class. Low scores will carry over into multiple subjects, especially as children move through grades. Math shows up in science classes and sociology classes. To fail them in math is to fail them in a string of future classes, the repercussions of which will grow increasingly challenging for students to overcome. This can translate into failure to advance to the next grade or dropping out of school entirely. By showing how a problem might snowball and impact actual lives, teachers will be less able to (incorrectly) compartmentalize a problem and see no need for change.

Resistance Reason 3: "We've never done that before"

High resistance to change

People are prone to resisting steps they've never taken before, as they have no proof they'll work or amount to anything but their wasted time. In this case, look for threads of the environment or past initiatives that relate, if even in a small way, to what you are suggesting. Anchor the unfamiliar to the familiar. Or merge your idea into one that already exists and is working.

Let's say a school has almost no relationship with the community and feels overwhelmed by the prospect of having to engage its members. As the coach, you see the opportunity for community members to assist in programs that help students learn about careers and career-relevant skills. Imagine the school has an early release day every month for teachers to collaborate and work on projects. You could suggest freeing up 45 minutes of that time each month to meet with a member of the community to brainstorm ways they could support student learning. Suggest accountability measures, such as *within four months, teachers must have a plan in place to collaborate with a community member*. By fitting a community engagement initiative into a pre-existing structure, it increases familiarity, which increases comfort and openness.

It's common to see this reason for resistance in environments where there is a high fear of failure. If this is the case, it is worth learning why. Have educators been punished in the past for mistakes? Are they not encouraged to take risks? Depending on the cause, this can require private conversations with leadership about how to change the culture to encourage risk-taking—no matter how small or cautious—so that educators will be more open to trying new things in the name of change and growth.

Resistance Reason 4: People were enthusiastic but then lost momentum

Medium/high resistance to change

Overcoming deflated enthusiasm can be tricky, especially if initial efforts didn't lead to expected results. In some cases, restoring momentum can be as simple as reminding teachers how far they've come up to this point, and enumerating and praising specific achievements where possible. In severe cases, disappointment in results to date can cause people to lose faith in themselves and/or their colleagues. In the most extreme cases, usually where it was a big feat to push teachers to try to change in the first place, people can default to negative attitudes, which can be even more entrenched if they were prevalent before change efforts sputtered.

In most cases, momentum is lost when results of change efforts do not materialize as quickly as people expected or wanted. Breaking through this resistance requires managing expectations, celebrating little wins, and changing habits to preclude a tendency toward abandoning efforts when the going gets even a little tough.

To combat unrealistic or self-defeating expectations, the Heath brothers advise teaching a growth mindset. As often as necessary, remind your educators that setbacks and even failure are a part of any big, important effort and change. Reiterate the thrust of Carol Dweck's growth mindset research—that learning and growth are pinned to one's underlying beliefs. If individuals or groups believe they are capable of only so much growth and change, then they will achieve only so much growth and change. If they believe their capacity for growth and change is limitless, then they will develop more perseverance and resilience, which will unlock more progress and growth. Those with a fixed mindset will be more easily discouraged by setbacks. Those with a growth mindset will see setbacks as nothing more than a natural part of the process, not indicators of some inherent personal deficiency or shortcoming. To help educators embrace a growth mindset, use stories from their past, or your past experiences, that highlight successes in spite of temporary setbacks and failures. Explain how failure is nothing more than an opportunity to learn and improve the process.

Amid setbacks and failures, help support momentum by reminding people that they are achieving objectives and are getting closer to goals every day. Make a point to celebrate wins, no matter how small, so that people are always aware that their efforts are having an impact. Praise the effort and then make time to talk through what can be learned from setbacks so that those, too, have meaning as they refine efforts going forward.

By building in these new conversations around setbacks and a growth mindset, you will help your educators create new thought habits. With your guidance, they can begin to see their capacity as individuals and groups as limitless, not tied to anything fixed about themselves. The growth mindset will help to change their thoughts about failure. This in turn will put new thought habits in their place, where a setback doesn't automatically trigger despair and the habit of giving up. Instead, the new and productive habit of looking for meaning and lessons from failure will take its place, which will provide them with the fortitude to "keep on trucking" toward their goals.

Resistance Reason 5: People are stuck in analysis paralysis

Medium resistance to change

Sometimes, when people are so inundated with data, they can't see a way out. In this case, the Heath brothers suggest picking an exit point, no matter how small or unsure. And then, similar to resistance reason 1, use emotion to convince people to take a leap and try a solution.

As an example, let's imagine a school has all kinds of data that show too little rigor in instruction across the board. To connect with teachers on an emotional level, focus on the long-term effects of low-rigor learning (e.g., our students will lack fundamental thinking skills and will fail to compete with their peers for jobs and livelihoods). A possible exit from paralysis could be to have all teachers in the school focus on asking rigorous, high-level questions in their classes every day for two weeks. Then, collect new data to see if it moved the needle. The exit from data overload won't always be obvious or clearly lit. But by starting somewhere, anywhere, we can begin breaking analysis paralysis. If the chosen exit point doesn't elicit results, then you have new information to change the conversation, which can open up new ideas.

Resistance Reason 6: "I'll get to that change tomorrow"

Medium resistance to change

Sometimes procrastination is at the root of resistance, which is usually a symptom of being overwhelmed. In this case, the Heath brothers say shrink the problem down so it can't overwhelm. When I confront this resistance, I put the larger timeline and bigger picture aside and ask teachers to think about one thing they can do this week. It's rare that people can find an excuse not to try one smaller task this week. If they still resist, make the task even smaller, or ask them, "What can you commit to trying this week?" What's key is building in accountability. If you ask people to try one small task this week, also ask them to report back to you, privately or in a meeting, about how it went. In that conversation, you can unpack and analyze their efforts as needed. The point, for now, is to get people to *do* the task, not assess it.

Resistance Reason 7: People are certain "it'll never work"

Medium resistance to change

Show them it will work. That's what's key to overcoming this resistance— prove people wrong, but with patience and empathy. Acknowledge their concerns and fears as to why it won't work, but don't let them stay there. Find examples of where the "it" is working. If educators are certain that students can't answer high-level and rigorous questions, find a classroom where they are. Invite teachers to observe this classroom to note specifically how the teacher is incorporating high-level questioning with success. Find ways to give voice to educators who are well developed in this area.

Let them explain in meetings or professional learning sessions how they meet with success. Or, as needed, look to other schools to find examples of success. If you find an example in a local school, go visit the school with those educators from your school who are showing resistance. If the example is farther afield, invite educators at that school to hold a video conference with your educators to walk them through how they made it work.

Resistance Reason 8: "We know we should be doing this, but we're not"

Medium resistance to change

Knowing isn't enough, as the Heath brothers say. When we know we should be doing something but we aren't, this often stems from exhaustion. This is another opportunity to break plans down into smaller, more manageable steps. Collaboration and accountability can be very powerful here. Where appropriate, suggest that people work in pairs or teams so that the work can feel less overwhelming and even somewhat social. Working with others also builds in natural accountability. Activities can be simple and lightweight in the beginning. As an example, you could suggest that small groups of educators do a classroom visit to observe a best practice. Then they can meet as a group for twenty minutes to decide on one simple thing each can try in their classrooms in the next week.

Resistance Reason 9: Most people agree change is needed, but nothing is happening

Medium resistance to change

When the starting gun has gone off and no one has left the starting line, this is typically because of two reasons: people cannot see the path forward, or they only see a roadblock. If the problem is due to the former, the problem comes from a lack of clarity. Begin by making the end goal explicit and understood. Vision cast as needed. Then back into a series of smaller goals that serve to light the path forward.

As an example, say you are working with the school to increase relevance in instruction. Explain what relevance is and why it's important, but also be sure to *show* them, to ensure total clarity and understanding of what you are asking them to achieve and do. Show videos of exemplary relevant instruction. Discuss research-based ways to boost relevance in instruction, and then model it. Then work together to break the end goal down into smaller yet still explicitly clear and definable steps.

If lighting the path still doesn't motivate people to take action, look for the roadblocks that could be standing in their way. These roadblocks can be structural, attitudinal, or logistical. Let's say one of the action steps you propose for relevant instruction is creating more interdisciplinary learning opportunities. Doing so will require educator planning and collaboration. Let's say your educators are clear on why interdisciplinary learning opportunities are so important, but they still haven't moved to make them happen. What might be in their way? Do they feel they have to come up with the entire module of lesson plans on their own? If so, help them find interdisciplinary class ideas that they can adapt to their needs. Do they have no time in their week to plan with colleagues? Work with the leadership team to find time teachers can devote only to this effort. Do they believe *they* are capable of this work but lack faith in their colleagues? Discuss the growth mindset with all educators, making a point to show that having a growth mindset about yourself isn't enough. You have to have it for your colleagues as well, or your fixed mindset about them could inadvertently thwart collective efforts.

When Your School Exhibits Low Resistance to Change

If this exercise has allowed you to see that your school is ready for change, that's great news. This will likely allow you to suggest initial changes that are larger in scope and ambition and can move at a relatively faster pace.

What's important to remember here is that it's nearly impossible for every last educator in a school to feel excited about and open to change. As you confront those individual hold-outs who are signaling, in explicit or implicit ways, that they are nervous about how you might make them change, refer to these resistance-to-change reasons and their suggested solutions. Hold private conversations with them to identify the root cause behind their resistance, so that you can help them break through it. This is crucial, because even a few people can begin to stand in the way of everyone else's enthusiasm about change. A small but vocal minority can derail the best-laid plans. Make time to hold one-on-one conversations with those in this minority. Your success relies on them coming around to change.

Completing Your School's Change-Readiness Profile Chart

Recall that after completing part one of the two-part change-analysis process, assessing your capacity to influence change, you began filling out the first part of the Change-Readiness Profile chart. We will now fill out the rest of it so that you have a complete profile picture. To do this, we'll refer back to the insights and data you collected in part two of the change-analysis process, assessing your school's readiness for change.

Look back to where your school fell on the sliding scale of readiness for change. Now, look at your notes from the resistance-to-change root-cause-assessment analytical process. How many times did you note your school demonstrated a resistance reason that had a medium resistance to change? How many times did you note your school demonstrated a resistance reason with a high resistance to change? Consider whether the total effect of the resistance reasons your school demonstrates pushes your school higher or lower (more resistant or less resistant) on the readiness-for-change scale. Do the resistance reasons you've observed in your school make your school appear more resistant to change? Or perhaps somewhat less resistant to change than you'd originally thought? Or about the same?

Ultimately, you are making a judgment call. The point of the two steps of the change-analysis process is to have the basis for that call be as informed and educated as possible. Based on your educated judgment call, you can now complete the Change-Readiness Profile chart. In the "Ambition of Change" and "Pace of Change" sections in the full version of the chart that follows, put an "X" in the two rows that align to your judgment call.

Visit www.leadered.com/coachingredefined to download the full Change-Readiness Profile chart.

RECAP: **Ambition of change** is defined as how challenging or simple goals should be. This is a function of your school's level of resistance to change. **Pace of change** is defined as the speed at which your school can handle implementing goals. It, too, is a function of your school's level of resistance to change.

Your School's Change-Readiness Profile: Completed
(Parts 1 & 2)

Based on the judgment call of your school's readiness for change, indicate the level of resistance in the Ambition of Change and Pace of Change sections of the chart. Mark an "X" in the two rows that align to your school's level of resistance to change. The corresponding adjacent cells, in the next column over, will tell you the appropriate degree of ambition and pace of change you would be wise to suggest in your school-wide improvement plan.

CHANGE-READINESS PROFILE		
Scope of Changes		
Your Capacity to Influence Change		**Recommended Corresponding Scope**
Large		Changes that are **larger** in scope
Medium		Changes that are **moderate** in scope
Small		Changes that are **smaller** in scope
Ambition of Change (degree of difficulty of goals)		
Your School's Resistance-to-Change Level		**Recommended Corresponding Ambition**
Low Resistance		**Challenging** goals
Medium Resistance		**Moderately** challenging (or an appropriate **mix** of moderately challenging and simple goals)
High Resistance		**Simple** goals
Pace of Change		
Your School's Resistance-to-Change Level		**Recommended Corresponding Pace**
Low Resistance		**Faster** pace for changes
Medium Resistance		**Moderate** pace for changes
High Resistance		**Slow** pace for changes

The completed chart is a composite picture of your school's Change-Readiness Profile. Let it guide you in the next chapters, as you work to build the school-wide improvement plan. Specifically, let it help you think through the appropriate mix of scope, ambition, and pace of the goals you suggest and intend to lead your educators through. Remember that honoring the degree of change your school can withstand today is not only a way to signal respect for your educators; it's also a way to set everyone up for the greatest success.

PONDER & POST

Studying the Change-Readiness Profile has helped me understand _____.

#coachingredefined

Chapter 5

Identifying and Prioritizing Improvement Needs

"Change is the law of life. And those who look only to the past or present are certain to miss the future."

President John F. Kennedy

You are now ready for step three of leading school-wide change, and you are one step from having a school-wide improvement plan in hand for your first coaching year. It can be daunting, even paralyzing, to try to figure out where and how to start leading your school through change, especially if a school requires several changes or is highly resistant to them. The process we will move through in chapters 5 and 6 might look dense on the face of it. But it's designed to help you break a complicated task into smaller, more manageable parts so that where to begin leading change becomes readily apparent. This methodical approach will help ensure the most well-thought-out and primed-for-success plan possible.

It is also designed to be a true co-creation. Ultimately, it is the information you've gathered on your listening tour and the first wave of classroom observations—which we will walk through in this chapter—that will drive the components of the school-wide improvement plan. Everything in the plan will come directly from the insights stakeholders have generously shared with you and school data, including the data that come from your observations. As a concrete document that you will share with all educators, the plan is built on inclusion and will keep everyone involved as, all together, you set out to achieve its goals.

The plan, as we will thoughtfully construct it, is also vital for a strategic leadership reason. The technical steps we will go through to identify improvement needs that align to your school's Change-Readiness Profile and to address them from a place of strength will ensure that your plan is built on positivity.

Leading from Positivity

In 2006, Alan Mulally was hired to replace Ford Motor Company's outgoing CEO. Mulally had rescued the Boeing Company (makers of the airplanes that often carry us around the world) from the brink of bankruptcy in his prior post as its CEO, and he'd been hired to pull off a similar trick at Ford. When Mulally took the helm at Ford in September 2006, the company had just endured an annual $12.6 billion loss and was fighting for its life (Gordon, 2017). Just two years later, the American economy fell into the greatest crisis since the Great Depression, dragging economies all over the world down with it (as if anyone needs a reminder).

Like so many companies across industries and countries, American auto companies were in dire straits. The U.S. government offered bailout money—with strings—to General Motors, Chrysler, and Ford, the "Big Three" American automakers. GM and Chrysler took the money and signed onto a range of government requirements around things like restructuring, mass layoffs, business closures, and salary caps. Ford, however, declined.

Mulally was after all in the middle of a multi-year turnaround plan, and he was not interested in changing course and losing momentum by agreeing to government terms and constraints. By 2009, three years after a $12.6 billion loss and one year after the greatest economic crisis in nearly a century, Ford was turning a profit, while GM and Chrysler were still beholden to the U.S. government. He'd also saved tens of thousands of Ford jobs around the globe. Mulally's turnaround of Ford is often regarded as one of the most significant leadership victories in business history. What allowed him to pull the company from the depths of despair in just three years while the global economy was in chaos?

Positive leadership—Mulally's unique and signature brand of leadership. Mulally defines "positive leadership" as ". . . the idea that there is always a way forward" (McKinsey & Company, 2013). In simplest terms, it means remaining positive as you lead. In practice, it means focusing on what's working rather than on what's not. It means looking forward, not backward; not placing blame but finding solutions; not conflating problems with people but always remembering people *have* problems, i.e., they are not a problem.

Mulally's intention was to rally everyone around something positive instead of alienating people by focusing on anything negative. By leading with positivity, he understood that teams can start from strength. It's far easier to get people to start from a place of strength than from a place of weakness. In focusing on strength, the conversation is less susceptible to descending into blame, scapegoating, or in-fighting. Positivity and strength are unifying and move things forward; negativity and weakness are fracturing and keep everything stuck.

In an interview about leading in the 21st century with McKinsey & Co., Mulally described positive leadership further:

> Critical to doing that (finding a way forward) is reinforcing the idea that everyone is included. Everyone is part of the team and everyone's contribution is respected, so everyone should participate. When people feel accountable and included, it is more fun. It is just more rewarding to do things in a supportive environment. (2013)

When Mulally arrived at Ford, departments weren't communicating with each other. They didn't know what the others were working on or toward, and there was rampant finger pointing and blame placing. The first thing he did was create the One Ford plan, which, at the core, was a vision for Ford's future. One Ford presented a picture of what Ford would grow into through clear steps and effort. It was designed to unite all departments around the same goals so trust could be repaired and everyone in the company could work with, not against, each other. Every last Ford employee was expected to know the One Ford plan, embrace it, and focus all work on achieving its goals. Everyone was also required to understand his or her role in achieving the goals, and Mulally focused on always reiterating that everyone was a valued and needed part of realizing One Ford. Essentially, everyone had to become "One Team." In the McKinsey interview, Mullaly continued:

> At the heart of our culture is the One Ford plan, which is essentially our vision for the organization and its mission. And at the heart of the One Ford plan is the phrase "One Team." Those are more than just words. We really expect our colleagues to model certain behaviors. People here really are committed to the enterprise and to each other. They are working for more than themselves. (2013)

When we adopt a mindset of positive leadership, we look for the positive. We are naturally focused on what's working and what our teams are doing well. This allows us to see where and how we can start change from a place of strength. Starting from strength creates the conditions necessary to change people's mind about change; when starting from what they are doing well already, people are motivated and more likely to believe they are capable of doing things better and of doing other things well, too. To start from strength is to start from promise. It provides something hopeful for people to buy into, rather than something negative to push against.

In the next chapter, we will create our equivalent of One Ford, the school-wide improvement plan. We will go through several steps to include the entire school in the process and ally everyone around common goals so that everyone can set out to achieve them as "One Team." But first, we have to do the work that ensures that you choose those goals that will address real improvement needs in your school *and* are of a scope of change and ambition level that your school can withstand.

In this chapter, you will identify improvement needs that, in the next chapter, you will turn into goals. Integral to this work is identifying what the school is currently doing well. This will help you pinpoint the goals that will allow you to start change from strength and positivity. Remember, goals cannot be positive if they are not meeting actual needs or are not aligned to the Change-Readiness Profile. Without first understanding the specific improvement needs that match your school's Change-Readiness Profile, we cannot guarantee that you will arrive at the goals that can rally your educators around positivity and unite them as a team.

Identifying Improvement Needs

Determining the right improvement needs and addressing them in the right order matters. Addressing the right needs at the wrong time could mean asking your educators to work to improve something before they've gained prerequisite skills. This will result in frustration and wasted time. Likewise, asking them to focus where little improvement is needed will result in frustration and wasted time. Tackling needs that are too big or too ambitious might be asking too much of your resistant-to-change school, causing them to lose trust in you and your process.

Based on your listening tour and review of school data, you likely have begun to build a list of improvement areas. In this chapter, we'll take this list a step further by taking any assumptions behind that list—particularly those that directly pertain to instruction—into the classroom to consider as you observe teachers at work. This will provide you with yet more data, sharpen your precision in identifying improvement needs, and support your case as you share your ultimate goals.

In this chapter, we will synthesize data collected so far on your listening tour and in your classroom observations, to arrive at a comprehensive list of improvement needs. We'll use observation data to find what's working well, which, eventually, will reveal your start-from-strength entry point for the improvement plan. Once you have a full list of improvement needs, you'll vet each against your school's Change-Readiness Profile to find the top contenders to become the goals of the plan in the next chapter.

Recall that everything that happens in your school impacts student learning directly or indirectly; both categories of inputs on student learning are fair game as improvement needs in your school-wide plan. First, you'll identify improvement needs that pertain to direct inputs on student learning, which will be determined by conducting the first wave of classroom observations. Then you'll return to notes from your listening tour to identify improvement needs that pertain to indirect inputs on student learning.

Identifying Improvement Needs Pertinent to Direct Inputs on Student Learning

To identify improvements for direct inputs on student learning, which are instructional needs, you need to see the teachers in action through a first wave of classroom observations. Once you are ready to begin one-on-one coaching, you will do additional classroom observations for the teachers you coach; these observations will dig deeper into the specific practice of each coachee. But for our purposes now, the first wave of classroom observations will give you an overview of the level and quality of instruction and learning happening in your school.

Rigor, Relevance, and Engagement Rubrics: A Powerful Tool to Transform Learning

For this first wave and all future classroom observations, I strongly suggest you use a rubric. Without some sort of instructional rubric or framework, you will be without a foundation or context to anchor instructional improvement conversations and frame your suggestions to educators. Rubrics unite parties around clear expectations and a common language to clarify and simplify all coaching conversations. Without some kind of rubric, it is like getting in your car to drive across the country with no map, plan, or ultimate destination.

There are several great rubrics out there, but for the purposes of explaining the work with teachers tangibly, we must decide on one rubric for the book. We will use the Rigor, Relevance, and Engagement rubrics (RRE) to frame classroom observations, identify improvement needs, and, eventually, walk through the nuts and bolts of coaching that can drive real change. In the next part of the book—where we will begin to dive into one-on-one instructional coaching—I will refer back to the RRE rubrics often. (Note that I will also provide considerations to vet and select an equally robust rubric, should you want to use a different one.) For now, though, I will provide an overview of the RRE rubrics. Think about how to use them in your first wave of classroom observations to identify instructional improvement needs that might end up as goals in the school-wide improvement plan.

The RRE rubrics appear in full in Appendix 3 and online at www.leadered.com/coachingredefined.

The RRE concept and rubrics are a product of the International Center for Leadership in Education (ICLE). They were designed to help educators, administrators, and coaches know the hallmarks of truly rigorous, relevant, and engaging learning. They are not scoring rubrics and were not designed to be evaluative; rather, they are a collaborative tool for planning and achieving the kind of instruction that creates for all students a robust learning environment capable of preparing them for long, successful futures.

What makes the RRE rubrics so powerful is that they are hyper-focused on student learning and guide teachers through small steps for instructional improvement. The rubrics have three categories: rigor, relevance, and learner engagement. Rigor captures the depth and complexity of thinking required for any learning task. Relevance speaks to its applicability to real-world and career-ready skills. Learner engagement was added to the rubrics as a means of sustaining rigor and relevance through intentional student motivation, agency, and accountability.

Each rubric category has three indicators—those hallmarks of powerful instruction that signal its presence and depth in instructional design and student learning. Each indicator is divided into four levels of growth, as evidenced in student learning and instructional design: 1-Beginning, 2-Emerging, 3-Developed, or 4-Well Developed.

The nine indicators divided across the three categories are:

1. Rigor indicators: high-level questioning, academic discussion, and thoughtful work
2. Relevance indicators: meaningful work, authentic resources, and learning connections
3. Engagement indicators: active participation, learning environment, formative processes and tools

The four levels of growth represented in the nine indicators are not meant to be evaluative in any sense of the word. They are meant to help you, as the coach, benchmark teachers' and students' progress toward instructional and learning goals, respectively; from there, you can launch a deeper conversation with teachers about planning, practice, and reflection on their road to continued growth.

As with all of the strongest rubrics, the RRE rubrics cut straight to the heart of what makes instruction powerful and effective, both in terms of what the instructional design looks like and entails and what the learning looks like and entails. It's simple, it's succinct, it's lightweight. It's easy for people to grasp and apply to their thinking and work. Importantly, it is without distractions that force the educator and coach to divert attention to factors not directly linked to instruction. Thanks to this combination of ideal attributes, I have found the RRE rubrics to be the most effective at changing instruction and, therefore, student learning.

Protocol for Classroom Observations

Doing a first wave of classroom observations will serve three equally important goals as they relate to the school-wide improvement plan. First, the data that comes from these observations will reveal the school's instructional improvement needs and provide validation to the conclusions you draw from your observations.

Second, the observations will give you coverage. If you were to suggest instructional change without having first gotten into classrooms, teachers would likely be defensive, claiming you couldn't possibly know what they need to change without having seen them teach. In observing instruction before declaring instructional improvement needs, you are taking yet another step to include people in the change process and maintain its status as a true co-creation.

Third, observations are an insurance policy against taking people at their word when it might not be warranted. On your listening tour, most people will be honest with you in their assessments of instruction because most people want to see improvements. But we do need to keep in mind that some people might have an agenda, or simply might not have the information they need to provide an educated assessment of instruction. As an example, an administrator might share an opinion about the school's overall instruction without having been in a classroom in months. Seeing instruction for yourself can only serve you well in serving your school to the best extent.

Most of the suggested protocols I lay out in this section will apply to any and all classroom observations you do as a coach. However, there are a few specific and self-evident points of protocol that will apply only to this first wave of classroom observations. The protocol of successful, respectful, and productive classroom observations fit into five categories: how many observations you should do and how much time you should spend in them; what to do before you start your observations; how to show respect when in the classroom; what to look for as you observe; and how to take notes as you observe that can serve as data to support your conclusions.

Protocol: Number and Duration of Observations

- As a general rule, the more classrooms you can get into, the better. Depending on the size of the school, it might not be possible to get into every classroom. Aim for at least 50 percent and get as close to 100 percent as you can. The more data you have from observations, the better. But you're human, and you don't want to spend so much time observing that you lose time getting to the work of making improvements. Use your best judgment.
- If you cannot observe all classrooms, prioritize observing the teachers you will be coaching.
- If you cannot observe all classrooms, aim to observe classrooms that represent a range of grade levels and subject areas, including the classrooms of the teachers you will be coaching.
- Spend a minimum of 30 minutes in each classroom. Less than 30 minutes isn't fair to teachers and will not give you an adequate picture of their instruction.
- If possible, spend the entire period in the classroom. Doing so will allow you to see how the beginning of the class connects to the end, whether the teacher does an assessment, and if so, how the data is discussed and handled with students.

Protocol: In Advance of Your Classroom Observations

- Familiarize yourself with the RRE rubrics (or the rubrics you intend to use). Doing so will allow you to keep your focus on the teacher and students once you're in the classroom, rather than on the rubrics.
- If you are not an administrator, give a copy of your rubrics to the administrator responsible for instructional improvement. Let the administrator decide if she will provide all teachers with the rubrics in advance of your classroom visit (and if she does, that is fine). Note: in advance of one-on-one coaching, provide every teacher you will be coaching with a copy of the rubrics.
- How much and what kind of notice you give to teachers in advance of your observations is likely a function of school policy. My preference is to let teachers know you will be doing observations over a period of, as an example, two weeks. You should feel comfortable notifying teachers of the specific weeks. But stop short of telling them on which days and at what times. I do not advise ever telling a teacher precisely when you will be observing.

Protocol: Showing Respect in the Classroom

- The most important thing to bear in mind is that you will be entering a classroom that belongs to a teacher and students, not to you. In welcoming you, they are helping you better serve their needs. Respect and gratitude on your part are paramount.
- Make sure the teacher knows when you've entered the room by waving hello or indicating your presence without disrupting the class. If you haven't yet met the teacher, try to introduce yourself so long as it doesn't interrupt the lesson.
- When you leave the classroom, thank the teacher and students for allowing you to join them, so long as it's not a disruption to the class.
- Sitting in the back of the classroom is ideal so that you avoid making the students nervous. With that in mind, try to sit where you can see the teacher and as many students as possible (even if you are looking at their backs; the point is to be able to assess their engagement). Ensure that students cannot see your notes.

- Try to make yourself as much of an observer in the classroom as possible. Try not to disrupt teaching or learning while you're in there.
- Taking video of class sessions can be a powerful tool for teachers to reflect on their practice. While this might be appropriate as you coach individual teachers, taking video is not appropriate in your initial wave of classroom observations; it makes people nervous and self-conscious. (Once it is appropriate in one-on-one coaching, always get your teachers' consent first and take care to avoid filming students.)

Protocol: What to Look for as You Observe Classrooms

- As you observe, above all, you will want to get an idea of who's doing the work, who's doing the thinking, the level of the work, and the level of the thinking. Looking for evidence in each of these four areas is the heart of a classroom observation. Prioritize looking for these characteristics of the instructional experience, especially if you are limited in time.
- Look for indicators that students are or are not engaged, e.g., students are asking and answering questions; students are concentrating on an assignment; some students have their heads on their desks; some students are playing on their phones, etc.
- If there's an opportunity to ask students what they're learning today and why, without disrupting the teacher or the learning, do so. Their answers will provide insights into how relevant and engaging the learning is.
- Look at artifacts of learning; look at what's on the walls or on the teacher's whiteboard. Use your phone to take pictures of such signals of the levels of learning in this classroom so you can consider later how effectively they promote rigor, relevance, and learner engagement. Always avoid taking pictures of students. Double check that the camera sound effect on your phone is turned off so it doesn't distract students or the teacher.
- If students are working on an assignment, try to take a picture of it so that you can later review it for rigor, relevance, and engagement.
- If you walk into a classroom whose students are taking a test or doing a silent reading, you can still observe. Look for clues as to

how engaged students are in the work. Without disrupting the students, ask the teacher if you can have a copy of the test or the reading so you can review it later for indicators of rigor, relevance, and learner engagement.

Protocol: Taking Detailed and Specific Notes that Can Serve as Data

- Taking detailed and specific notes will be vital to generating accurate data from your observations. If you are focused on looking for all nine indicators of the RRE rubrics, you will be distracted from what's happening in the classroom. Instead, focus on taking notes of your observations. Immediately after you leave the classroom, compare your notes to the rubrics. Then write down the growth level (1-Beginning, 2-Emerging, 3-Developed, or 4-Well Developed) of each indicator you saw present in the classroom. Be sure to do this *right after* the observation, while your memory is fresh. To do this, I use the Teacher Visitation Form, which follows.

Visit www.leadered.com/coachingredefined to download the Teacher Visitation Form.

Teacher Visitation Form

Goal of Visit:	
Teacher Visited:	Day / Time:
Teacher Actions	**Student Actions**
Goal of Visit:	
Teacher Visited:	Day / Time:
Teacher Actions	**Student Actions**

- Write down what you see, both the positive and the negative. You will want to, and need to, refer back to what is positive to help you prioritize improvement needs, so that you can start from strength.
- To that end, write down evidence to support what you observe. That is, write down exactly what you hear teachers and students say (as accurately as you can) and exactly what you see happening, e.g., the questions and answers you hear; who's asking questions; who's answering questions; the tools students use, how, and why; the tools the teacher uses, how, and why; how students are or are not showing their engagement; etc. This will help you avoid making assumptions, especially when you refer to your notes later when your memory is not as fresh. Ultimately, when you draw conclusions from your observations about current levels of instruction and the corresponding improvement needs, your notes will function as data. The more precise your notes, the more accurate and objective your conclusions will be, and the more convincing an argument for change you can build.

Drawing Objective vs. Subjective Conclusions: A Matter of Notes

I cannot stress this last protocol point enough. Objective conclusions of your instructional analysis, and the corresponding improvement needs, come from specific and detailed notes. Subjective conclusions of your analysis and improvement needs can result from unclear notes that leave you to make assumptions. If you cannot validate your conclusions with hard evidence, you will appear subjective. This will undermine all the trust you've worked so hard to establish with your educators. When you share your analysis and improvement suggestions, teachers will always ask you for evidence. The stronger the data you've created that you can reference, the more likely they will be to trust you and your conclusions and suggestions.

To help you grasp this point, here are examples of specific notes that lead to objective conclusions and vague notes that can lead to assumptions and, therefore, subjective conclusions.

Specific Notes → Objective Conclusions	Vague Notes → Subjective Conclusions
The teacher asked students the sum of 21 + 34.	The teacher asked low rigor questions.
In their study of the 1960 presidential election, students chose from several authentic resources; e.g., newspaper articles, speeches from and interviews with the candidates, encyclopedias, YouTube footage of the debates, and history textbooks.	Students used authentic resources.
Four students had their heads down; at least six were playing on their phones; nine whispered to classmates throughout the class.	Students were disengaged.

Make a concerted effort to develop a habit of taking detailed notes as you observe. You will thank yourself as you move to the next step—converting this qualitative information into quantitative data that you can then analyze.

Analyzing Classroom Observation Data to Identify Instructional Improvement Needs

To optimize your understanding of this section, reference Appendix 3 and read the RRE rubrics in full. As a quick reference for walking through the observation-data analysis process, the first indicator of the rigor category of the RRE rubrics follows. Notice that it shows what the meaningful work indicator looks like as student learning and as instructional design at each of the four growth levels:

As a matter of protocol, make a habit of analyzing a teacher's growth level across all three RRE categories (rigor, relevance, and learner engagement) immediately after your classroom observation. Write down the growth level the data says your teacher has reached for all nine of the indicators: 1-Beginning, 2-Emerging, 3-Developed, or 4-Well Developed. (You will usually see some degree of all nine indicators; but where you don't, simply do not assign a number to it.) Be sure to keep your notes

Relevance Rubric

Support teachers in building effective instruction based on relevance of experiences to learners. The three indicators for relevance are: meaningful work, authentic resources, and learning connections.

Meaningful Work	1 – Beginning	2 – Emerging	3 – Developed	4 – Well Developed
Student Learning	• Student work is procedural and structured, reflecting a basic understanding of information learned during the lesson/unit. • Student work focuses on class-specific content, with an emphasis on building skills, developing comprehension, or other foundational skills.	• Students think critically about content and apply information learned to address a specific task. Student work demonstrates originality. • Student work requires application of knowledge learned during the lesson/unit.	• Students think critically about content and apply information learned to address a range of cross-disciplinary tasks. Student work demonstrates creativity and originality. • Student work requires real-world predictable and/or unpredictable application that has a direct connection to a career in the related field of study.	• Students think and act critically to curate content and apply information learned to address a range of cross-disciplinary tasks which are both creative and original. • Student work requires the ability to select, organize, and present content through relevant products with multiple solutions.
Instructional Design	• Lesson provides students an opportunity to demonstrate foundational understanding of content.	• Lesson provides students an opportunity to complete a specific task that requires application of knowledge.	• Lesson provides students an opportunity to select from a range of real-world, relevant tasks, using critical thinking about new learning to complete the task.	• Lesson inspires students with an opportunity to think critically about new learning to create their own real-world, relevant tasks.

and analysis separate for each teacher, rather than merging them without record of names and growth levels for each person. You will need this information to identify exemplars to be shared with other teachers, in your one-on-one coaching, and as a record of which teachers might need extra help or support.

Once you've done sufficient classroom observations for your first wave, you will analyze all the data you collected as a composite. You can do this quantitatively or qualitatively—either is fine, and you could even do both. In this chapter, we will complete a qualitative analysis. If you are a numbers person, please see Appendix 4. In this appendix, I explain how to calculate the data you've collected to arrive at a quantitative picture of the school's current and general growth across rigor, relevance, and learner engagement.

Whether you take a qualitative or quantitative approach to analyzing your data, you will be looking for three main things:

1. How strong or weak the school is in all nine indicators across rigor, relevance, and learner engagement.
2. How strong or weak the school is, generally, in each category.
3. In which of the three categories the school is strongest or weakest.

Even if you take a qualitative approach, doing some simple and quick addition will help. In each of the nine indicators, add up how many times you counted each growth level. As an example, you could find that for the thoughtful work rigor indicator, you counted three teachers at level

1-Beginning, four at level 2-Emerging, five at level 3-Developed, and two at level 4-Well Developed. Doing these quick calculations would begin to show you how advanced the school is in each indicator. In turn, this will begin to show you the school's strongest and weakest indicators in each category.

Then you want to add up how many times you identified teachers at each growth level within each rubric category. As an example, you could find that for the rigor category, you identified teachers at level 1-Beginning 12 times, at level 2-Emerging 12 times, at level 3-Developed 10 times, and at level 4-Well Developed eight times. This would begin to paint a picture of where, in which general rubric category, the school is strongest and weakest.

With your classroom-observation experiences and these quick calculations in mind, think through these questions, which will help you identify the school's instructional needs:

- In general, how strong or weak is the school in achieving high levels of rigor in the classroom?
- Of the three rigor indicators, where is the school strongest? Where is it weakest?
- What do you see as the instructional improvement needs for rigor?
- In general, how strong or weak is the school in achieving high levels of relevance in the classroom?
- Of the three relevance indicators, where is the school strongest? Where is it weakest?
- What do you see as the instructional improvement needs for relevance?
- In general, how strong or weak is the school in achieving high levels of learner engagement in the classroom?
- Of the three learner-engagement indicators, where is the school strongest? Where is it weakest?
- What do you see as the instructional improvement needs for learner engagement?
- Of the three RRE categories, in which one is the school strongest? In which one is it weakest?
- In terms of the greatest improvement needs, which category would come first? In that category, which indicator would come first?

- In terms of the improvement need where it would be easiest to achieve quick gains (start from strength), which category would come first? In that category, which indicator would come first?

Using these guiding questions, write a general analysis of what the data is saying about how the school is doing in each of the three rubric categories as well as a general analysis of the school's instruction relative to the rubrics (e.g., the school is strongest in rigor and in need of most help with relevance).

Working from an Example: Fictional Public School 1

Let's bring this process to life with our fictional school, Public School 1, or PS 1. We'll imagine that it's a medium-sized middle school and that you were able to observe 14 of its teachers. To help us grasp its needs, we'll work from the example observation data and data-analysis charts that follow for PS 1.

In the chart, input how many times you observed each indicator level for all indicators within each RRE category. From there, calculate the percentage rate of each level per indicator and each level within a category at large. Beneath the calculations, you will see a fictional analysis of PS 1 based on the data and calculations.

(If this sounds daunting, fret not. In Appendix 4, I will explain in detail how to calculate the data represented in the chart that follows. I will also direct you to download an Excel spreadsheet you can use to auto-calculate your observation data if you use the RRE rubrics. Calculating percentages is a simple process that draws a more precise picture of what the observation data reveals.)

From PS 1's observation analysis, we can identify and list all the school's research-validated instructional improvement needs, which we will next turn into a master list of improvement needs. For our fictional school, the instructional improvement needs would be:

PS 1: Master List of Improvement Needs

- Increase rigor in all classrooms
- Increase level of thoughtful work (rigor)
- Increase level of high-level questioning (rigor)
- Increase level of academic discussion (rigor)

RRE Rubrics: Total Classroom Observation Data & School-Wide Instructional Calculations and Analysis (Example) PS 1 Middle School

RIGOR	Level observed in classroom	1—Beginning	2—Emerging	3—Developed	4—Well Developed	Row totals
Indicator: Thoughtful Work	level # of occurrences	3	5	4	2	14
	% of indicator	21.43%	35.71%	28.57%	14.29%	100.00%
Indicator: High-Level Questioning	level # of occurrences	7	4	1	2	14
	% of indicator	50.00%	28.57%	7.14%	14.29%	100.00%
Indicator: Academic Discussion	level # of occurrences	2	4	4	4	14
	% of indicator	14.29%	28.57%	28.57%	28.57%	100.00%
General Rigor Assessment: column totals	*total level # of occurrences*	*12*	*13*	*9*	*8*	*42*
	% of all 3 indicators	*28.57%*	*30.95%*	*21.43%*	*19.05%*	*100.00%*

RELEVANCE	Level observed in classroom	1—Beginning	2—Emerging	3—Developed	4—Well Developed	Row totals
Indicator: Meaningful Work	level # of occurrences	4	4	4	2	14
	% of indicator	28.57%	28.57%	28.57%	14.29%	100.00%
Indicator: Authentic Resources	level # of occurrences	3	4	7	0	14
	% of indicator	21.43%	28.57%	50.00%	0.00%	100.00%
Indicator: Learning Connections	level # of occurrences	6	6	1	1	14
	% of indicator	42.86%	42.86%	7.14%	7.14%	100.00%
General Relevance Assessment: column totals	*total level # of occurrences*	*13*	*14*	*12*	*3*	*42*
	% of all 3 indicators	*30.95%*	*33.33%*	*28.57%*	*7.14%*	*100.00%*

LEARNER ENGAGEMENT	Level observed in classroom	1–Beginning	2–Emerging	3–Developed	4–Well Developed	Row totals
Indicator: Active Participation	level # of occurrences	0	3	4	7	14
	% of indicator	0.00%	21.43%	28.57%	50.00%	100.00%
Indicator: Learning Environment	level # of occurrences	1	1	6	6	14
	% of indicator	7.14%	7.14%	42.86%	42.86%	100.00%
Indicator: Formative Processes and Tools	level # of occurrences	3	1	8	2	14
	% of indicator	21.43%	7.14%	57.14%	14.29%	100.00%
General Learner Engagement Assessment:	*total level # of occurrences*	*4*	*5*	*18*	*15*	*42*
column totals	*% of all 3 indicators*	*9.52%*	*11.90%*	*42.86%*	*35.71%*	*100.00%*

Rigor Analysis:

Generally, teachers' growth levels are pretty evenly spread in their understanding of and competence in achieving high levels of rigor in the classroom. Yet, rigor is a clear opportunity for growth. Most teachers need help improving levels of rigor in their classrooms. Currently, teachers are strongest in academic discussion and weakest in high-level questioning.

Relevance Analysis:

Of all three categories of the RRE rubrics, teachers demonstrate the weakest evidence of growth on relevance. As of now, they are strongest with authentic resources and weakest in learning connections.

Learner Engagement Analysis:

Of all three categories, teachers showed the greatest growth with learner engagement. They are, more or less, having equal success with active participation and learning environment. The most room for improvement is with formative processes and tools.

General Analysis:

In terms of the scope of improvement needs, the needs are from largest to smallest scope: relevance, rigor, and learner engagement. The school needs most help with relevance, as many teachers struggled to demonstrate an understanding of all three relevance indicators in instruction and learning. In terms of current instructional successes, the most positive starting point with the most likely quick and easy wins would be learner engagement. From there, the next most positive starting point would be in rigor, since more of the school's teachers are having some success with rigor right now. Because relevance will need the most effort and improvement gains, it will be the most challenging.

- Increase relevance in all classrooms
- Increase level of meaningful work (relevance)
- Increase level of authentic resources (relevance)
- Increase level of learning connections (relevance)
- Increase learner engagement where needed
- Increase level of active participation (learner engagement)
- Improve learning environment (learner engagement)
- Improve use and level of formative processes and tools (learner engagement)

Identifying Improvement Needs Pertinent to Indirect Inputs on Student Learning

By and large, the needs that fall under the category of indirect inputs on student learning are those that relate to school culture, school operations, and school-wide instructional programs. Examples that would fall here include, but are not limited to: access to technology; community engagement; social-emotional learning initiatives; equity; systematic supports for struggling students; professional learning; teacher empowerment; openness to innovation; leadership attitudes; teacher attitudes; administrator-and-teacher relationships; communication channels and effectiveness.

To identify improvement needs in this category, refer back to your notes from the listening tour in chapter 3. Which did you note among areas that impact student learning that were in need of improvement? Add them to your master list of improvement needs.

Using our fictional school, we will make up what these needs are and add them to the master list:

PS 1: Master List of Improvement Needs

- Increase relevance in all classrooms
- Increase level of meaningful work (relevance)
- Increase level of authentic resources (relevance)
- Increase level of learning connections (relevance)
- Increase rigor in all classrooms
- Increase level of thoughtful work (rigor)
- Increase level of high-level questioning (rigor)
- Increase level of academic discussion (rigor)

- Increase learner engagement where needed
- Increase level of active participation (learner engagement)
- Improve learning environment (learner engagement)
- Improve use and level of formative processes and tools (learner engagement)
- Grow the number existing community-business partnerships to grow student opportunities for real-world, career-ready learning
- Grow the range and frequency of teacher-led professional learning opportunities for educators
- Share student-learning outcomes and progress with parents in greater detail and with more frequency
- Emphasize academics over sports in school communications and announcements

Aggregating and Prioritizing Improvement Needs

The next step is to match all improvement needs to the level of change your school can handle today. First, we must imagine PS 1's Change-Readiness Profile (that we learned about in chapter 4). Let's imagine that PS 1 has a high resistance to change and that your capacity to influence change is medium. Therefore, the school can handle changes that are moderate in scope, simple in level of ambition, and slow in pace.

We'll refer to PS 1's Change-Readiness Profile to vet each improvement need against two inputs of the profile: scope of change and ambition of change. You will not vet improvement needs against pace of change. This is because the Change-Readiness Profile will dictate the pace of change for any and all improvement goals, which we will address that in the next chapter.

> Refresh: **Scope of change** is <u>defined</u> as the size—how big or small—of changes you can make. It <u>depends</u> on your capacity to influence change, which is a <u>function</u> of your current level of decision-making power at the school, your reputation, and how long you've been working in the school. **Ambition of change** is <u>defined</u> as how challenging or simple goals should be. This is a <u>function</u> of your school's level of resistance to change.

To align improvement needs to change readiness, we will fill out the Improvement Needs & Change-Readiness Profile Alignment. An example of this chart follows, filled out for PS 1. It's helpful first to see the chart, and then I will explain the straightforward process of filling it out for your school.

CHANGE-READINESS PROFILE (Example) PS 1		
Scope of Changes		
Your Capacity to Influence Change		Recommended Corresponding Scope
Large		Changes that are larger in scope
Medium	**X**	**Changes that are moderate in scope**
Small		Changes that are smaller in scope
Ambition of Change (degree of difficulty of goals)		
Your School's Resistance to Change Level		Recommended Corresponding Ambition
Low Resistance		Challenging goals
Medium Resistance		Moderately challenging (or an appropriate mix of moderately challenging and simple goals)
High Resistance	**X**	**Simple goals**
Pace of Change		
Your School's Resistance to Change Level		Recommended Corresponding Pace
Low Resistance		Faster pace for changes
Medium Resistance		Moderate pace for changes
High Resistance	**X**	**Slow pace for changes**

Visit www.leadered.com/coachingredefined to download the Improvement Needs & Change-Readiness Profile Alignment template that you can use for your own school.

We begin by putting an "X" in the cells at the top of the chart that align to the school's scope of changes and ambition of changes, i.e., moderate in scope and simple in ambition. These capture the maximum levels of intensity the school can handle in scope and ambition, or the school's change threshold.

Then we list each improvement need in the chart. For each improvement need, we'll use our experience and best judgment to determine the scope of change that would be required for each, as well as the level of ambition each would take to achieve as a goal. If you're unsure, consult your PLN or trusted colleagues who've had experience managing change or who are intimately familiar with the school's educators. In the chart, we'll then put an "X" in the cells that match the school's improvement need's maximum scope and ambition, its change threshold, i.e., moderate and small in scope and simple in ambition.

Keep in mind: an improvement need cannot go beyond the school's change threshold. In our example, PS 1 can handle changes that are moderate in scope; therefore, it can handle changes that are small in scope, but cannot handle changes that are large in scope. The school can handle only simple ambition; therefore, it cannot handle goals that are moderately challenging or challenging. When you put an "X" in each cell that falls within the change threshold, what will emerge is a picture of which improvement needs currently do and do not meet the school's Change-Readiness Profile.

As stated in the chart's key, the two columns with a darker border represent the school's change threshold, the most intense level of change the school can withstand. The light blue shading refers to the columns that fall within the school's change threshold (moderate and small in scope and simple in ambition). The rows in italicized font indicate those improvement needs that are within the school's change threshold but are not in total alignment with the maximum threshold; they are small in scope as opposed to medium in scope. Lastly, the bolded font and bold-bordered improvement needs are those that are in total alignment with the change profile: they are both moderate in scope and simple in ambition.

Per the analysis stated with the chart, there are four improvement needs that totally align to PS 1's change profile: 1) Increase learner engagement; 2) Increase level of academic discussion (rigor); 3) Share student learning outcomes and progress with parents in greater detail and with more frequency; and 4) Emphasize academics over sports in school communications and announcements. These will be the needs that, in the next chapter, we will convert into goals and then vet for their potential to start school-wide improvement from strength.

Please visit www.leadered.com/coachingredefined to download the Improvement Needs & Change-Readiness Profile Alignment template that you can use for your own school.

IMPROVEMENT NEEDS & CHANGE-READINESS PROFILE ALIGNMENT
(Example) PS 1 Middle School

		Scope of Changes			Ambition of Changes		
		Large in scope	Moderate in Scope	Small in Scope	Challenging	Moderately Challenging	Simple
Your school's Change-Readiness Profile is: →			X				X
Improvement Need ↓	The need/change is: ↗						
Increase rigor			X			X	
Increase level of thoughtful work (rigor)			X			X	
Increase level of high-level questioning (rigor)			X			X	
Increase level of academic discussion (rigor)			**X**				**X**
Increase relevance			X		X		
Increase level of meaningful work (relevance)			X		X		
Increase level of authentic resources (relevance)			X			X	
Increase level of learning connections (relevance)			X		X		
Increase learner engagement			**X**				**X**
Increase level of active participation (learner engagement)				X			X
Improve learning environment (learner engagement)				X			X
Improve use of formative processes & tools (learner engagement)				X			X
Grow the number existing community business partnerships to grow student opportunities for real-world, career-ready learning		X			X		

Grow the range and frequency of teacher-led professional learning opportunities for educators	X			X
Share student-learning outcomes and progress with parents in greater detail and with more frequency		X		X
Emphasize academics over sports in school communications and announcements		X		X

Note: Our fictional PS 1 school can handle changes that are **moderate in scope** and **simple in ambition**; changes that meet these levels meet the school's **change threshold** or maximum capacity for change. Changes that are small in scope fall *within* its change threshold.

Note: The pace of change input of your school's Change-Readiness Profile is omitted here. No matter the improvement needs that align to the scope and ambition the school can withstand, and thus those that will become goals in the school-wide improvement plan, the pace it can withstand will dictate the pace of the goal, not the other way around.

Key:

• The darker borders around the "moderate in scope" and "simple" columns represent the school's change threshold, or the maximum capacity of change the school can withstand (i.e., excluding, in this case, needs that are small in scope); for PS 1, that is moderate in scope and simple in ambition.

• Light blue shading indicates which improvement needs fall *within* the school's Change-Readiness Profile threshold or maximum capacity for change, i.e., moderate to small in scope and simple in ambition.

• The rows in bold font and with a bold border represent those improvement needs that totally align to the school's Change-Readiness Profile threshold.

• The rows in italicized font represent those needs that fall *under* the school's Change-Readiness Profile capacity, meaning only up to the point of needs small in scope.

Analysis: In this example, the school can handle changes moderate in scope (and therefore small in scope, as well) and of simple ambition. The improvement needs in total alignment with the school's change-readiness capacity are:

1. Increase learner engagement;
2. Increase level of academic discussion (rigor);
3. Share student learning outcomes and progress with parents in greater detail and with more frequency;
4. Emphasize academics over sports in school communications and announcements.

If, after going through this process with your school's improvement needs, you do not have any improvement needs that totally align to your school's Change-Readiness Profile, that is OK. Work with those that at least fall *within* the change threshold, even if at a lower intensity than your school can withstand. In our example, those would include the italicized improvement needs that are only small in scope. Bear in mind that the italicized improvement needs can be used in conjunction with needs that are in total alignment to the school's change profile if they help you achieve an appropriate mix of scope, ambition, and pace, to stay within the change threshold.

If you find yourself in a situation where all improvement needs are larger in scope and ambition than your school can withstand, don't panic. This is common in schools with both a very high resistance to change and a long list of big improvement needs. In this scenario, you will want to find the need that most closely aligns to your school's Change-Readiness Profile and turn it into multiple smaller needs. Break it into as many smaller component parts as it takes to identify at least one improvement need that does align to your school's Change-Readiness Profile.

Thank you for sticking with me through this highly technical process. I assure you that when you do this for your school, your educators will thank you and respect you for your thoughtfulness and care in identifying improvement needs that land in that sweet spot—where they are both important and real, *as well as* aligned to how much change the school can handle right now. They will also thank you when, in the next chapter, you build from the needs that hit their sweet spot to find your starting goal—that goal that will allow you to start from strength.

You're now ready to create your "One Ford" school-wide improvement plan and rally all your educators around positivity to function as a true "One Team."

PONDER & POST

One way I can lead with positivity and strength is _____.

#coachingredefined

Chapter 6

Building and Implementing the School-Wide Instructional Improvement Plan

"Leadership requires two things: a vision of the world that does not yet exist and the ability to communicate it."

Simon Sinek, author, motivational speaker, and organizational consultant

In 2006, Alan Mulally was on a plane back home to Seattle after taking meetings in Detroit with Ford executives who were recruiting him to take over the CEO role. It's said that it was on this flight that Mulally crafted a framework to save Ford from bankruptcy. As the first step, he wrote, "Clear, compelling vision going forward." Once he became Ford's CEO, Mulally would formulate that framework into the One Ford plan to unite the entire company around the same goals and, therefore, make it a fact that everyone at Ford was on the same One Team (Gallo, 2012).

While One Ford was a plan, it was first and foremost a vision. Before Mulally led the company through the process of implementing the plan, he used it to vision cast. Recall the instructional coach's real values from chapter 2. Vision casting is a skill you will use again and again as a coach. You will use it on yourself throughout all your coaching work to ensure you stay pointed in the direction of growth and personal mastery. You will use it throughout your co-creation and coaching with each individual educator. In your collaboration with others, it will likely show up for the first time as you introduce the school-wide improvement plan. The plan will serve as a functional plan; and it will also serve as the launch pad for the entire team banding together to realize a specific vision of growth, change, and improvement.

In this chapter, we will tackle the final step of leading school-wide change. This involves the final sub-steps that go into building the school-wide improvement plan. We will convert improvement needs into goals and then prioritize those goals so that you start from strength. I'll guide you through the process of winning buy-in to keep everyone feeling included in change and vital to its success. Lastly, I will show you how to cast a vision of school-wide improvement and lead the implementation process such that you maximize your chances for success.

Turning Aligned Improvement Needs into Goals

To begin, let's return to the list of improvement needs we determined align to PS 1's Change-Readiness Profile in the last chapter. We'll convert these into the goals, one of which we will use to start change from strength.

Turning needs into goals is a straightforward process. It comes down to two main factors: applying best practices pertinent to an improvement need and adapted to your school as necessary; and phrasing the goals as a casted vision that can be imagined, embodied, and observed. Put another way, goals should be clear, specific statements that capture a vision of the best practices you hope the educators will achieve. The art of vision casting your plan starts with how you word its goals; they should be written in such a way that educators can read them and imagine themselves doing what the goals lay out.

To bring specificity to goals, you will rely on two more of your coach's real values: lifelong learning and commitment to instructional skill building. One of the improvement needs from our fictional PS 1 school is to share student-learning outcomes and progress with parents in greater detail and with more frequency. Turning this into a goal requires knowing some best practices around it. As needed, rely on research or experience to identify appropriate best practices for each goal. Consult trusted sources or your PLN to help you bring specificity to your goals.

Research about sharing student-learning outcomes and progress with parents might say that, as a best practice, student progress should be data rich and inform parents of the plan that a teacher and a student have crafted for continued improvement. Your experience might tell you that for middle school students, bi-monthly progress reports have been effective at updating parents regularly enough without overwhelming them. Such best practices and insights will help bring enough detail to your goal that an educator can visualize putting into practice.

When it comes to specifying direct instructional improvement goals, the same process of finding best practices applies. Instructional rubrics, though, are also helpful, as they often have the exact language that shows what highly effective instruction and the intended learning results look like at proficiency.

Remember, though, to adapt any best practices to your school's culture, protocol, or requirements where necessary. To work against culture is to set yourself up for frustration, slow progress, or no progress. Culture is changed, after all, through steady improvements from the inside out.

To walk through an example, we'll use the aligned improvement needs from PS 1. We found four needs that were in total alignment with the school's change profile, each of which we'll turn into goals that qualify as a vision cast.

Start from Strength & Build on Positivity

Not every goal will necessarily be addressed immediately in the school-wide improvement plan. Some might even have to wait until the next school year. Your first task with the goals you've articulated is to determine which one or ones will allow a positive entry point to change. The positive entry point will dictate the strategic order in which to tackle your goals such that you strike the right balance between focus and continually building and maintaining positive momentum.

CONVERTING IMPROVEMENT NEEDS INTO GOALS (Example) PS 1 Middle School		
Improvement Need	→	Goal
Increase learner engagement	→	Teachers will build upon their developing skills for all three indicators of learner engagement: active participation, learning environment, and formative processes and tools. Teachers will broaden their suite of instructional tools and best practices to achieve a Well-Developed level with ease in all three indicators. Students will be capable of monitoring their own class participation, as enabled by a learning environment that has defined learning procedures but maintained flexibility in how students apply them. Formative processes are frequently used to differentiate instruction just-in-time.
Increase level of academic discussion (rigor)	→	Teachers will become skilled and facile in applying a range of best practices to elevate the level of academic discussion in class. The teacher will become more of a facilitator and overseer of dialogue. Meanwhile, students will drive conversation that is less reliant on Q&A and more reliant on engaging in a thoughtful inquiry of a concept, through which students share evidence-based opinions and provide respectful feedback to each other. Students stay focused and use content-rich vocabulary.
Share student learning outcomes and progress with parents in greater detail and with more frequency	→	Teachers will develop a habit of sharing student progress toward the current learning outcomes with parents through an emailed report twice a month. The report will be a form sheet that requires data to show a student's growth or current point of struggle. It will also include an overview of the plan the student and teacher have devised to overcome struggle and/or continue growth in the next two weeks. Parents will be encouraged to sign up for the school's app, which informs parents of any recorded grades.
Emphasize academic accomplishments in school communications and announcements	→	Academic achievements (at the individual, class, or school level) and notable academic events will constitute at least 51% of time/space in all student and community channels of communication, including but not limited to: weekly PA announcements; student newsletter; community newsletter; publicly shared social media posts; signs and posters on the school's community-space walls. They will also be included in all pep rallies.

Starting from Strength: Finding Goal #1

The plan for school-wide improvement will fall flat if you start from a place of weakness or negativity. Recall Mulally's definition of positive leadership: ". . . the idea that there is always a way forward" (McKinsey & Company, 2013). A way forward is going to be much more easily accessed from current forward momentum. If we are to use positive leadership, we will need to find what's working and begin making changes from there.

To determine the goal(s) that will allow you to start from strength, think through the following three considerations:

1. Refer back to your listening-tour notes to recall what your school is doing well today in terms of indirect and/or direct inputs on student learning. Do your goals link to any of these current successes? If there is not one program or initiative that's working well as a whole, find a part or feature of a program/initiative that is working well and that you might be able to link to a goal.

Let's use PS 1's goal around emphasizing academics over sports in school communications and announcements. (Note: for efficiency, I will refer to our goals in this conversation in wording similar to when they were still only instructional needs. But please know this is just for brevity, and that in the plan, we will write them fully as vision-casted goals.) Imagine that you learned on your listening tour that the school makes a PA announcement once a week about sports. You also noted when walking the halls that there is a bulletin board in the cafeteria regularly updated with sports information. Lastly, you read a few issues of the monthly student newsletter, which is put together by students, also featuring sports. You conclude that there are currently several channels of communication in use, but without attention to academic achievements. You see opportunity in praising current use of communication channels and suggesting that they embed academic news into them.

For PS 1, we will say that there is an opportunity to start from strength for the goal of emphasizing academic achievements alongside sports achievements.

On the other hand, let's say that in terms of the goal of sharing more student progress with parents, you do not presently see any low hanging fruit to start from strength. Currently, the school has no procedures in place for teachers to interact directly with parents outside of once-a-semester parent-teacher conferences. As a goal on its own, it would not present an opportunity to start from strength.

2. In terms of instructional improvement goals, which one or ones can you start by linking to a related area where teachers are already somewhat proficient or advanced?

PS 1 has two instructional goals: increasing learner engagement and improving academic discussion (rigor). If we review the RRE Rubrics: the Total Classroom Observation-Data & School-Wide Instructional Analysis chart from the last chapter (that chart that captured our analysis of instruction and learning after our first wave of classroom observations), we can see where there might be opportunities to start improvement from strength in learner engagement and rigor.

Our observation data and analysis showed us that of all three rubric categories, PS 1 is strongest in learner engagement. Within learner engagement, the school is more or less equally strong in active participation and learning environment, and weakest in using formative processes and tools. An argument could be made that starting with any indicator of learner engagement is starting from strength, as you can frame any goal as building upon current success in engaging students in their learning.

In terms of academic discussion, recall that observation data and analysis showed a relatively even spread across all four growth levels for all three rigor indicators. In other words, the school is doing OK with rigor, *and* improvement is clearly needed. Presently, academic discussion is the strongest indicator in the school's classrooms. Therefore, there is no other momentum in this category from which academic discussion could launch; it would have to build upon itself, which might not be strong enough. While academic discussion could be used as a positive entry point to general improvements in rigor, it would likely benefit from first piggybacking off of more positive momentum built elsewhere.

3. Which goal might allow for an easy and relatively quick improvement or "win" that will boost confidence and build momentum where there is little to none?

This consideration is most relevant in schools that have poor performance metrics across the board and a high resistance to change. These are the schools where no improvement needs align to the school's Change-Readiness Profile, and therefore have to be broken down into a series of smaller needs. In turn, those will be turned into smaller goals. The idea here is first to tackle the goal that will afford a quick, easy win to begin changing people's opinions of change and encouraging them to see themselves as capable of it. Of course, you will still need to start from strength, however small.

Let's say you're in a school that must boost literacy scores before they can consider any other student learning improvements, yet there are no obvious glimmers of hope in current literacy data. When there are no instructional or learning strengths, look for something structural or logistical that is working. Is there an instructional process to which you can pin initial changes?

Perhaps the school has a pretty good track record of attendance in a weekly instructional meeting, but the meetings are unfocused, unstructured, and are not offering value to teachers. Start with the meeting. Praise teachers for showing up to meetings week after week, as it shows they care. Then, until further notice, make the focus of every meeting a literacy strategy that all teachers will be required to practice in the next week. Build in accountability by asking each to be prepared to report back on how it went in the next meeting. Be sure to celebrate wins and praise efforts in every meeting to build positive momentum. Move onto a new literacy strategy once teachers demonstrate proficiency in the prior one.

Only in schools that are exceptional and everyone is enthusiastic about change do I advise *considering* starting from a place of weakness. Even in schools where performance is good and most people are ready for change, it can be discouraging to start from a place of failure or deficit. There is no easier way to squash all the goodwill you generated on the listening tour and damage the trust and relationships you have begun to nurture than to start from struggle.

Reflecting on the three considerations, note all of your goals that have great potential to start change from strength. You might find that you have only one goal you can start from strength, and thus, your entry point to change is clear. If you have more than one, you'll need to consider them relative to each other and to your school's Change-Readiness Profile, which we'll walk through next.

For PS 1, we found two goals with the potential to start from strength: increasing learner engagement and emphasizing academics in school communications. Revisiting the school's Change-Readiness Profile (included in chapter 5), we recall that the school has a high resistance to change and your capacity to influence change is medium. In other words, the school's change threshold is moderate in scope and simple in ambition; it can tolerate changes only at a slow pace. Using your judgment, you might decide that before beginning to change things in the classroom (which could feel very personal to teachers with a high resistance to change), you might begin changing things in the hallways and announcements.

Building on Positivity: Ordering Goals to Maintain Momentum

For PS 1, our first change goal will be around bringing academic achievements into majority focus in the school's announcements, student newspaper, and across its PA system. But how do you know when to begin achieving other goals, and in what order? And how fast? Answering these questions will be necessary to build a comprehensive and fully thought out school-wide plan.

This decision is part continued analysis of the goals, as measured against your school's Change-Readiness Profile, and part educated judgment call. As you plan the goals to move through in the order that your school can withstand in a year, you'll seek to strike a balance between focus and maintaining positive momentum. Another way to say this is that you want to strike a balance between not getting distracted and not thwarting momentum by taking on a goal the school is not ready for.

Given that our fictional PS 1 teachers have a high resistance to change and your capacity to influence change is medium, they will be best served if the process of meeting goals moves at a relatively slow pace. The goal of emphasizing academic accomplishments in school communications and announcements will afford some quick, easy wins. Therefore, you can consider starting work on a second goal soon after sufficient milestones have been passed on this first goal.

With PS 1, the obvious second goal choice is learner engagement, as it has plenty of start-from-strength opportunities. Let's say you have reason to believe that, even after some positive momentum gained from the first goal, most teachers will still resist change in their classrooms. So, you make the decision to begin improving learner engagement through its strongest indicator today, which is active participation. The start to your second goal, then, is improving active participation such that all teachers can grow to a Well-Developed growth level. From there, you can move onto the other two learner-engagement indicators in an order that maintains positive momentum.

What will be your third goal: improving academic discussion (rigor) or devising a process for teachers to share student learning outcomes and progress with parents? Recall that there was no start-from-strength entry point for the latter goal. So, let's select improving academic discussion as our third goal. At this point, there will be sufficient positive momentum from learner engagement successes to move onto academic discussion; you can link success in achieving across-the-board growth in learner engagement to doing the same for academic discussion.

Once teachers reach Well-Developed in academic discussion, you will face a question: should you focus on rigor in general, despite the fact that improving in the other two indicators were not goals that totally aligned with your school's change profile? Or should you move onto the next goal that did align, developing a process for teachers to regularly share student-learning progress with parents? You will inevitably face this kind of question as you prioritize your goals for the improvement plan. In most cases, answering it will be a judgment call largely based on which approach you feel will keep momentum positive and not thwart progress.

In our example, we make a judgment call to focus on rigor; we determine that interrupting rigor improvement to introduce an entirely different goal that has no positive entry point would thwart momentum. We reasonably expect to generate sufficient positive momentum in guiding all teachers toward rigor proficiency that the school can then handle an entirely different goal that will require introducing some new protocol and structure. In other words, by that point, the success to date in and of itself will be an entry point to a new goal.

For PS 1, we now have what we believe are the goals the school can manage in year one and in this order: 1) Emphasize academics in school communications; 2) Increase learner engagement in all three indicators;

3) Increase rigor in all three indicators (Note: this change from increasing rigor only in academic discussion is based on the judgment call we just made); 4) Develop a process and protocol for teachers to share detailed student progress updates with parents regularly.

As you can see, this is a qualitative process more than a quantitative one. Use your best judgment. Where you're unsure or hesitant to make a judgment call, talk to a trusted advisor or someone at the school with more experience working with its educators than you've had.

The example we walked through touched on only a handful of the many different factors and possible scenarios when prioritizing goals for a school-wide improvement plan. As a guide, here are questions to ask yourself as you rank, order and evolve the goals that you will address in one year, with the intention of helping you think through other possible factors and scenarios:

- Can the school handle working toward more than one goal at once?
- What is the ideal pace for each goal?
- Are there other improvement needs that are smaller in scope or ambition than the school's change threshold that the school could potentially work on simultaneously with another goal?
- Are there too many goals for the school to handle realistically in one year? If so, which one(s) could or should be saved for next year?
- Are there too few goals to fill the school year? If so, which additional improvement needs should also be turned into goals for this year?

Sharing Goals with Educators

We have one last step before we get to writing the improvement plan, which is to share your goals with all educators. Recall that as part of his One Ford and One Team initiative, Alan Mulally made sure that everyone in the company felt included, and needed, in the change process. You will, of course, get stakeholder buy-in for the final plan. But it's wise first to get buy-in for the goals you've established, as they are the foundation of the plan. Doing so is yet another signal of respect, which will fortify trust in you and your change process. It also demonstrates that you want all the educators involved in the process and see them as an integral part of it.

If you are not an administrator, first run your goals by someone who can approve them before sharing them with educators. Be prepared to cite the data that validates your decisions around which goals to address and in what order.

Once you and an administrator are in agreement about goals, I suggest holding a school-wide meeting to share your goals with the entire staff. Outline your goals and explain how you arrived at each and why you have decided to move through them in a specific order. I encourage you to reference your RRE observation-data analysis with the staff. Do not hesitate to be transparent about what you observed and the conclusions you drew in your classroom observations. The data will validate your conclusions about the current state of instruction at the school as well as the improvement needs you see.

This is also an opportunity to begin vision casting for your goals. Frame each of them around what's positive. That is, explain that you have chosen goals because they build from strengths (or, for later goals, will build upon strengths gained by that point). Emphasize what the school is currently doing well and that this shows you that the school and its teachers have great potential and a growing track record. As you describe your goals, use vivid, specific language of what they will look like in practice. Describe what achieving this goal will mean for teachers and students.

In addition to beginning the work of unifying all educators around shared goals, positivity, and strength, there is a tactical benefit to detailing goals with them: hearing their ideas. As I outline and explain my goals for the school, I ask teachers for ideas to achieve these goals. In more cases than not, they suggest great ideas that I hadn't thought of. Write them down when they suggest them to you, as you will often put them into the school-wide improvement plan. In doing this, you take yet another step to ensure that your process of leading change and instructional improvement is a true co-creation.

As you explain goals to both administrators and teachers, ask them to make sure you aren't missing any critical considerations that might preclude certain goals from happening in the near term or might require a reprioritization of them. I was recently asked to help a school system improve math performance. After doing my listening tour and identifying needs, it was evident that there was a pervasive culture of low student and teacher expectations. When it came time for me to present my goals to administrators, I prioritized improving culture before an exclusive focus on math instruction. Afterward, the superintendent pulled me aside and respectfully asked that for now, we focus only on math. He confided that the school was under intense pressure from multiple stakeholders to improve math scores in the year.

Such scenarios will come up. What matters is that you let go of your preference in timing and sequencing rather than letting go of the goals you know will unlock the greatest growth potential in the school. What this principal and I decided was that for the school year, we'd have a laser focus on math scores. And in the next year, we'd begin pursuing goals to improve the culture and lead the school toward growing into a place of high expectations for all.

Trust your research and data. Trust this process to lead you to the appropriate goals for your school. And trust yourself and your educators to get to them, even if the timeline must change due to realities or special circumstances.

Building the Yearlong, School-Wide Instructional Improvement Plan

At long last, you are ready to write the school-wide instructional improvement plan. Thank you for moving through the many steps and methodical approach to this process. Each has helped you arrive at this point, as prepared as possible, to create a plan custom tailored to your school's needs and change profile. It has you as prepared as you could be for great success.

Before we get into the nuts and bolts of the plan, always keep this in mind: you are building a *yearlong* plan. You don't have to turn your school into an exemplar overnight! It will likely take a few years. Turning a big ship around is no hasty process. You simply have to start smart, keep reassessing progress, and update the plan or make new plans as needed. One year at a time, and one goal at a time.

On that point, you will revisit this plan throughout the year. As things evolve and grow, you might find that you need to change parts of the plan, reorder goals, prioritize new ones, and put original ones on the back burner. You might also find your educators are moving faster or slower than you expected. In the case of the former, you will likely be able to address more goals in the first year than you'd thought. In the case of the latter, you will need to plan for ways to better support your team so that progress, even if slowed, can be maintained. Flexibility is important. However, never deviate from the ultimate goal: improving instruction and learner outcomes. To some degree, always be sure to be working on at least one goal that keeps student interests first.

Lastly, always remember the principal purpose and power of your plan: Having a plan and sharing it with educators are critical steps in uniting the entire school around a shared vision and common goals such that everyone can feel part of one team.

School-Wide Instructional Improvement Plan Template

How you document your plan is up to you. I use a template, which I will share here, that I fill out for every goal. Use a format and approach that works for you. Take care, however you format yours, to address each of the sections I include in my template to ensure all the necessary details for success are in place: goal; goal time frame; strategy; tactics; action steps; step time frame; resources; progress indicators; and reflection statement. In the generic template that follows, I explain each of these steps.

Visit www.leadered.com/ coachingredefined to download the following Yearlong School-Wide Instructional Improvement Plan Template.

First, a refresher in how to determine and differentiate goals, strategies, and tactics: Begin by identifying the goal, or the <u>result</u> you'd like to achieve to support school-wide instructional improvement. Then we determine an appropriate strategy, or <u>how</u> you will go about achieving that goal. Lastly, you identify the tactics, or <u>what</u> you will <u>do</u> to implement the strategy and work to achieve the goal.

Note that the word "strategy" is used differently in the school-wide improvement plan from when we discuss "instructional strategies." Often, instructional strategies, as we are accustomed to using the term, will appear in the "tactics" section of the improvement plan, as instructional strategies are often the "what" that can fulfill "how" to achieve a goal.

Yearlong School-Wide Instructional Improvement Plan: Template

Goal: *The goal is the RESULT you'd like to achieve to support school-wide instructional improvement. Your first goal will be the goal you determined allows the school to start from strength; it is the goal that links an improvement need that fits your school's Change-Readiness Profile to something the school is doing well today, so that you are starting change efforts from a positive place.*

Build the goal as a vision-casted goal, such that all staff and stakeholders can envision what the school, they, instruction, and student learning will be like upon goal achievement.

Goal time frame: *Be realistic as you set the time frame within which you will ask educators to achieve this goal. It is at this point that you will consider the pace of change you determined your school can withstand. Again, refer to your school's Change-Readiness Profile.*

Keep in mind that toward the end of one goal, you will often begin implementing the next one; the degree of overlap between goals will be a function of the school's Change-Readiness Profile. Also, keep in mind that you might find you can speed up the goal time frame or you need to slow it down. The progress indicators and reflection questions will help you maintain a pulse on how well the school is progressing toward goals and if the pace is supporting or thwarting progress—by being either too fast or too slow.

Strategy: *Where the goal is the RESULT you want to achieve, the strategy is HOW you intend to achieve it. Bigger goals can have multiple strategies.*

Tactics: *Tactics are WHAT you will do as you implement the strategy to meet the goal. Please note that instructional strategies (as we're accustomed to using the word "strategies") can often be listed here as tactics because instructional strategies can be "what" you do to fulfill "how" you will achieve a goal.*

Action Step	Step time frame	Resource(s)	Progress Indicator	Reflection Questions / Statements
Break your strategy and tactics down into action steps. List here the first step you will take to begin to meet this goal. Repeat this for as many steps as are required to meet a goal.	By when will this step need to be completed? In your plan, list specific dates here. In our examples, we will use generic "weeks 1–2," and so on, where week 1 is the first week of plan implementation, not the first week of the school year.	What resources are needed to complete this step?	What indicators will you monitor to show progress toward the goal?	I created this column of the chart just for me and any administrators with whom I reflect on progress; I do not include this column when I share the plan with the school. When I build the plan, I will include reflection questions here to consider as each step of the plan is implemented. At the time of any next step and with administrators, we will consider the questions and make notes here.
Include additional steps as needed and fill out the corresponding cells accordingly.				

Let's build the template for our fictional middle school, PS 1, to help you think through and familiarize yourself with completing the template for each goal. We will build the template for PS 1's first two goals, so that we see an example of what this can look like for goals that pertain to both direct and indirect inputs on student learning. To refresh our memories and frame our thinking, PS 1's Change-Readiness Profile is:

CHANGE-READINESS PROFILE (Example) PS 1		
Scope of Changes		
Your Capacity to Influence Change		*Recommended Corresponding Scope*
Medium	**X**	**Changes that are moderate in scope**
Ambition of Change (degree of difficulty of goals)		
Your School's Resistance to Change Level		*Recommended Corresponding Ambition*
High Resistance	**X**	**Simple goals**
Pace of Change		
Your School's Resistance to Change Level		*Recommended Corresponding Pace*
High Resistance	**X**	**Slow pace for changes**

Before we read through the plan for PS 1's first and second goals, a few things to keep in mind:

- While I try to provide a realistic amount of detail, these examples are somewhat more generalized than your goal charts will be. Yours will include specific dates, more specific resources, and they might include specific people and names.
- Remember that the reflection questions/statements are for you (and the principal or other key stakeholders); they will not be shared with the school.

- All the step time frames I lay out in the charts assume a certain pace of teacher growth. Know that step time frames will always be unique to a school and might need to be adjusted (forward or backward) based on the pace of growth as the plan is implemented.
- In the plans, you will see comments in brackets. These are for your clarity; these are not comments that would be in the plan or read by educators.

As you fill out your plan for each goal, consult trusted colleagues or your PLN as needed. Seeking insights from those who've done similar work can be of huge help in choosing strategies, tactics, and action-step breakdowns, as well as possible resources that might help you achieve goals.

Common Goals, Strategies, and Tactics: Possibilities to Consider for Your Plan

While each school-wide instructional improvement plan is unique, in my experience, I often see some goals appear again and again. In an effort to help you complete your improvement plans, I'm including a chart with the most common goals I see, titled Common Improvement-Plan Goals, Strategies, and Tactics Per Resistance-to-Change Level. I also include an example strategy to meet each goal and tactics that can serve each strategy, as calibrated to low-, medium-, and high-resistance schools.

In chapter 3, I mentioned that I had the honor to be included in the Successful Practices Network and AASA's study of the nation's 25 most innovative districts/schools. A team of educators—of which I was one—spent time in each school/district to understand what about their environments enabled innovation that was truly transforming instruction and learning. The result was 25 case studies (available from SPN and AASA) to share the wisdom of these schools/districts with all educators.

Many of the strategies and tactics I include in this chart come from my own experience. Please know that many come from the innovative thinking and doing from these 25 schools/districts that are helping to lead our entire education system into the future. The suggestions in this chart are real and they work.

Yearlong School-Wide Instructional Improvement Plan

(Example) PS 1 Middle School: Goal 1, Emphasize Academics in School Communications

Goal #1: Academic achievements (at the individual, class, or school level) and notable academic events will constitute at least 51% of time/space in all student and community channels of communication, including but not limited to: weekly PA announcements; student newsletter; community newsletter; publicly shared social media posts; signs and posters on the school's community-space walls. They will also be included in all pep rallies.

Goal time frame: Plans will start in week 1 (where week 1 is week 1 of plan implementation, not of the school year). They will evolve and remain in effect for the duration of the school year.

Strategy:

Strategy #1

Build excitement, respect, and appreciation for academic achievement. Ensure everyone in the school understands and believes in the importance and power of academic achievement on student lives such that they want to champion academic achievement when they see it.

Strategy #2

Through formal leadership and engagement opportunities, inspire people to participate in efforts to emphasize academic achievement within and outside of the school.

Tactics:

Aligned to Strategy #1

(Because the school has a high resistance to change) The principal and coach develop an early-stage calendar to use any and all school communication channels—PA announcements; signs and posters in the school's community-space walls, pep rallies, social media—to broadcast academic achievements to all key stakeholder groups (staff, students, parents/ guardians and community) on a fixed schedule and to build positive growth momentum.

The principal will make weekly PA announcements about academic achievements to build momentum.

All staff will be encouraged to use social media to broadcast academic achievements to parents/ guardians and community members.

Students will be encouraged to use the student newspaper and class web pages to share their academic achievements and those of their classmates.

Students and teachers will be encouraged to make signs to hang on community walls that celebrate academic achievements.

Aligned to Strategy #2

The principal and coach will begin recruiting teachers to join or volunteer for the Academic Achievement Announcement Committee (AAAC).

Once formed, the AAAC will take over creation and management of the academic achievement announcement calendar. They will build out the calendar for the rest of the school year and aim to regularly reach all key stakeholder groups through strategic communication channels.

The AAAC will build a formal but simple process for students and staff to submit academic achievements for mention through any and all communication channels.

AAAC will collaborate with the administrator who handles to school's PR to inform this person when they have an achievement worthy of PR outreach for community awareness.

Action Step	Step Time Frame	Resource(s)	Progress Indicator	Reflection Questions / Statements
Step 1: Principal and coach develop early-stage academic achievement communications plans. As needed, they reach out to staff to help broadcast these achievements through various channels.	Weeks 1–2 (where week 1 is week 1 of plan implementation, not of the school year)	Communications channels.	By week 3, there will be at least one academic achievement announcement made through any one communications channel.	In this early stage, which communication channels will reach the most people in all key stakeholder groups?

Action Step	Step Time Frame	Resource(s)	Progress Indicator	Reflection Questions / Statements
Step 2: The principal will begin weekly academic achievement PA announcements.	Weeks 2–3	PA announcements; communications with staff to solicit announcement material.	By week 2, the principal will have reached out to teachers and invited teachers to share prospective achievements for her PA announcement. By week 3, she will be making the weekly announcement.	Are our efforts to solicit high-quality academic achievement announcement material effective? How could they be improved to make more teachers more willing to contribute?
Step 3: The principal and coach will facilitate at least one academic achievement announcement per week through at least one communication channel (in addition to the weekly PA announcement), aiming to reach each stakeholder group at least once a month. (Note: In week 5, the principal and coach will begin to work on goal #2, as sufficient momentum has been generated at this point.)	Weeks 4–12	Conversations with staff to solicit achievement information. All communications channels as needed.	By week 8, there will be at least one weekly academic achievement announcement (in addition to the principal's weekly PA announcement) through a range of communication channels. At least once announcement per month will be intended to reach all stakeholder groups.	Are our early-stage efforts building enough momentum to, in week 10, begin recruiting teachers for AAAC? If not, what can we do to have more success? Which teachers show an interest in joining this effort?

| Step 4: The principal and coach will begin recruiting staff and asking staff to volunteer for AAAC. The AAAC will be formed within one month, and training and planning meetings will be had as needed. | Weeks 10–13 | Conversations with staff. Training and planning meetings. | Conversations to form the AAAC will begin in week 10. By the end of week 12, the AAAC will be formed. By week 13, planning and training meetings will commence. | Are our efforts to market the AAAC to teachers effective? Have we made the experience sufficiently appealing? Have we made it clear how important this effort is to student growth and for cultivating a culture of praise, celebration, and growth mindset?

Are students indicating that they are hearing / seeing / reading announcements? In turn, are they showing more interest and curiosity about academic achievements? |
| Step 5: The AAAC will meet as needed to build an academic achievement announcement calendar through the end of the school year. The calendar will aim to reach each stakeholder at least once per week and strive to, by week 30, account for 51% of all school announcements. The AAAC will get approval and buy-in for their calendar from leadership. | Weeks 13–15 | Meetings and conversations. | By week 14, the AAAC will have a first draft of the calendar. They will seek leadership buy-in and make adjustments accordingly by week 15. | Are we providing enough support and guidance to AAAC members? Do they feel there are enough communication channels available to reach all key stakeholder groups weekly? |

Action Step	Step Time Frame	Resource(s)	Progress Indicator	Reflection Questions / Statements
Step 6: AAAC will establish a process for staff and students to send academic achievements for prospective announcement every week to a point person(s). Once established, AAAC will clearly communicate to the school the process so that they can begin engaging in it.	Weeks 15–17	Team discussion and brainstorms; communication channels; whatever might be needed to build their process of staff and student engagement in academic achievement communications.	By week 16, AAAC will present the plan for their engagement process to leadership. They will adjust plans accordingly. By week 17, the system will be communicated to the entire school and will launch, such that all staff and students begin to engage in the process.	Are we providing enough support and guidance to AAAC members? Is the process they come up with simple enough to spur widespread staff and student engagement? Do they need more resources to create or simplify their process?
Step 7: AAAC will implement and manage the calendar on an ongoing basis. An AAAC team member will volunteer to begin tracking all school announcements to track the percentage of announcements that are and are not academic in nature. One AAAC team member will volunteer to keep an eye out for academic achievements that are worthy of formal PR outreach. When such situations arise, they will communicate to the administrator (in the school or district) in charge of PR.	Weeks 18–end of the school year	Meetings as needed. Utilization of all available and strategic communication channels to meet all key stakeholder groups according to the calendar.	By week 18, the AAAC will be implementing their calendar. Academic announcements will be made weekly through a range of channels. Staff and students will become ever more familiar with the process to submit their ideas for announcements. By week 26, all staff and students will express familiarity with the process and will be actively engaged. By week 30, at least 51% of all school announcements will focus on academic achievement.	Are AAAC members struggling to keep their schedule? If so, how can we help them? Is a meaningful portion of staff and students engaged in the process?

Keep in mind that for any goal there will likely be several strong strategy options. In fact, some goals—especially larger ones—will require more than one strategy. For every strategy, there will likely be several strong tactic possibilities as well. Please do not let this chart limit you. It is intentionally simplified for brevity. Let the school's change profile, circumstances, available resources, and culture dictate which strategies and tactics can best serve your goals. Let this chart simply help you think, provide ideas where they align with your needs, and spark ideas where they don't. Let it also be a guide to differentiating tactics based on the level of resistance to change in your school.

Finally, as a school grows more comfortable with change, you can use more advanced tactics. If your school has a high resistance to change, the idea—and hope—is that the tactics you use at the outset will begin to soften their resistance. As you see evidence of that, you can look to tactics suggested for medium resistance to change and begin using some of them.

Winning Key Stakeholder Buy-in & School-Wide Support for the Plan

Congratulations! You have built the school-wide instructional improvement plan. You are now ready to gain key stakeholder buy-in, introduce it to all educators in the school, and win their approval. This is the fun part, where you get to talk the talk of positive leadership, where you will inspire and rally the entire school around a vision of growth, change, and improvement for students and their futures.

Solicit Key Stakeholder Approval

Before sharing the plan with the school, seek feedback and input on the plan from key stakeholders, such as a lead administrator, if you are not on the administrative team, or additional members of the team if you are. Doing so, again, will signal your respect and make sure you are not missing details or realities that could impede your plan's success. Are there rules or regulations in place that would render any aspects of your plan impossible in this school? Might someone else have insights into why something in your plan might get significant pushback from certain

Yearlong School-Wide Instructional Improvement Plan (Example) PS 1 Middle School: Goal 2, Learner Engagement

Goal #2: Teachers will build upon their developing skills for all three indicators of learner engagement: active participation, learning environment, and formative processes and tools. Teachers will broaden their suite of instructional tools and best practices to achieve a Well-Developed level with ease in all three indicators. Students will be capable of monitoring their own class participation, as enabled by a learning environment that has defined learning procedures yet maintains flexibility in how students apply them. Formative processes are frequently used to differentiate instruction just-in-time.	**Goal time frame:** Plans will start in week 5 (where week 5 is week 5 of plan implementation, not of the school year). Unless teacher growth necessitates a change, plans will last for four months, or through week 20. Ongoing support in the area of learner engagement will take place through individual coaching as needed after week 20.
Strategy: Strategy #1 Guide teachers to further grasp the importance of learner engagement on student learning and toward growing their capacity and comfort using a range of engagement strategies to improve student outcomes. Start from the school's current engagement strength—active participation—to emphasize teachers' successes to date and shore up their confidence in moving toward growth in the other two engagement indicators. Strategy #2 Engage teachers as instructional leaders in supporting colleagues' and the school's ongoing growth in the area of learner engagement.	**Tactics:** Aligned to Strategy #1 The coach will lead professional development in the area of learner engagement over a four-month period. PL will include a general instruction of learner engagement (to establish common language) and an initial deeper focus on active participation. PL will include regularly scheduled learning sessions. After each session, teachers will meet with their PL teams to discuss learnings and commit to trying a new active participation strategy in the upcoming week. In their next PL team meeting, they will be expected to share with each other how it went and discuss issues and solutions together. The coach will attend PL team meetings in full where possible to lead them and offer support.

Strategy (Cont.):	Tactics (Cont.):
	In an ongoing basis, the coach will collect qualitative and quantitative data where possible (from periodic classroom walkthroughs, formal observations, meetings and observing teachers' discussion, etc.) about growth. Once the majority of teachers have demonstrated sufficient growth in active participation, PL will move onto learning environment and formative processes and tools (and repeat aforementioned tactics).
	The coach will incorporate school-wide learner-engagement goals into one-on-one instructional coaching with the teachers, as needed to support and tailor growth.
	<u>Aligned to Strategy #2</u>
	The coach will reach out to a teacher showing strong instructional leadership potential in the area of learner engagement to ask if she would like to begin leading PL sessions.
	The coach will co-lead learner engagement PL sessions with the new instructional leader, gradually handing over more responsibility to them. The coach will remain in attendance at PL sessions even once the leader is leading sessions in full.
	The coach will reach out to teachers on every PL team who show instructional leadership potential to see if one would like to serve as the team instructional leader and team learning manager. (Note: both roles are explained in Chapter 11.) The coach will co-lead meetings with the team instructional leader and gradually release all responsibility to her. At that point, the coach will pop into team meetings to remain an available resource.

Action Step	Step Time Frame	Resource(s)	Progress Indicator	Reflection Questions / Statements
Step 1: The coach reaches out to teachers to ask how they perceive their instruction relative to learner engagement. She supplies them with reflection questions on learner engagement to frame their thinking. (The coach is comparing their perceptions to hers from the initial wave of classroom observations in chapter 5 and any additional observations that might have been conducted since.)	Week 5 (where week 5 is week 5 of plan implementation, not of the school year)	RRE rubric for learner engagement; observation data; Coaching & Observing Learner Engagement: Reflection Questions (Note: We discuss these, and they are listed, in chapter 10)	By the end of week 5, all teachers have provided their perceptions of their instruction relative to learner engagement.	Where do the coach's perceptions of teachers' overall instruction relative to learner engagement align? Where don't they align? What does this say about what needs to be the focus of PL?
Step 2: The coach and principal meet to discuss PL learning plans on learner engagement, including the ideal frequency of PL sessions and PL team meetings. They will be reviewing teachers' perceptions of their instruction and observation to inform PL plans.	Week 6	Teachers' responses to reflection questions; observation data	By the end of week 6, there will be a PL plan and calendar in place for learner engagement. The coach will be prepared to lead the first PL session in week 7.	Based on the school's current skill in learner engagement and teachers' perceptions of it, what is the appropriate cadence of PL? What resources will be needed to achieve the PL plan?

Action	Weeks	Resources	Milestone	Reflection Questions
Step 3: The coach begins PL sessions focused broadly on learner engagement (and developing common language) and deeply on active participation (taking care to emphasize the positive work taking place in this indicator so far). The principal will attend and participate in early PL sessions and as many as possible going forward.	Weeks 7–10	RRE rubric for learner engagement; Coaching & Observing Learner Engagement: Reflection Questions; Teaching Channel videos; professional reading materials; additional resources as needed to meet teacher learning needs	By the end of week 7, the first PL session will have taken place.	Are teachers engaged in PL sessions? What is the evidence? Is the coach providing them sufficient opportunities to give feedback and shape PL? Are PL leaders implementing their feedback into future PL sessions and plans such that it better meets their needs? Are the outcomes of PL clear and known by all?
Step 4: PL teams meet after each session to discuss learnings. In meetings, all teachers commit to trying one new active participation strategy in the upcoming week. PL teams meet again after trying new strategies to discuss how it went. The coach attends as many PL team meetings as possible to offer guidance and support.	Weeks 8–10	RRE rubric for learner engagement; Coaching & Observing Learner Engagement: Reflection Questions; Teaching Channel videos; professional reading materials; additional resources as needed to meet teacher learning needs	By the end of week 8, all PL teams will have had their first meetings. In week 9, all teachers will have implemented a new active participation instructional strategy.	What is the evidence that teachers are growing their active participation instructional skills? What is the evidence of impact on student learning? Are teachers using the common language around learner engagement? Are PL and team meetings productive and focused? If not, how can the coach and PL leaders plan better so that they are? Which teachers are showing instructional leadership potential?

Action Step	Step Time Frame	Resource(s)	Progress Indicator	Reflection Questions / Statements
Step 5: With each teacher the coach is currently coaching one-on-one (and who are in need of additional learner engagement support), the coach and teacher will co-create learner engagement goals, and the coach and teacher will begin coaching cycles accordingly. Throughout, the teacher will reflect on her practice relative to learner engagement goals. Together, the coach and teacher will reflect on the teacher's progress toward individual professional learning goals and adjust coaching as needed, so that the teacher remains fully supported and growing.	Weeks 7–10	RRE rubric for learner engagement; Coaching & Observing Learner Engagement: Reflection Questions; professional reading materials per coaching modality and to tailor coaching; the coaching cycle (note: this is outlined in chapter 7)	By the end of week 8, the coach will have co-created learner engagement goals with all teachers she's coaching (in need of additional learner engagement support). The coach and teacher will have scheduled their first coaching cycle meetings.	Which teachers being coached are in need of additional learner engagement support? Which are ready to move onto other areas of instruction? What evidence shows that coaching is helping teachers improve instruction and student learning relative to co-created goals? How can the coach better support individual teachers? Which teachers are showing instructional leadership potential?
Step 6: The coach and principal conduct walkthroughs to observe progress toward learning engagement growth, particularly in the area of active participation. The coach and principal	Weeks 7–10	RRE rubric for learner engagement; observation data; Coaching & Observing Learner Engagement: Reflection Questions; objective data from walkthroughs	Throughout weeks 7–10, the principal and coach will have aimed to walkthrough all classrooms at least twice.	Have teachers adapted learnings and instructional strategies form PL (and coaching where applicable) to their classrooms? Are students responding positively to the changes the teachers are making?

Action Step	Step Time Frame	Resource(s)	Progress Indicator	Reflection Questions / Statements
will set up individual meetings with teachers (which can be conducted together or on a "divide and conquer" basis) to discuss what was observed during walkthroughs. The coach and/or principal will provide to each teacher positive and constructive feedback and suggestions for continued learner engagement growth.				Where is there growth in active participation? Based on the walkthrough data, what are the next steps toward further growth?
Step 7: The coach begins approaching teachers to take on instructional leadership roles for PL related to learner engagement. The coach will begin providing guidance and support about instructional leadership to teachers who accept roles.	Week 10–11	RRE rubric for learner engagement; observation data; Coaching & Observing Learner Engagement: Reflection Questions; coaching for newly appointed instructional leaders to practice leading PL sessions and meetings	By the end of week 10 or 11, instructional leaders will have committed to the roles. The coach will have scheduled time to coach them to lead PL sessions and meetings.	If the teachers we ask to assume instructional leadership roles decline, who are our backups? Or do we need to move through more PL weeks and more teacher growth to leave time to spot more teachers with instructional leadership potential? How can we best coach and train teachers to function as instructional leaders?

Step	Timeline	Tools/Resources		Reflection Questions
Step 8: The coach will begin handing over responsibility to instructional leaders in PL sessions and PL team meetings. The coach will co-lead sessions and meetings until instructional leaders are ready for additional responsibility.	Week 11–20	RRE rubric for learner engagement; observation data; Coaching & Observing Learner Engagement: Reflection Questions; ongoing coaching as needed for new instructional leaders to improve skills	Same for steps 3–7	How are instructional leaders managing their new roles? Which instructional leaders are ready for more responsibility? Which might need more support, and what kind of support do they need? Have PL sessions and team meetings remained productive and effective under new instructional leadership?
Step 9: As there is sufficient evidence of participation growth, repeat steps 3–7 as calibrated for a deep focus on the learning environment and formative processes and tools indicators for learner engagement. (Given that PS 1 is strongest in active participation, more time is given to PL on learning environment and formative processes and tools.)	Weeks 11–15 for one indicator Weeks 16–20 for the other indicator	Same for steps 3–7	Same for steps 3–7	What does the data reveal in terms of school-wide improvement in the area of active participation? How many teachers are reaching Well Developed? Do enough leaders believe the school is ready to move onto PL in the next learner engagement indicator? If so, which one? If not, how does this plan's timeline need to be adjusted accordingly? What is the impact on the other goals we intended to work toward this year?

Step 10: Once the majority of teachers are Well Developed in all three areas of learner engagement, the coach and principal will begin work on goal 3. (This will likely be planning work, such that teachers might not engage in goal 3 until a week or two later, depending on the goal.) The coach will continue to coach learner engagement for teachers still working toward their professional goals.	TBD; perhaps any time after week 18

Common Goals, Strategies, and Tactics Per Resistance-to-Change Level

Improvement Goal (The RESULT you want to achieve)	Strategy (HOW you will achieve it)	Low Resistance to Change: Tactics for Corresponding Strategy (WHAT you will do to achieve the goal)	Medium Resistance to Change: Tactics for Corresponding Strategy (WHAT you will do to achieve the goal)	High Resistance to Change: Tactics for Corresponding Strategy (WHAT you will do to achieve the goal)
Get a critical mass of educators to join school-wide improvement plans.	Build trust through relationships so educators will grow comfortable following your lead through change.	Simultaneously begin implementing school-wide change efforts while also focusing on those few holdouts who are resisting change. Identify their reason for resistance and use appropriate tools and tactics to help them push through. Acknowledge their fears and concerns and reassure them that you will support them through change and at a pace comfortable for them.	In terms of implementing a school-wide instructional improvement plan, begin with smaller goals so you can devote time to building relationships with those teachers resisting change. Identify their collective reasons for resistance to change and use the appropriate tools and tactics to help them push past it. For those holdouts showing openness to change, partner them with educators already pursuing plan goals, so that they get involved, grow comfortable, and begin to see themselves as vital to school-wide improvement.	Spend extra time building relationships (particularly with teachers you coach and key stakeholders) before launching change initiatives. Identify collective reasons for resistance to change and use the appropriate tools and tactics to help educators break through their resistance. Acknowledge that initial change will be made through the educators you coach, so invest in those relationships to build trust and bring them into alignment and agreement with your vision.
Increase the use of data to make instructional improvements.	Facilitate opportunities for educators to collaboratively review and analyze data so that they feel empowered and comfortable making instructional decisions based on data.	Identify teachers who show strong data-analysis skills and who are already using data to drive instructional decisions. Ask them to collaborate to create a data-analysis protocol that other teachers can use. Plan time for teachers to meet, study, and analyze data per a data-analysis protocol. Ask them to outline steps for instructional improvements based on the data and then share their process and plans for teachers to help other teachers learn. Ask educators with strong data-analysis skills to lead PL sessions on using a data protocol, analyzing data, learning which data to follow and collect, and how to use data to personalize instruction. Provide guidance and support to these teachers leading PL, as needed.	Make all things data the focus of PL for two months. Lead PL sessions on using a data protocol, analyzing data, learning which data to follow and collect, how to use data to inform instructional changes, and how to use data to personalize instruction, etc. Build in accountability by asking all teachers to try a new data strategy in advance of a PL session. Ask them each to share their experiences at least once in the two months. Attend all teams' weekly meetings once in the two months to lead a mini-class on data specific to that team. In the meeting, guide teachers through a data analysis. Based on what the data says, teachers will come up with at least one instructional strategy to apply to improve in the area that the data revealed was in need of improvement. Return to their next weekly meeting to discuss with them how it went.	You analyze relevant student data. Then you lead a meeting (with teams or all teachers as appropriate) where you explain your analysis process, discuss the insights you culled, and explain how you would use the data to inform a change in instructional practices. Follow this up with a discussion and Q&A. With all teachers you coach, devote a coaching cycle to data analysis. Provide for all teachers a data protocol to frame and guide their thinking around data and data analysis. Guide each teacher through an analysis of data from their classrooms. From there, make a plan to apply data to an instructional improvement. Make that improvement the focus of the next coaching cycle.

| Grow the number of instructional leaders in the school to support overall and ongoing instructional growth. | Empower strong teachers to share their strengths, formally and informally, to nurture their leadership skills and help them see themselves as instructional leaders capable of supporting overall school instructional improvement. | Where teachers are already leading PL sessions, offer planning support, check to see if they need additional resources to succeed, and regularly pop into their sessions to be a resource.

Identify and tap exemplary teachers who show leadership potential. Ask them to begin to co-lead PL sessions with you. Gradually hand over more responsibilities to them such that you feel comfortable with them leading entire sessions. As needed, attend full sessions or reduce your attendance to brief pop-ins. | Identify exemplary teachers who show leadership potential. Suggest to them that they begin to offer guidance to colleagues in small, informal ways, e.g., when she is doing a class session that can serve a colleague's current improvement goals, the teacher can invite the colleague into her class to observe; or when the teacher has a skill a colleague is seeking, she can pop into the colleague's class for a few minutes after school to discuss.

When a teacher has developed ease in leading her colleagues toward improvements here and there, ask her to co-lead a PL session with you. Gradually release more PL session responsibilities to her until she's ready to brief pop-ins so that she knows you're still there to support her.

Replicate this approach with all teachers who demonstrate leadership potential. | Focus on building strong relationships with the teachers you coach. Only when one begins showing meaningful growth and is approaching self-directed coaching, ask her if she will share an instructional strategy in an upcoming PL session. Where her growth aligns with a colleague's current improvement goals, ask the teacher to pop into the colleague's classroom after school to help her with a specific skill or instructional strategy. As this teacher grows more comfortable supporting colleagues, ask her to co-lead a PL session with you. Gradually release more responsibility in leading PL sessions to her.

Replicate this approach with all teachers showing growth and leadership potential. Over time, teachers will grow to see each other as resources. As they see more teachers taking on instruction roles, invite those with an interest to discuss with you how they can get involved. |
| Expand the number and frequency of use of research-validated instructional strategies in all classrooms. | Support educators in the use of research-validated instructional strategies through PL sessions, focused practice, and collaborative learning opportunities. | Require that all teachers use at least two research-validated instructional strategies each week. At their weekly team meetings, every teacher is expected to briefly explain a strategy they used, and teachers will then discuss. | Once a teacher you coach has achieved mastery using a research-validated instructional strategy, invite teachers whose current learning goals align with this strategy to observe the teacher using it in a class. After, lead a discussion with those teachers who observed the class as to what made the strategy effective. | Aim to recommend one research-validated instructional strategy at a time with all the teachers you coach, at a pace customized to each teacher, until each has mastered it, one at a time. When a teacher masters one, invite others to come observe the teacher's class when she plans to use it. After, lead a discussion with those teachers about what made the strategy effective. |

Improvement Goal (The RESULT you want to achieve)	Strategy (HOW you will achieve it)	Low Resistance to Change: Tactics for Corresponding Strategy (WHAT you will do to achieve the goal)	Medium Resistance to Change: Tactics for Corresponding Strategy (WHAT you will do to achieve the goal)	High Resistance to Change: Tactics for Corresponding Strategy (WHAT you will do to achieve the goal)
		Establish a practice and process of an "open door" policy so that teachers can do a quick observation of colleagues when they are using a research-validated instructional strategy they want to learn about. In a shared Google Doc, teachers are required to list a research-validated instructional strategy they plan to use in an upcoming week and at what time. It is then understood that they are inviting any and all teachers to come observe that class session. Teachers will develop a habit of routinely checking this Google Doc and popping into colleagues' classrooms when they want to learn a new research-validated strategy. As you observe teachers, note which ones are successfully implementing research-validated instructional strategies. Invite them to lead a PL session to explain how they apply it to improve learner outcomes.	Make research-validated instructional strategies the focus of all PL sessions for two months. In each session, walk through three research-validated strategies, showing videos of their use (taking care to include videos of an ineffective application of strategies). After each video, engage teachers in a discussion about what made the strategies successful, what did not, and why. Require that teachers try at least one of the strategies in the two months. They will be expected to share their experiences in their next team weekly meeting.	Ask all teachers to research one research-validated instructional strategy. Ask them to be prepared to explain what they learned, particularly how to apply it to drive meaningful student growth, in their next team meeting. The idea is to introduce teachers to more research-validated strategies. Then ask that all teachers apply one of the strategies discussed in that meeting in their own classrooms in the next two weeks. They will be expected to share their experiences trying the strategy in the next team meeting to spur discussion and share new learnings.
Create a culture of self-reflection so that all teachers routinely and habitually reflect on their instructional practice to support ongoing learning.	Use specific learning tools and opportunities that promote deep thinking and reflection about one's instructional practice. Use team learning opportunities to help teachers feel supported in their attempts to create a self-reflection habit.	Provide teachers an opportunity to read professional-learning materials on their own. Ask them to reflect on how they relate to their own teaching practice. Specifically, ask them to consider what they can take from the materials to improve their practice. In weekly team meetings, encourage them to share learnings from their experiences of applying them in classrooms. Show videos of teachers inside the school using best practices. Ask teachers to then reflect on what the	Provide teachers an opportunity to read professional-learning materials on their own. Teachers will meet to decide how they can apply the information to their current classroom practices. After they have done so, they will meet again to discuss how it went and what they learned. Show videos of teachers (from inside the school, other schools, or Teaching Channel videos) using best practices. Ask them to reflect on what the teacher did that they believe they	Design a coaching cycle around the reading of a PL material, which you will select for individual teachers, such that the reading supports a current growth goal. Ask the teacher to reflect on how the reading relates to her practice. In the next coaching meeting, ask her to share with you what she thinks she can use from the article to make an instructional improvement. Show teams of teachers videos of best practices. Ask them to reflect together on how the videos compare to their

	teacher did that they believe they can apply to their own instructional practice. Where appropriate, have teachers video their own classes so that they can watch their own instruction on video and reflect on what they see and how they can make improvements. Give all teachers a weekly writing prompt to reflect on their instructional practice. Set the expectation that each is required to write their responses in a private journal every week. Set an expectation that once a month, each teacher is expected to speak at their next team meeting or a PL session about what they reflected on.	can apply to their own instructional practice. Give the teachers you coach a weekly reflection prompt. Ask them to report on their reflection in your next coaching meeting with them. As appropriate and where you see benefit to other teachers, ask them to share a reflection in their next weekly team meeting.	instructional practices. Ask them to come up with one idea from the videos they can all try in the next two weeks. As you develop trust with the teachers you coach, begin giving a weekly reflection writing prompt to those who are growing more comfortable being vulnerable with you. Ask them to share their reflection in your next coaching meeting with them.
Create more equitable learning opportunities for all students.	Encourage teachers to plan instruction collaboratively, such that teams who share students develop a more comprehensive sense of how their students are learning not just in their classrooms, but also in the school at large; together, teachers can create plans to support all students more, consistently more equitably, and more effectively.	If the school is not using a common planning protocol, invite instructional leaders to create one. Provide support as needed. Once the protocol has been approved, they will share it with all teachers. Create an expectation that all teams will have a weekly common planning meeting. They will use qualitative and quantitative data to discuss their shared students and grasp which ones are currently in need of more support. Together, teachers will devise a support plan for those students for the upcoming week. In the next meeting, they will discuss results of these plans and repeat the process again for the upcoming week.	Host a PL session about how collaborative planning can provide more equitable learning opportunities for all students. Require that all teacher teams devote their next team meeting to discussing how they could collaborate to bring equity to students. They will be expected to share ideas in the next PL session. Provide all teams with collaborative planning protocols. Attend team meetings to go over the protocols with all teachers, taking care to have reached all teams and components. Walk teachers through all components, answer questions, and check for understanding. Remain available to support teachers as they begin using the protocols.	Host a two-month PL process on collaborative planning and how it can bring equity to all learners (PL will include discussion about planning protocols). Throughout, create accountability measures and expectations for teachers to bring ideas to PL sessions. After the PL process is over, require that teachers devote one weekly team meeting a month to collaborative planning. Attend all of them to offer support, clarify thinking, and answer questions.

Improvement Goal (The RESULT you want to achieve)	Strategy (HOW you will achieve it)	Low Resistance to Change: Tactics for Corresponding Strategy (WHAT you will do to achieve the goal)	Medium Resistance to Change: Tactics for Corresponding Strategy (WHAT you will do to achieve the goal)	High Resistance to Change: Tactics for Corresponding Strategy (WHAT you will do to achieve the goal)
			Teams will devote two of their weekly team meetings a month to common planning time. Attend all of them as often as you can initially. Make sure teams understand the role of data to inform how all shared students are learning, growing, struggling, and in need of additional support. Remain as available as possible to teams, both in and out of meetings, to support them as they learn to use collaborative planning to better meet the needs of all students.	
Create a culture of positivity among educators.	Use frequent celebrations, socializing opportunities, and praise—of and amongst educators—to make the school feel like a positive, affirming environment.	Create an expectation that all teachers will praise a colleague at least once a month in common educator spaces or communication channels, e.g., brag boards in the teacher's lounge, teacher newsletters, social media groups, blank banners above classroom doors where others can write a complimentary note to the teacher, etc. Identify teachers with a naturally positive attitude. Tap them to create a multi-channel system of praise that all teachers can participate in. This could be creating a Twitter hashtag celebrating teachers; building an email distribution list specifically for praise; launching a column in the school news-letter specifically for teacher praise from students and formalizing a pro-cess of article submission; a campaign where each teacher is encouraged to write one thank-you note a month to show gratitude for support offered, knowledge shared, encouragement given, a kind gesture, etc.	Encourage all teachers to praise a colleague twice a month in common educator spaces or resources, e.g., brag boards in the teacher's lounge, teacher newsletters, social media groups, etc. Lean on your tribe to initiate efforts to build momentum. Share with the principal when you see teachers achieve goals, learn something new, persevere through challenges, etc. The principal will then mention these achievements in her weekly PA announcement. Plan social events and gatherings so that the staff can begin to bond and get to know each other as people. Some ideas include: hosting a catered meal for staff and their spouses/partners; holding rejuvenating yoga classes in the gym; hosting mini spa sessions; doing a movie screening; inviting members of the staff to teach a class about an area of expertise, e.g., cooking, painting, crafting, etc.	As the coach, commit to frequently and habitually praising teachers when you see them succeed, grow, and learn by providing verbal compliments, sending them an email, or giving them a handwritten note. Whenever you use the guided observation coaching modality or when you encourage two teachers to collaborate, ask the teacher who learned from the other to write a quick, handwritten thank-you note. Make one team planning meeting a month somewhat more casual so that—in small groups—staff can begin to interact with each other more as people, less as colleagues, and in a somewhat less formal-feeling environment. Some ideas include: delivering pizza and soda to the meeting; celebrating all team member birthdays from that month with cake (taking care to fold in the summer birthdays at some point).

Plan social events and gatherings so that the staff can bond and interact more as friends, less as colleagues. Some ideas include: hosting a catered meal for staff and their spouses/partners; holding rejuvenating yoga classes in the gym; inviting members of the staff to teach a class about an area of expertise, e.g., cooking, painting, crafting, etc.; arranging a cooking class with a chef and in the kitchen of a local restaurant; arranging a staff "field trip" to a museum with a guided tour; doing a staff community service day; etc.	To show genuine care, give voice to all staff, and listen to each, survey them to learn their outside interests, favorite things, and areas of passion: how they like to spend their free time; their favorite candy bar; their favorite movies and books; etc. Based on how they answer, create moments of positivity and opportunities for relationship building. For example, when a teacher achieves a goal, leave her favorite candy bar and a handwritten note of praise on her desk. Where groups of teachers share an interest, arrange a social event around it, e.g., a mini book club for the avid readers (where books are for pleasure, not professional learning); a movie screening for the movie buffs; a museum day for the art lovers; etc.

administrators or educators? In vetting your plan, such concerns can be brought to your attention, allowing you to make the necessary changes before it's too late. Once you've adapted and improved your plan based on feedback, make sure you've gotten sign-off from anyone who needs to approve the plan.

Introduce & Vision Cast the Plan to All Educators

Before you begin implementation, you will strive to win a critical mass of support for your plan among educators—the very people whom you will be asking to change, and the very people whom you want to unite as one team. Arrange and lead a school-wide meeting where you will introduce your plan to the entire staff. To win their support, strive to strike an emotional chord and appeal to their humanity. To achieve this, vision cast.

Share a copy of the plan with educators, or broadcast it on a screen, so they can reference it while you walk them through it. As you explain the plan, you will want to articulate not only the vision for each goal but also for the entire plan. Articulate in vivid detail what instruction and learning will look like when each goal is in successful practice. Explain the results that will follow achievement of each goal.

Then, take it a step further and vision cast the results of the plan at large. In this grander vision, you are telling a story—one that starts with everyone uniting as a team and working toward the same goals. Detail the manifold productive ways the plan will help educators become stronger, more effective resources to their students. Draw its goals back to how achieving them will fulfill for students the hope of better, more fruitful, and happier futures. Paint a clear picture to help educators *see* the satisfying and fulfilling places of growth that working together to meet the plan's goals will take them—as individuals and as a team.

All the while, take every opportunity to focus on the positive. Make a point to list and celebrate the school's successes to date, no matter how small. Reiterate that these successes will serve as the launching pad for even greater success. Make it unequivocally clear that you believe in every educator at the school, and his or her capacity for limitless growth. Remind them they are all needed, all vital pieces of the change puzzle, and that the school cannot improve without them.

If you are selling the plan to educators with high resistance to change, refer back to chapter 4 to review why people resist change and apply suggested communication tactics to push through resistance reasons. Weave them in as often as necessary to chip away at their resistance. Important to softening any resistance to change is keeping in mind the lessons of New Coke. Always talk about the school as ours, not yours. Remind educators you are there to serve their needs, not yours. Make it clear you do not want to take anything away from them but rather add to their toolkit of knowledge, best practices, and wisdom so that they can add joy and fulfillment to their work as educators.

You will also want to take the time to explain the technical features of your plan clearly and patiently. Describe the thinking and rationale that went into all components. Make known what is expected of educators as you begin implementing the plan, including all benchmarks, timing, how you will measure progress toward goals, and what this will mean for them. List the resources you've allocated to facilitate meeting each goal, and make sure they feel the resource plan will sufficiently support their success in this effort.

Lastly, make time for questions and concerns. Be open to their feedback and take relevant suggestions or concerns seriously. As needed adapt the plan and update the school when and why the plan changes based on their input.

Ongoing Messaging Campaign of the Plan

Winning school-wide support for your plan will likely not be done after just one meeting. Nor will explaining your plan, its vision, and the expectations of all educators. That is OK. You will want to lead a messaging campaign for about two weeks after you introduce the plan to the school. In this time, focus your energy on continuing to unite the school around the plan and its vision. You will also want to give educators this time to digest the information, raise concerns, ask questions, and offer ideas. To that end, make it clear that educators will have a set amount of time to offer feedback on the plan before you all begin implementation.

Operate the ongoing messaging campaign however best fits the culture of the school: you can hold school-wide meetings, a series of smaller group meetings, communicate via email, hold webinars, or a mix thereof. (If you need to form groups, make sure they include a combination of people open to change and resistant to change, as those open to change can often serve as motivators to those who are hesitant.) Remain available after any meetings for questions and remain accessible and responsive over email.

Remember the tribe you identified early on and noted after your listening tour? That team of people who show leadership potential and a desire to get involved in change efforts? Lean on them to help you get your message out there. Where appropriate and prudent, ask them to lead sessions to further explain parts of the plan and field questions. When someone in your tribe has expertise that pertains to a specific goal, make them the point person fellow educators can approach when they have questions or concerns about that goal.

For those who remain resistant to change even after your efforts to win them over, meet with them individually to indicate you care about their engagement in the change process and want them to feel seen, supported, and part of the team that needs them. Refer again to chapter 4 to review why people resist change to identify why each individual holdout is holding out. Let the corresponding tools and tactics guide how you talk to each holdout and inform the ways you can nudge them to break through their resistance.

Most importantly: let all educators know that you understand that change is emotional, change is personal, change is human. Reassure them that you are there to support and advocate for them all along the way. Keep the experience positive and keep everyone's eyes on the vision that together, as a team, you will realize: providing a learning environment for students that gives ALL of them the greatest chance at successful lives and futures.

Managing Plan Implementation & Change Throughout the Year

Once you've reached a critical mass of educator support for the plan (which will typically take up to two weeks), you can begin implementing your first goal. As you do, recruit members of your tribe to help you manage all the moving parts. Always use your judgment about where you can delegate tasks to empower your tribe and where you need to remain in charge. That said, you will be simultaneously coaching individual teachers, and at times you will need to ask your tribe to support you in managing school-wide change. As an example, you can ask some of them to track data for each goal and report back to you about progress, red flags, victories big and small, and concerns.

Establish a communication plan to keep educators updated on progress, when they hit major milestones, any issues that come up, or any changes to the plan. This can be a monthly meeting, a bi-weekly email, or some other kind of regularly scheduled communication—use your judgment about what best suits educators' needs and suits school protocol.

Should you run into setbacks or fail to meet benchmarks, hold sessions with key stakeholders as needed to unearth to the root cause of the issue (recall the Five Whys discussed in chapter 3—a powerful tool to unpack a problem to reach the root cause). Adapt and refine the plan as needed to get back on track and maintain positive momentum.

Throughout the entire year, celebrate all wins, big and small, with the school as you meet benchmarks and reach goals. Broadcast positive news, data, and anecdotes as often as you can to keep spirits high and momentum strong. Always be sure to remind educators how far they've come. This will also help maintain a collective positive attitude and continue to expand a school-wide growth mindset.

Celebrate failures for what they are—nothing more than information that will help the entire school improve the process. In reframing failures as lessons, you will shore up resilience across the school and also encourage people to take measured risks in the name of school-wide improvement. And of course, remind educators that you are not expecting miracles in one year. Instead, you are all working together toward thoughtfully defined and paced goals for one year to begin to realize a vision. Then, you will repeat the entire process next year and keep working toward these goals or begin working toward new ones—together, as a group of educators who believe in limitless growth.

A Final Note: Communication is Key

For years, McKinsey has studied organizational transformation, specifically why it fails and why it succeeds. For recent research on the topic, the company looked at 24 transformation actions—actions taken by leaders and managers in organizational change processes—and found that communication is the action most closely linked to success (2015).

McKinsey found three types of communication in particular that are key drivers of change success: 1) open and frequent communication about progress; 2) open communication about how change will impact each individual's day-to-day work; and 3) consistent communication of the change story (2015).

For us, this translates into: 1) ongoing progress reports, celebrations of wins, and championing lessons learned from setbacks; 2) setting clear expectations about how changes will impact school operations or individual instruction day-to-day and week-to-week, as well as what's expected of each individual in the implementation process; 3) consistently reiterating and vision casting the plan as a story of all educators uniting around shared goals and as a single team—for students and their long, bright, successful futures.

Above all, your communications plan throughout the year should remain your top priority when it comes to driving change at the school level. Establish some sort of formal and structured process to communicate in all three of these ways, regularly and openly. Your school's improvement is counting on it.

PONDER & POST

I plan to communicate progress toward the school's instructional vision by _____.

#coachingredefined

PART 3

Instructional Coaching: Best Practices of Great Coaches

"You manage things; you lead people."

Grace Murray Hopper, former U.S. Navy Rear Admiral

Congratulations on completing part 2 of this book and learning to lead school-wide instructional change. I know many readers picked up this book expecting to start with what we are going to get into now—leading instructional change on the individual level. However, in completing part 2 of the book, you are well on your way to becoming a coach *redefined*. You have become part of a field-wide movement to change instruction for the betterment of all students. For many of you, this means you've likely stepped out of your comfort zone. True growth only comes when we do. Thank you for taking that leap of faith with me. I assure you it will be well worth it, for your own growth and for all those fortunate enough to co-create with you.

In chapter 7, I will walk you through everything you need to know to lead transformational one-on-one coaching: from preparing for the first meeting; to meeting each teacher where he or she is, always, and guiding growth from there; to general wisdom to keep in mind throughout. In chapters 8, 9, and 10, we will dig into everything that goes into rigorous, relevant, and engaging instruction and learning, respectively, and how to coach all your teachers to achieve it. Finally, in chapter 11, I will guide you through the process of building a sustainable learning system so that the school and all its teachers can grow capable of leading their own lifelong learning (and, therefore, relying less and less on you).

Before we launch into these chapters, a few housekeeping items about rubrics.

Selecting a Powerful Instructional Coaching Rubric

In chapter 5, I introduced you to the Rigor, Relevance, and Engagement (RRE) rubrics. We will continue to use RRE to showcase coaching in action in the ensuing chapters. Please trust that this process works no matter the rubric you choose or must use.

As I mentioned, what I like so much about the RRE rubrics is that they keep a sharp focus on what directly matters to instruction and learning. They don't bother educators with things extraneous or ancillary, so therefore, they can make a real impact. Yet there are many other strong rubrics out there. If you are curious to consider others, I would suggest vetting them to make sure that they, like RRE, keep a strict focus on what drives meaningful teaching and learning.

Guidelines to vet instructional rubrics:
- Does the rubric focus solely on powerful instruction?
- Does it tie directly to those components of instruction that have a meaningful impact on student learning, such that they can meaningfully change instructional design and student learning?
- Is it free of factors that risk distracting both teacher and coach from keeping a focus on powerful instruction?
- Is the rubric simple and easy to use?
- Is it clear and unlikely to confuse educators?

Use Distinct Rubrics for Coaching and Evaluation

The relationship between coaching and evaluation is a bit tricky. We will talk more about it in the next chapter, but in short: you want coaching and evaluation to be totally separate; but coaching must align to evaluations. Teachers will often feel that coaching is wasting their time if it isn't helping them improve their evaluation results. Yet for coaching to work, teachers must understand that the coaching relationship never bleeds over into evaluation.

One way to show that the two processes are separate is to make sure you use two different rubrics. Some of the most widely used instructional design frameworks are also widely used for teacher evaluation. When the same tool is used for both coaching and evaluation, it can breed mistrust in the coaching process.

We've established why trust is a non-negotiable in the coaching relationship. If the educator does not trust the coach, he won't allow himself to be vulnerable and open to change. As such, coaches must always keep an eye out for landmines that can blow up all the effort you've put into establishing trust and cultivating mutually respectful relationships with all of your educators. Conflating coaching and evaluation is one such landmine.

I've seen it again and again—if a teacher does not see coaching as pure coaching, but instead sees it as part of the evaluative process, the potential for true transformation of coaching is stymied. The teacher has more difficulty seeing past the way he will be evaluated and will only want to use coaching time to meet evaluation thresholds. Nor will he be able to view the coach solely as a person there to champion his growth. When the two processes are conflated in the educator's mind, he can perceive coaching as some sort of punishment or remedial effort rather than the growth opportunity it is. Furthermore, if the educator has any inkling the coach is going to report back to an administrator, he will have a tendency to clam up, put up defenses, and miss out on all the growth potential of the coaching process.

Whenever possible, use a coaching rubric that is different from the one used to evaluate your educators. In my experience, administrators often don't consider that using the same rubric for coaching and evaluation can negatively impact the coaching process. If you're asked to use the same rubric, where appropriate, appeal to administrators to allow you to use a distinct rubric. Explain to them how important it is to avoid jeopardizing the trust that is so invaluable to the co-creation coaching process.

A Final Thought: Use Rubrics That Plan for Future-Focused Instruction and Learning

It's no longer enough to view what we do as preparing students for college. We have to prepare them for long futures—aware that for many students, college might not be the most practical decision. In an economy where the cost of college is skyrocketing and wage and job growth is stalling in several industries, higher education is growing less accessible and less practical for many of our students. This is not at all to say that we should deemphasize college-ready instruction and learning; it's to say that we must place greater emphasis on career-ready instruction and learning.

In education, we hear "college and career ready"—in that order—all the time. I prefer to say *"career and college ready."* Everyone needs a career. Not everyone will need a college degree.

This is especially true when there are numerous well-paying jobs out there that do not require a four-year college degree. Our job as educators is to weave career conversations and skills into instruction and learning whenever we can. Our job is to help students gain broad exposure to myriad career paths and the skills required of them. Our job is to help students discover their strengths and how they might align to different career paths—those that require a college degree *and* those that do not. To me, a truly future-focused education is career and college ready—in that order.

Career skills are changing at a head-spinning rate. Or rather, they tend to evolve quickly, becoming more complex from prior career skills as the working landscape changes. Automation and technology mean that students must grow into adaptable, lifelong learners capable of thinking deeply and flexibly, applying old skills to new situations, and always gaining newly relevant skills.

As part of your ongoing business learning, stay aware of the career skills you see being discussed as valued today and on the horizon for tomorrow. Always consider how you can fold them into your instruction. A resource I keep tabs on is the World Economic Forum's annually published list of skills needed to thrive in the workforce. At the time of this writing, they have listed as the most valued career skills by 2020 (Gray, 2016):

1. Complex problem solving
2. Critical thinking
3. Creativity
4. People management
5. Coordinating with others
6. Emotional intelligence
7. Judgment and decision making
8. Service orientation
9. Negotiation
10. Cognitive flexibility

Please see Appendix 5 for descriptions of each of these skills; we will revisit them in the ensuing chapters. In the descriptions of these high-level skills, you will find that several social-emotional skills and other careers skills go into them. There is also overlap on this list, as certain skills feed into other skills.

Most of these skills are found and nurtured at the intersection of rigor, relevance, and learner engagement. Some are a bit more black and white; critical thinking is tightly aligned with rigor, but is also found in relevant learning. Judgment and decision-making features prominently in engaging learning and is also required in relevant learning. But by and large, honing these skills into strengths requires a rigorous foundation, relevant application, and engaging learning opportunities. Career skills come through *all* of these components of future-focused learning, not just one or some.

Above all: please keep your students' futures—and guiding them toward long, productive, healthy ones—in mind as you consider a rubric.

Now that we've gotten those rubric matters out of the way, let's get coaching.

Chapter 7

Great Coaching: Diving into the Details

"So often people are working hard at the wrong thing. Working on the right thing is probably more important than working hard."

Caterina Fake, Co-founder of Flickr and Hunch

This should come as no surprise, but I am a big believer in instructional coaching. This is not just because I enjoy watching others grow. It is not just because I've seen it change teachers' and students' lives again and again. It is not just because I've witnessed countless gratifying moments where educators discover capacity and potential they didn't know they had. It's not just because when done effectively, it guides educators to become lifelong learners. It's not just because I know anecdotally and from my experience that great one-on-one instructional coaching works. It's because the research says it works, too.

Linda Darling-Hammond, Charles E. Ducommun Professor of Education Emeritus at the Stanford Graduate School of Education and President and CEO of the Learning Policy Institute (LPI), has studied what is necessary for professional learning (PL) to be effective. In a paper co-authored with two LPI colleagues, she outlines what a meta-analysis of 35 rigorous studies indicated must be in place for PL to work. In summary, elements for success are that the PL: focuses on content-specific instructional strategies; relies on active, hands-on, and engaging learning embedded in the classroom context; is collaborative and allows teachers to observe each other and share best practices; includes expert coaching tailored to individual needs; carves out time specifically for feedback and reflection; and is of a sustained duration (Darling-Hammond, Hyler, & Gardner, 2017).

Coaching, when done expertly, meets all of these requirements. It is arguably the most efficient (including cost-effective) form of PL. It offers an unparalleled opportunity for educators to improve their practice while mitigating wasted time and resources. And when it is *redefined*, as it will be under your stewardship, learning truly is limitless.

Popeyes & Servant Leadership: The Real Power and Potential of Coaching

I will add one more reason why coaching is the most effective form of PL. It is a reason sometimes seen in the business world—and seen with my own two eyes every time I sit down with a teacher. Coaching makes individual teachers feel seen, valued, and important. Most coaching is done one-on-one (and sometimes in small groups). Getting that level of personalized attention and support—when it is delivered the way we great coaches deliver it—lets teachers know they are worth this level of attention. It lets them know they matter. Most importantly, it reminds them they matter to students. Without them, there would be very little student learning and very little hope.

In 2007, the Popeyes' board of directors asked one of its members, Cheryl Bachelder, to become the company's CEO. In the seven years prior, the restaurant chain had gone through four CEOs, and its stock price had dropped from $34 to $14. Nearly all Popeyes locations are franchised, and franchise owners were furious with corporate's lack of attention, which translated into their own flagging profits (2016).

When she arrived at her post as CEO, Bachelder, a fast-service restaurant industry veteran, conducted a listening tour—something we coaches *redefined* are familiar with. In talking to key stakeholders, from the corporate office to those working the till at individual franchise locations, Bachelder learned that franchisees and their teams had felt unsupported by corporate leaders in their efforts to grow their own store sales. She learned that corporate executives had fallen victim to short-term thinking and lack of unified strategy. There was inattention to new product innovation, and no consideration was given to building brand awareness or coordinating advertising. The result was angry franchise owners who felt they had to go it alone to drive sales, which misses the point of the franchise business model. The hope, though, was the chain's food, long known by many to capture a unique Louisiana flavor, born from cherished cooking traditions.

Bachelder and her team decided to make a bold decision. In an industry and a business environment that long praised "customer first" thinking, Bachelder committed to a "franchisee first" approach to leadership. She'd come to this bold, and in its time, against-the-grain conclusion not only because she saw how ignored Popeyes' franchisees felt, but also because of a watershed moment she'd had earlier in her career.

In an article Bachelder wrote in the *Harvard Business Review* (2016), she recounts how she was once touring a franchise to talk to that location's team about the importance of serving guests (customers) well. She writes:

> I met a young man who was not excited about my "lesson." He asked who I was. "I'm Cheryl," I said. "Well, Cheryl," he said, "there's no place for me to hang up my coat in this restaurant, and until you think I'm important enough to have a hook where I can hang up my coat, I can't get excited about your new guest-experience program." It was a crucial reminder that we are in service to others—they are not in service to us.

Without Popeyes franchisees, there would be no Popeyes. Without the teams that franchise owners manage, there would be no Popeyes. Bachelder recognized the personal risk and commitment each franchisee takes on to own something of their own while creating value for Popeyes' shareholders. They take out second mortgages on their homes to buy franchises. They work seven days a week when needed. They learn to manage teams to run the best franchise possible. And it matters to them. Because they depend on their stores' profits to feed their families.

Franchise owners and their teams were important and mattered to the company, and Bachelder was determined to make sure they all knew this. It became her mission and purpose to serve her franchisees and their teams so they had everything they needed to run their locations optimally. In addition to addressing systemic issues, Bachelder also focused on restoring trust and conveying her respect for the entire franchise network of owners and staff. She repeatedly showed them she was not an authority, but a leader there to serve their best interests so that, in turn, they could serve their customers' best interests. This brand of servant leadership imbued all decisions made at the corporate level.

And it worked. In the ten years that Bachelder led Popeyes, her team repeatedly solved structural and operational problems that had for years been standing in the way of franchise profitability. In doing so, they unleashed potential at the individual-store level that franchisees could then harness to drive their own stores' growth and revenue. Together, the corporate team and individual franchisees achieved an incredible company-wide turnaround. Along with a range of positive sales metrics, the company saw annual global sales growth from 2008 to 2015 averaging 8.4 percent (Schwantes, 2017).

Popeyes holds an important lesson for us as coaches. Everything we as educators do must, ultimately, focus on student outcomes. Students must always be top of mind each time we sit with teachers and plan their growth. But we must also treat teachers as the important people they are, not simply middlemen on the way to improved student outcomes.

To do this, we must embody true servant leadership as coaches. We must let each teacher we have the honor of working with know that they matter. We must make them feel whole and seen, cared for and respected, needed and valued. And we must let them know that we view them as humans worthy of our respect. Only then can they hang their coats, so to speak, and become excited to get to work to serve students.

The Coach's Servant Leader Wisdom

Before you sit down for your first meeting with an educator you will be coaching, re-read chapter 2, The Coach's *Real* Values. In fact, re-read that chapter as often as you need in your coaching work. Eventually, all of the values will become part of who you are as a coach and how you automatically conduct yourself with each teacher. Keep the values fresh in your mind until they and you are one.

In addition to those values, I offer up some succinct points of wisdom to bear in mind as you begin each coaching relationship and set out to serve teacher growth:

- Keep students first—while also always acknowledging that their learning cannot happen without your teachers' growth. Make your teachers feel seen, needed, valued, and respected. Serve the best interests of students and teachers simultaneously.
- Recall that this is a co-creation. You are not an authority figure, but a partner and guide in the teacher's growth journey. This rests on always working to establish trust and build a relationship.
- Co-creation requires that you must get to know each teacher and build a sincere relationship. Knowing about a person, knowing of a person, and knowing a person are all different things. You cannot lead those whom you do not know. Actively listen to each teacher to learn about her and know her.
- Connect. On the relationship-building point, I like to start and end every coaching session on a personal note—e.g., by asking teachers about their weekend or how their kids are—to show them that I see them as whole people with lives beyond work.
- Be flexible. Change plans as needed but never lose sight of the big picture: teacher growth that drives student learning.
- Be humble. Remember your charge is to walk alongside teachers on their path to growth, not to push or pull them where you want to go.
- Be honest. To be a great coach means to have sensitive conversations with teachers. Compassionate and diplomatic constructive criticism is part of coaching. Always take care to surround criticisms with honest credit and compliments.
- Fearlessly admit when you don't have an answer and welcome your teachers' ideas and thoughts. You will earn your teachers' respect in doing so.
- Keep moving forward. Failure—yours and the educator's—is not a setback but rather, a vein of precious information to mine as you go forward.
- Finally, you are leading adults, not teaching children.

Let's go a bit further into that last point. Until it's muscle memory, remind yourself seconds before you start each coaching session that you're about to lead an adult. This is especially important for us former teachers who have "teaching kids" muscle memory. Letting our teacher habits cause us to talk to and treat adults like children is a sure way to make them feel insulted, disrespected, and dubious.

While there are several key differences in how adults and children learn, in my experience the three most significant to keep in mind as you coach are:

- Where children rely more on adults—and their knowledge and experience—to direct their learning, adults prefer self-directed learning, as enabled by the breadth of knowledge and experience they can bring to it.
- Where children are usually motivated by external factors that pertain to reward and punishment (report cards, fear of not passing or advancing grade levels, etc.), adults are more likely to be motivated by internal factors, sometimes linked to extrinsic incentives (e.g., a raise or promotion). Often, adults learn to build skills that can make them more valuable in their careers, for self-improvement, to grow their confidence, to satisfy interests and curiosities, to name some.
- Where children tend to be open to a range of learning styles and approaches, most adults know how they prefer to learn. This sometimes requires that we guide adults to try other learning styles if their preferred style is presenting a learning barrier. (Gaetano, 2016)

For a chart that compares additional differences between how children and adults learn, please review the Peak Performance Center's article titled "How Children and Adults Learn" (nd).

The Mechanics of Coaching

What to coach? Which modalities of coaching and tools to coach with? When to coach? How to coach? We're now ready to dig into the nuts and bolts of coaching.

The Coaching Cycle

Every time you coach, you will be completing a coaching cycle—all those necessary components to lead learning that drive teacher- *and* student-growth. There are several takes on the coaching cycle out there. Many are valid and constructive while some are narrow and fixed. In general, a good coaching cycle will be both broad and specific enough—broad enough to allow for flexibility in tailoring coaching to each individual and coaching modality, and specific enough to make sure it hits the crucial components that move instruction forward. Coaching is and must always be adapting to meet your teacher where he is—every time you sit down with him. Yet however you slice it, the coaching cycle must include at least three general steps:

1. Design: Based on a pre-determined and SMART goal, you and your teacher get on the same page about the action you or the teacher will be taking in step two and why. You will be designing the process that will unfold in this coaching cycle to help the teacher meet the goal in question. This includes discussing any tools or resources that will be utilized.
2. Develop: This step speaks to the specific action your teacher will take to actively practice and develop skills and strategies. This will always come through one of four coaching modalities described in the next section.
3. Discuss: After you and the teacher have reflected upon the action taken in step two, you meet to discuss key takeaways and insights, ideas and tools for improvement going forward, and next steps.

Every coaching cycle is built from a goal (which we will discuss later in the chapter) and is a function of step two, the skills and strategies your teacher will be developing. Keep in mind for now that step two will dictate the design process necessary, as well as what to reflect upon for discussion in step three. Based on the goal at hand, you will select one of the four coaching modalities to use in step two. Those modalities, as explained within each one's corresponding coaching cycle, follow.

The Coaching Cycle Per Coaching Modality*

Coaching Modality 1, Observation: The coach observes a lesson. You observe classroom instruction with a specific focus on the teacher's predetermined instructional goals. You use a rubric to align expectations and help ensure that your observation is objective.

When to use this modality: At large, observation is an information gathering modality. Use this modality when you want to confirm or deny your assumptions about what the teacher needs to do and what kind of support or tools she needs to do it. Observation is also useful to establish whether what you and/or the teacher thinks is happening in the classroom actually is. It's also the most appropriate modality when you want to take note of things happening in the classroom (e.g., who's doing the work, who's doing the thinking, what's the level of work, what's the level of thinking) and elements of the environment. All told, observation will inform the strategies you suggest in step three.

What this modality looks like as a cycle:

1. Design: The teacher has planned the lesson. You meet with the teacher, and she explains her lesson plan to you and how she intends to achieve the goals you two have established for this lesson. You offer feedback or suggestions and ask clarifying questions as needed. You outline precisely what you will be observing and looking for in the class that relates to the goal at hand.

2. Develop: You observe the class session using a rubric to identify areas of strength and possible areas of additional skill development opportunity relevant to the goal. Your objective is to look for elements of the class that pertain mainly to the goal at hand; this allows you to have an intentional focus for the observation, which will, in turn, lead to a more focused follow-up meeting. You take care to record objective notes as you observe (refer to chapter 5 to refresh your memory on objective vs. subjective notes).

3. Discuss: After you and the teacher have had time to reflect on how instruction and learning went and how well the teacher met

---

* Coaching cycles and modalities © 2019 by Reflective Learning, LLC.

her goals in the observed class, you meet to discuss your observations and listen to learn her insights after her own reflection. You look to see if your assessment of the class aligns with that of the teacher's. You are looking for clues about how she is thinking about her instruction: if she can accurately see what, related to the goal, went well or did not; if she can recognize where and why students struggled; and if her thinking demonstrates understanding about how to take the needed steps to achieve her goal. If it doesn't, seek to understand why. Together, plan for ways to set new goals to integrate new strategies in order to continue to improve instruction and student learning.

Coaching Modality 2, Lesson Planning: The coach guides lesson planning. You guide the teacher through the process of planning a lesson that will help a teacher grow specific skills and drive specific student learning. You take care to guide the teacher to include all the components necessary for her to be able to meet predetermined goals.

When to use this modality: Our ultimate goal with coaching is to help teachers learn how to teach at higher levels. Sometimes a teacher's thought process might be impeding her progress. In this case, planning a lesson together can be a great modality. It allows you and the teacher to talk strategy, research, and problem solve together. Your goal as the coach is to guide the teacher toward thinking about how to make a more focused and intentional lesson pertinent to the goal.

What this modality looks like as a cycle:

1. Design: Together, you plan the lesson as you stay focused on influencing how the teacher thinks about intentional lesson design. This includes articulating: the teacher's personal goals; student learning goals; the essential question to frame the lesson and the tasks to help students understand the essential question; the learning task; the high-level questions that will be asked in the lesson; the types of interactions planned for between and among students and the social-emotional skills involved; and how she will monitor student learning and provide feedback.

2. Develop: The teacher conducts the lesson. Depending on the circumstances at hand, you can decide to observe the class or not observe the class; in certain cases, you'll find it's not necessary. Use your judgment. Alternatively, the teacher could video the class and you could watch it later.

3. Discuss: After the educator teaches the lesson and has had time to reflect on it, you have a follow-up meeting to see if the lesson met its intended goals. Where it did, you set new goals. Where it didn't, you and the teacher determine a plan to help the teacher increase skill in this area to meet the intended goals in the next lesson.

Coaching Modality 3, Modeling: The coach models a lesson or strategy. You model a lesson or a specific strategy within that lesson or in front of the teacher, or a group of teachers.

When to use this modality: Modeling is effective when you and the teacher are discussing something new or you determine that the teacher could benefit from seeing something a new way.

What this modality looks like as a cycle:

1. Design: You ask the teacher his learning goals and the content he intended to focus on in the class you will be modeling, demonstrating respect for the plans he had in place. From there, you plan the modeling on your own. You meet briefly with the teacher to explain what you will be modeling and why (pertinent to the predetermined goal).

2. Develop: You model an entire class session or only a specific strategy in the educator's classroom (or in a meeting) for him to observe and study. The teacher takes notes about evidence of specific instructional techniques and the student learning they are intended to elicit such that he develops capacity to identify and implement hallmarks of higher-level instruction.

3. Discuss: After you both have time to reflect on what was modeled, you and the teacher meet to discuss what he observed as you modeled, including any outstanding questions or new realizations he might have. You set a goal for him to apply this strategy in a future class session and set a timeline to discuss, afterwards, how it went.

Coaching Modality 4, Guided Observation: The coach guides a teacher through a classroom observation. You have the teacher observe the classroom or part of a class session of a colleague who is highly skilled in an area pertinent to the teacher's goal.

When to use this modality: First and foremost, I only recommend using this modality if you believe the culture is conducive to it. This modality can work beautifully in an environment where teachers are supportive of each other, it's OK to send teachers into classrooms, and there are teachers on staff having success with a strategy that is a growth opportunity for another teacher. I particularly like this modality in a school where there's value in bringing teachers together to promote resource sharing; guiding teachers to observe colleagues' lessons can serve to further unify teachers and see each other as experts and resources to each other. Practically speaking, it also shows those teachers doing the observation what steps go into success with a specific strategy.

What this modality looks like as a cycle:

1. Design. You and the teacher meet to discuss why she will be observing another teacher. You offer guidance as to what specifically she should look for and focus on, relevant to her goal.
2. Develop: The teacher does the observation. Use your judgment as to whether or not you should accompany the teacher. If the goal is related to rigor, and the teacher lacks understanding of what rigor is, the coach should join. If the teacher is ready for self-directed learning, there's no need to join. Use your judgment based on what you know about the teacher and her needs and goals.
3. Discuss. You and the teacher meet to discuss what she noted in her observation. Make a point to ask the teacher to select an observed strategy she could adapt for her classroom. Once she's committed to trying it, establish a timeline for her to do so and a time for you to meet again to discuss how it went.

Completing the Coaching Cycle with Individuals or Groups

The second, third, and fourth coaching modalities and cycles can be done with individual teachers or groups of them. You could have a group of teachers plan classes together followed by a group discussion. You could also have a group of teachers watch you model a class or strategy, followed by a group discussion. Lastly, a group of teachers could go observe the same classroom, also followed by a group discussion.

In most cases, potential groups are evident in a school. Most elementary school teachers are grouped by grade, middle school teachers by content and grade, and high school teachers by department. It's rare that I am forming my own groups for coaching. If and when I do, I aim to group people who have the same learning needs. An obvious exception is when goals pertain to interdisciplinary instruction. In such cases, of course, group people according to the disciplines at hand and, if possible, shared learning needs.

Ultimately, deciding to group teachers is a matter of experienced judgment and the coaching goals at hand. When deciding whether to complete a coaching cycle with individuals or groups, consider the following:

- What is typical at the school? Is it typical for teachers to plan lessons collaboratively? Is it expected that they plan in groups? If so, it is best to honor the customs in place.
- Do teachers have common planning time that you could use to coach lesson planning or lead a modeling session?
- Do the teachers tend to work better as teams or alone? Do they get along? Does the school culture support a healthy and safe professional learning environment?
- Do teachers have similar needs and goals such that it makes sense to deliver coaching in a group?
- Is there anything sensitive in nature that will come up for any one teacher in a coaching session that necessitates the cycle be completed with just the teacher and coach?

Timing the Coaching Cycle The timing and frequency with which you meet teachers and address each stage of the coaching cycle will vary given the circumstances in your school and your relationship to it. If you are an on-staff administrator, you will likely meet more frequently with your teachers and complete each coaching cycle relatively swiftly. For someone like me, who travels to see various clients and spends a few days a month with each, my timeline is different.

That said, here are some loose guidelines to adapt to your circumstances:

- The frequency with which you meet a teacher will depend on her needs. As a general rule of thumb, strive to complete two coaching cycles a month with a teacher. However, a teacher who is struggling might require four coaching cycles a month. One who is already a strong self-learner and is achieving at high levels might need to complete only one coaching cycle per month. Use your judgment. And recognize that the same teacher might need more frequent support for this topic or strategy and less frequent support for another one. Frequency isn't fixed, but rather, is dependent on ever-changing teacher needs.
- Strive to complete step one, the design stage, at least a day before moving onto step two, the development stage. This allows you and your teacher to digest what was decided upon in design, and for you both to reflect on implementing plans.
- The timing of step three is a delicate balance. You want to allow at least one day to pass in between steps two and three, but you don't want to allow so much time to pass that step two is no longer fresh in your mind or the teacher's. For the discussion in step three to be most productive and constructive, you and the teacher will benefit from sufficient time to reflect on how things went: Was the design sufficient? Did it help the teacher get a maximized impact in step two? Did the teacher meet the goal? What did the teacher do well? Where did the teacher show need for support? What tools and resources can you recommend to the teacher to drive improvement? At a minimum, aim to complete steps two and three in the same week, whenever possible.

Gradual Release Coaching Model

You will often find yourself coaching, to some degree and in some way, in all three steps of the coaching cycle, and the teacher's needs and goal at a moment will inform which modality to use in the cycle. But what of the simplicity or complexity with which you coach? If the objective of coaching is to meet each teacher where she is, so that you can lead her growth from where she currently is—not where you want her to be or where she has already been—how do you determine this starting point? To answer this question, we first need to get acquainted with what I call the Gradual Release Coaching model (GRC).

If I had to sum up the goal of coaching in one sentence, I would say it is to get the teacher to think so deeply about her practice that she can continue her ongoing learning primarily on her own. The objective of coaching is not to make a teacher dependent on you; it's the exact opposite. Great coaches aim to meet each teacher where she is, provide the appropriate support from there, steadily guide the teacher toward growth and improvement, and eventually release her to her own ongoing learning.

GRC ensures that coaching and learning are personalized to the teacher at every point in time. It ensures that you are guiding the teacher in the way that will drive the most growth on a specific topic or strategy. It ensures that the teacher is doing most of the thinking and most of the work, with scaffolding as needed. And it helps mitigate the common mistake of delivering a type of coaching that won't resonate or work with a teacher because it's too far from where she currently is.

We know that we cannot explain fractions to students without yet confirming they understand division. We also know that we cannot ask a student confronting a complicated physics principle for the first time to direct his own learning. In both cases, we first need to scaffold, teach the foundational components, and ensure comprehension of them. Nor could we ask the student to self-direct his learning if he's never done so before. Doing so requires guiding the student to practice and gain the skills of autodidactic learning.

The risks of any of these approaches are too high. At best, teaching students new content before they grasp its foundational pieces or skills is a recipe for frustration. At worst, it can make students feel incapable and lose belief in their potential and, therefore, lose interest in the subject at hand. By asking students to learn in a manner for which they don't yet have the foundational knowledge or learning skills is demoralizing, counterproductive, and can be destructive to one's confidence.

It is for this reason that more and more schools are moving toward a personalized and proficiency growth model of learning. This is a change I, for one, am thrilled to see. For it is this kind of learning—that meets each individual learner exactly where she is and provides for her the exact content she needs through the exact learning model best suited for that moment—is the most effective. And it's the same kind of learning we will use with the adults whom we coach.

That is the Gradual Release Coaching model.

The Spectrum of Gradual Release and Its Four Points of Coaching What kind of coaching a teacher needs to be able to improve from a specific point, in a specific way or on a specific topic, is a spectrum. And there are four progressive kinds of coaching that sit as points on this spectrum of GRC. Determining where on the spectrum a teacher currently sits is part art, part science. You will make this determination through a combination of thoughtful questions and observation data, all of which we will dig deeper into soon.

First, let's familiarize ourselves with the four points of coaching on the GRC spectrum:

Spectrum Point 1: Instructive Coaching

- What it is: In instructive coaching, you are using the most hand-holding and being most explicit in walking the teacher through information and foundational knowledge. This is the coach-to-teacher equivalent of direct instruction with students. Through instructive coaching, we seek to give the teacher all the information needed to begin to gain comprehension of a specific topic or instructional strategy.
- When we use it: we use instructive coaching when a teacher shows minimal background, or foundational knowledge or understanding of a topic or instructional strategy, and/or does not grasp the importance of a topic or instructional strategy.

Spectrum Point 2: Illustrative Coaching

- What it is: In illustrative coaching, we show illustrative examples of what a specific topic or instructional practice means and looks like in practice or when applied. This can include reviewing and analyzing exemplar lesson plans, assessment exemplars, and videos. After showcasing any example, it's important to discuss with the teacher how she can go on to implement the topic or strategy in her classroom.

- When we use it: we use illustrative coaching when a teacher understands what a topic or instructional strategy is and/or grasps the need for and importance of it, yet struggles to visualize how it could be used effectively.

Spectrum Point 3: Guided Discovery Coaching

- What it is: guided discovery coaching is when we provide select information or prompts for a teacher to take and research or address independently and, eventually, share what she learned with you and discuss any questions.
- When we use it: we use guided discovery coaching when the teacher has a firm grasp on background and foundational knowledge, understands the importance and need of a topic or instructional strategy, and is motivated to learn on her own.

Spectrum Point 4: Self-Directed Coaching

- What it is: Self-directed coaching is when we begin to release the majority of the responsibility of learning to the teacher. We suggest or introduce concepts to the teacher, then leave it to her to learn what she needs to learn to be able to adapt the knowledge, and implement the strategies in her classroom. We remain available for support, suggestions, guidance, and check-ins as needed.
- When we use it: we use self-directed coaching when the teacher has a firm understanding of, and comfort with the common language around, rigor, relevance, and engagement; has shown a desire and ability to learn on her own; and, you are quite confident, has the best interests of students at heart.

Ultimately, this spectrum represents how we serve teachers at each stage of their growth and development. Practically speaking, it provides guidance for us, as coaches, to identify when a teacher is ready for more autonomy in her thinking and work, and when she can assume more responsibility for her own learning. While it must be a great coach's goal to have the teacher do as much work and thinking as possible, and to assume as much responsibility as possible for her learning, GRC ensures that you only give a teacher what she can handle at a given time so you can avoid squashing her momentum or demotivating her.

Where a teacher falls on the GRC spectrum will keep changing. A teacher could prove highly competent in all things rigor. You might find that you can start her growing in rigorous instructional capacity from the self-directed coaching point. Yet, this same teacher could struggle even to see the importance of relevance, and you might find that she requires instructive coaching to begin grasping the value of it. Within the indicators of relevance, you might find that she is naturally better at one than the other two, and you may choose to toggle back and forth on the spectrum as you work to grow her instructional capacity in relevance. In some cases, you will find you need to use a hybrid, or mix, of any two adjacent points on the spectrum: some instructive and some illustrative coaching, as an example, for this same teacher who has some, but not total, grasp on the importance or need for a relevance indicator.

What matters is that you keep your eye on moving the teacher up the spectrum toward self-directed coaching and, one day, fully self-directed learning. The goal of the GRC model is to steadily release the teacher to do more of her own thinking and more of her own work so that, eventually, she can do all of it. Nurture those skills whenever possible—whenever the teacher is ready. Once she grasps the more advanced learning skills for one topic or strategy, you will find that she begins to apply them in other topics or strategies more readily.

Merging the GRC Spectrum & The Coaching Cycle Practically speaking, where a teacher sits on the spectrum will inform your approach to coaching in all three steps of the coaching cycle. Consider GRC as an overlay to the coaching cycle. You might be using the lesson-planning modality with a teacher capable of managing her own learning. Thus, you will use self-directed coaching to guide how you design the cycle with this teacher; how you expect she will use her development time; and how and what you discuss with her after you've both had time to reflect on the actions she took.

Or you might be using the modeling-a-lesson modality with a group of teachers who sit on spectrum point two. As you design the cycle, you may focus on using a range of illustrative examples (i.e., videos to showcase how this lesson can be done well or ineffectively) to help the teachers gain clarity and understanding of the goal and lesson at hand. This will help them grasp what it is they will be aiming to do in their own classrooms. The illustrative examples will also guide discussion, or discussion might warrant use of additional illustrative examples to reinforce their new learnings. (In the next three chapters, we will go over many scenarios to bring to life the art of overlaying different spectrum points on different coaching modalities.)

The Gradual Release Coaching Rubric How do you determine where a teacher is on the GRC spectrum? For years, I determined where on the spectrum a teacher was by considering and synthesizing my classroom-observation data together with some softer observations about her attitude about the class session observed, attitude toward change, reflection skills, and self-awareness of her practice. So that you do not have to climb into my head, I formalized this analytical and synthesis process into the GRC rubric.

Using it requires completing an initial classroom observation (which you did as part of building the school-wide instructional improvement plan) and asking specific questions in your first meeting with the teacher. I will outline those questions in the next section.

First, let's walk through the GRC rubric. It is not meant to be evaluative; rather it is to help you sense what kind of coaching will best meet a teacher's needs at a given time. It's broken down into two sections and eight total indicators: 1) About the Teacher, which has three corresponding indicators (perception alignment; reflection skills; resistance/openness to change); and 2) About Instruction, which has five corresponding indicators (goal-setting aptitude; goal-meeting success; rigor aptitude; relevance aptitude; and learner-engagement aptitude—these last three deriving from the RRE rubric). To use the rubric, you will synthesize classroom observation data and insights the teacher shares in response to specific questions. Based on this information, you will note where on the spectrum the teacher falls for each indicator.

Note: the first time you place a teacher on the GRC spectrum, you will be considering the rigor, relevance, and learner engagement indicators, as you will be setting out to determine a teacher's understanding of all three of these concepts to inform where you will start your coaching with her. Once you get into setting goals with the teacher and completing coaching cycles, you will likely address only one of these indicators at a time.

Therefore, in future attempts to place the teacher on the GRC spectrum, you will often find that you use only one of these three indicators and disregard the other two. Use only the indicators of the GRC rubric that are relevant to the need or goal.

Visit www.leadered.com/coachingredefined to download the Gradual Release Coaching Rubric.

Ideally, the teacher will always be advancing up the spectrum in the About the Teacher section. Ideally, the teacher is growing more trusting of you and your change process, more willing to critically reflect on her practice, and more willing to be honest about where she is in it, at a given time. You will likely see more back-and-forth movement in the About Instruction section, as this can vary widely for different topics and instructional strategies.

Ultimately, you will get a general picture of where the teacher falls on the spectrum for a specific topic or instructional strategy. This is where the *art* of coaching comes in. You could find that for learner engagement, a teacher is all threes in the instructional section of the rubric (excluding, for this analysis, the rigor and relevance indicators). Yet in the teacher section, he is all ones. How do you merge this seemingly dichotomous information? Use your experience, judgment, and sense of the person sitting before you. Keep in mind that your number one goal is to establish trust and build the relationship on a foundation of trust.

In a case such as this, it would likely insult the teacher—who is largely competent in learner engagement—to deliver instructive coaching. Yet it would be a disservice to him to start with guided discovery if he doesn't yet have the reflection and self-awareness skills to handle this much responsibility for his learning or a belief that he needs to change at all. Landing somewhere in the middle would be ideal. You might apply some very light and brief instructive coaching about the differences between instruction and learning at levels 3 and 4 in the RRE learner engagement indicators. Then you could share video clips of instruction, which the teacher can use as a tool to reflect on learner engagement in his current instructional practice. The expectation would be that together in your next meeting, you would discuss his reflections and what he can do to boost engagement even more in his classroom.

Let the rubric be a guide, not a rule.

Gradual Release Coaching Rubric

ABOUT THE TEACHER	1—Instructive	← Hybrid →	2—Illustrative	← Hybrid →	3—Guided Discovery	← Hybrid →	4—Self-Directed
Perception Alignment: The extent to which the teacher's view of her instructional practice appears to align with yours	Your perception of the teacher's instruction and the teacher's perception of her instruction are opposite.		Your perception of the teacher's instruction and the teacher's perception of her instruction are somewhat aligned.		Your perception of the teacher's instruction and the teacher's perception of her instruction are mostly aligned.		Your perception of the teacher's instruction and the teacher's perception of her instruction are totally aligned.
Reflection Skills: The extent to which the teacher can objectively analyze her instruction (based on indicators of effective instruction) and apply new insights to improve instruction	The teacher reflects minimally on her instructional practice.		The teacher understands the importance of reflecting on her practice but does not know what to consider or analyze for a productive reflection process.		The teacher routinely reflects on her instruction with an understanding of what to analyze but struggles to apply insights to improve her practice.		The teacher routinely reflects on her instruction and consistently applies insights to improve instruction.
Resistance/Openness to Change: The teacher's attitudes toward change, learning, and/or growth	The teacher doesn't see the need for change, learning, and/or growth.		The teacher sees the need for change, learning, and/or growth but would benefit from guidance on where or how to start.		The teacher is eager to be more proactive in her own change, learning, and/or growth.		The teacher is currently proactively changing, learning, and/or growing on her own.
ABOUT INSTRUCTION	**1—Instructive**	**← Hybrid →**	**2—Illustrative**	**← Hybrid →**	**3—Guided Discovery**	**← Hybrid →**	**4—Self-Directed**
Goal-Setting Aptitude: The teacher's understanding of and skill for setting SMART instructional goals	The teacher does not set instructional goals in advance of lessons.		The teacher knows that she must set instructional goals in advance of lessons but doesn't know how to do so.		The teacher is regularly setting instructional goals in advance of lessons, but they are not always SMART goals.		The teacher is adept and habituated at setting SMART goals in advance of every lesson.

	Instructive	Hybrid Instructive-Illustrative	Illustrative	Hybrid Illustrative-Guided Discovery	Guided Discovery	Hybrid Guided Discovery-Self Discovery	Self-Directed
Goal-Meeting Success: To what extent and frequency the teacher meets instructional goals	The teacher does not set instructional goals and therefore cannot gauge success meeting them.		The teacher struggles to identify the success of instruction because goals are not always set in advance and/or are not always measurable or actionable.		The teacher can usually cite data that indicates that most of her classes meet instructional goals.		The teacher can regularly cite data that shows that all (or nearly all) of her classes meet instructional goals.
Rigor Aptitude: The extent to which the teacher shows an understanding of rigorous instruction and learning	The teacher cannot define rigorous instruction and learning accurately, nor can she identify any indicators of rigor.		The teacher is familiar with rigorous instruction and learning in general terms and can identify some indicators of rigor.		The teacher demonstrates an understanding of rigorous instruction and learning and can identify many indicators of rigor.		The teacher demonstrates an understanding of rigorous instruction and learning and can identify most or all indicators of rigor.
Relevance Aptitude: The extent to which the teacher shows an understanding of relevant instruction and learning	The teacher cannot define relevance accurately, nor can she identify any indicators of rigorous instruction or learning.		The teacher is familiar with relevant instruction and learning in general terms and can identify some indicators of relevance.		The teacher demonstrates an understanding of relevant instruction and learning and can identify many indicators of relevance.		The teacher demonstrates an understanding of relevant instruction and learning and can identify most or all indicators of relevance.
Learner-Engagement Aptitude: The extent to which the teacher shows an understanding of engaging instruction and learning	The teacher cannot define learner engagement accurately, nor can she identify any indicators of engaging instruction or learning.		The teacher is familiar with engaging instruction and learning in general terms and can identify some indicators of learner engagement.		The teacher demonstrates an understanding of engaging instruction and learning and can identify many indicators of learner engagement.		The teacher demonstrates an understanding of engaging instruction and learning and can identify most or all indicators of learner engagement.

Spectrum of Gradual Release

If you are focusing only on one of these areas of instruction and learning, use only that indicator and disregard the other two as needed for your rubric analysis.

You can and would benefit from revisiting this rubric as often as you need until you develop an instinct for placing teachers on it. Keep in mind that the rubric is useful each time you and your teacher set and meet another goal and complete another coaching cycle.

Placing Your Teacher on the GRC Spectrum In this section, I list a series of questions per both GRC rubric sections. Questions are designed to help you place the teacher on the rubric and, therefore, eventually on the spectrum. Answering all of them will help you serve teachers best—by meeting them exactly where they are.

In brackets after each question, I note to which GRC rubric indicator the question aligns. As you read this section, refer back to the rubric to refresh your memory on how each indicator is defined. You will begin to see how answers could point you to a specific spectrum placement in each indicator.

In your first meeting with your teacher, you will ask all of these questions. As you progress through different goals, use your judgment as to which questions need to be asked again. Each time you get answers to the questions you decide to ask, you can reposition the teacher on the GRC spectrum for a given topic or instructional strategy.

Note a third category of questions: starting from strength. As a coach *redefined*, you recognize this concept. While it doesn't pertain to the rubric, it is important to ask this question, especially early on in your co-creation with a teacher. For reasons you will understand from part 2 of the book, and just as we did for school-wide improvement, you will always start from strength with individual teachers. Make a habit of asking the teacher what strengths he demonstrated in a specific lesson. We'll dive deeper into this aspect of coaching later in the chapter.

About Instruction Rubric Questions (to be asked of the teacher):

- What were the instructional objectives of the lesson? (goal setting aptitude)
- Do you feel your instructional goals were met? (success in meeting goals)
- Were you satisfied with the level of rigor in the lesson; why or why not? (rigor understanding/skills)

- Were you satisfied with the level of relevance in the lesson; why or why not? (relevance understanding/skills)
- Do you feel the students were productively engaged during the lesson? How do you know? (learner engagement understanding/skills)

Note: you will also be applying any and all observation data you have for the teacher, pertinent to the class session in question, at this point. Factor observation data and where you placed the teacher on the RRE rubrics for the category (i.e., rigor, relevance, or learner engagement) into placing the teacher on the GRC spectrum. By and large, RRE observation data will drive your placement on the GRC spectrum in the rigor, relevance, and learner engagement indicators.

About the Teacher Rubric Questions (to be asked of the teacher):
- How did you feel about your lesson? (perception alignment)
- If you taught the lesson again, what might you adjust and why? (reflection skills)
- How did this lesson compare with a typical lesson you teach? (reflection skills)
- How do you feel about this process of co-creation coaching? (resistance/openness to change)

Starting from Strength Question
- What do you feel were the lesson's strengths? (window to start from strength)

The Coaching Protocol: A Pre-Step to Your First Coaching Meetings

Before you start meeting with the teachers you coach, you will want to make sure they all have what I call "the coaching protocol." This is a list of expectations of everyone involved in coaching—you and each of your teachers. A sample of a coaching protocol I have used many times follows. Please tailor it or build a new one to fit your school's needs.

SAMPLE COACHING PROTOCOL

(Name of school) will implement instructional coaching during the 20XX–20XX school year. The purpose of instructional coaching is to increase student achievement through the implementation of engaging rigorous and relevant instruction. For instructional coaching to have the greatest impact, everyone should have a clear understanding of his or her roles and responsibilities.

Role of School Administrators

Administrators will:

- Take an active role in promoting instructional growth at (name of school).
- Be committed to helping students reach their fullest potential by supporting all teachers' professional growth.
- Routinely conduct classroom walkthroughs, analyze student-learning data, and be an instructional leader.
- Meet with the coach to provide guidance on professional learning needs of school staff
- Provide teachers summative feedback after formal observations.
- Support coaches as they nurture the individual growth of teachers.
- Ensure that coaches and teachers work collaboratively and effectively.

Role of Coach

The Coach will:

- Take an active role in promoting instructional growth at (name of school).
- Observe teachers.
- Analyze student-learning assessments.
- Review lesson plans and offer constructive feedback.
- Provide resources and resource ideas to teachers.
- Provide constructive and personalized feedback to teachers.
- Provide instructional support for school administrators and teachers as they strive to meet the individual learning needs of students.

Role of Teachers

The Teachers will:

- Take an active role in promoting instructional growth at (name of school).
- Analyze student-learning data with regularity, to inform instruction.
- Regularly participate in professional learning.
- Lead professional learning (when appropriate).
- Actively seek ways to increase student achievement.
- Turn in completed lesson plans to the coach.
- Commit to meeting with the coach to actively seek the best ways to meet students' individual learning needs.

Such a protocol must be in place before you get started. Without clear and shared expectations, little issues can escalate and totally derail any hope of a productive coaching experience with teachers who don't engage wholly. The protocol builds in accountability and lets each participant know exactly what they must do in good faith to get the most out of coaching. The teacher will take comfort in knowing that you, the coach, are also beholden to certain behaviors and actions. This, in theory, will put them at ease and make them more open to abiding by their expected behaviors and actions.

As the coach, the protocol also gives you recourse. In some cases, the coach has little authority to take action if a teacher simply refuses to participate in coaching or use the time seriously. The protocol creates options for action when the teacher isn't holding up her end of the bargain—actions that the teacher has been made well aware of and knows to anticipate.

If there is no coaching protocol at your school, make your case for one to a supportive administrator. If appropriate, offer to draw up a first draft then work collaboratively with that administrator to make any improvements.

Whenever and wherever possible, have the administrator distribute this protocol to teachers; or, if you are an administrator yourself, ask the principal to pass it along on your behalf. This protocol will always be taken most seriously when it doesn't come from the coach, but rather, from a person with the authority to act if a teacher doesn't do what's expected for their own growth.

In advance of your first meetings with teachers, make sure they've all received the protocol. In your first meeting, walk through the protocol. Make it clear to them that you are wholeheartedly committed to the expectations placed on you; you are, after all, there to serve. Ask them if they have any questions about the expectations placed on them, and reiterate that, if they are to grow and learn from your time together, this protocol is there to assist to that end. It is there to make sure their time isn't wasted (and yours isn't either) and that they get the greatest benefit possible from the powerful process that is coaching *redefined*.

Preparing for Your First Coaching Meeting

Classroom Observations

You likely observed the classrooms of all the teachers you are responsible for coaching in the first wave of classroom observations we walked through in chapter 5. If you have not, be sure to complete at least one classroom observation for every teacher you'll be coaching, prior to your first meeting with each. What you observe, and the rubric data you collect from it, will serve as the foundation for the discussion in that first meeting.

If you feel you didn't get enough useful data from your classroom observation of a given teacher, feel free to do another one before your first meeting. When we do our first wave of classroom observations for the school-wide plan, we do enough that it's OK if some observations yield no useful data. But when it comes to the teachers we coach, we must start the relationship with a basic understanding of how they teach.

Revisit chapter 5 as needed to refresh your memory on how to conduct a classroom observation. Recall the importance of drawing objective conclusions vs. subjective conclusions about a teacher's performance. Keeping data objective is a way to avoid appearing judgmental and, instead, establishing the trust that is so vital to successful coaching.

Sharing Rubrics with Teachers

Before you set out to begin work around the RRE, or another instructional rubric you might select to use, share it with each of the teachers you coach. As a best practice, meet with them in person as a group to share the rubrics and discuss all components of it. In your meeting, explain that the co-creation process on which you are about to embark will be grounded in these rubrics. Let them know that the rubrics hold the indicators of powerful instruction and learning, and that you'll be looking for these indicators in their classrooms. Make extra clear that the rubrics and your work are by no means tied to evaluation. Reassure them that any and all conversations about identifying where on the rubric an educator presently is will be used only to help you know where to begin or pick up your work together. Reiterate that it is a launching point for scaffolded and limitless growth.

Discuss any questions the educators have about the rubrics until everyone confidently grasps them. (And if not, you can tackle this in your first individual meetings.) One of the ways to reassure them and help win buy-in for the rubrics you will be using is to show video clips of teaching and then asking them to discuss certain aspects of the rubric. You can ask questions such as:

- What did this teacher do well, based on the rubric?
- What could they improve, based on the rubric?
- What resources/strategies might you recommend to the teacher?

In doing this, teachers begin to see what the coaching experience might entail. This is comforting to them, as it shows that the coaching experience will be guiding, and non-threatening.

It's inevitable that in this meeting (or at some point as your coach), someone will ask if the rubrics and the coaching process are tied to evaluation. It's also common for teachers to express concern that when they are coached, they will be asked to work on things that have nothing to do with what they're evaluated on (which does happen, and is a surefire way to frustrate teachers and undermine trust). I cannot emphasize this enough: say as many times as needed that coaching is in no way tied to evaluation. And also reassure teachers that when coaching is approached as a best practice—as we are doing as coaches *redefined*—it will naturally drive growth that will help teachers improve their evaluations.

Only by being totally transparent about the content and intent of the rubrics will you avoid undermining trust and work to cultivate even more of it with your educators. Such transparency is yet one more signal of your respect for them as people and as professionals.

Conducting Your First Coaching Meeting

In a way, what will unfold in your first meeting will loosely replicate the process we went through in part 2 but on a much smaller scale. You will begin by getting to know the teacher—really listening to learn about her. You will aim to get a sense of her openness to the coaching process. You will do a needs assessment. And finally, you and the teacher will set a first goal together. Rest assured that the steps you take to get to the point of setting goals will be much lighter weight than the process you went through in part 2. After all, they will all take place in one meeting. That said, do keep the process of part 2 in mind as you complete your first meeting with teachers. Its context and explanation will make you more effective in these meetings.

The Coach's Promise

In an interview on the EntreLeadership podcast—one of my go-to resources for improving my leadership skills—Popeye's Cheryl Bachelder explains why she thinks her servant leadership has been so effective (2017). Her answer was simple: "Good intent."

In chapter 1, I shared with you what I say each time I sit down with a new instructional coach I'm coaching. I introduce myself with the same promise to them: "I'm here to serve you. I'm here to understand where you are and what you need, and to walk beside you as you improve your ability to better guide teachers so that their students will become better learners."

Adapt this promise to the teachers you coach and in a way that is and sounds authentic. There's no better way to begin showing your good intent—and start from service and positivity—than to declare it up front when you meet a teacher.

Listening to Learn About the Teacher

Show your teacher you want to know her so that you can best serve her. Recall what we learned in chapter 2, The Coach's *Real* Values: take notes as you listen. This will demonstrate that you care about what the teacher is saying. Notes will also help jog your memory later, as you reflect on what you've begun to learn about the teacher.

Suggested questions to get acquainted with your teacher and begin to establish trust:

- What are your professional hopes and dreams?
- What would you like to accomplish together?
- What are your greatest strengths as an educator?
- What causes you stress or worry about your job?

- How would you like to be supported and coached?
- In a perfect world, what resource or tools would you have to make your work easier?
- As you ask these questions, you are looking for:
- How open or resistant the teacher appears to coaching. This will inform how much time you would be wise to spend establishing trust and building a professional relationship before setting out to achieve big, ambitious goals.
- What matters to the teacher in her profession.
- Where she has felt supported or unsupported in the past.
- What she hopes to get out of your co-creation.

Discussing the Classroom Observation

To start this part of the meeting, make sure the teacher feels comfortable with the instructional rubrics you will be using. Ask her if she has any questions about them and take time to answer each one. If you did not get the opportunity to introduce the rubrics to a group of teachers in person, use a few minutes to show the teacher videos of instruction. Then ask the teacher rubric-based questions so that she grows familiar with how you will be using them to guide her instruction.

Next, you'll want to discuss your classroom observation of her. It is at this point that you will ask the teacher questions that pertain to the GRC rubric, which I'll repeat here. First, a note to keep in mind: I advise against telling the teacher specifically where you placed her on the RRE rubrics in rigor, relevance, and learner engagement. You will use this information to inform your needs assessment and steer the conversation around goal setting. But to share the numbers you assigned to the teacher, especially in this first meeting, might feel too threatening and judging and, therefore, could undermine trust. In terms of where you placed the teacher on the RRE, you will be looking to see if your perceptions of the class session observed align with her perceptions of it. If they don't, you will want to understand why, as this will help you more precisely place her on the GRC rubric and identify what she needs.

Questions to ask about the observed class to begin locating the teacher on the GRC spectrum are:

About Instruction Rubric Questions

- What were the instructional objectives of the lesson? (goal setting aptitude)
- Do you feel your instructional goals were met? (success in meeting goals)
- Were you satisfied with the level of rigor in the lesson; why or why not? (rigor understanding/skills)
- Were you satisfied with the level of relevance in the lesson; why or why not? (relevance understanding/skills)
- Do you feel the students were productively engaged during the lesson? How do you know? (learner engagement understanding/skills)

About the Teacher Rubric Questions

- How did you feel about your lesson? (perception alignment)
- If you taught the lesson again, what might you adjust and why? (reflection skills)
- How did this lesson compare with a typical lesson you teach? (reflection skills)
- How do you feel about this process of co-creation coaching? (resistance/openness to change)

Starting from Strength Question

- What do you feel were the lesson's strengths? (window to start from strength)

In addition to looking for clues to help you place the teacher on the GRC rubric, you will be looking for:

- How much work the teacher is doing vs. how much work the students are doing
- How much thinking the teacher is doing vs. how much thinking the students are doing.
- How willing the teacher appears to be vulnerable in the coaching process.

Identifying Improvement Needs

Based on your initial classroom observation, you probably have a sense of the areas in which the teacher can improve. How the teacher responds to questions about her practice and the observed class may also reveal improvement opportunities. And, as we did in part 2, let her degree of openness or resistance to change and coaching inform how ambitious your initial goals can be. Refer back to the steps in part 2 to offer guidance, if and where helpful, as you do a needs assessment with the teacher.

Ideally, you will identify needs and set at least one goal in this first meeting. You might want more time to reflect on the teacher's bigger needs or full scope of them. That is OK. As you see potential needs come up in this listening-to-learn meeting, jot them down. Refer back to them as needed to begin planning how you might address future needs and meet future goals. But strive to home in on at least one need in this meeting to serve as the first shared goal, if even small.

Note: so that the examples and scenarios we walk through in the next three chapters can be most concrete and constructive for you, all the needs and goals we use will pertain to RRE, i.e., rigor, relevance, or learner engagement. Know, though, that improvement and goals can also pertain to content areas.

For our purposes, I'll include reflection questions (many of which you will recognize from chapter 5) to help you pinpoint a teacher's current improvement needs. You might find that you won't be able to answer all these questions for all three RRE categories in the first meeting. That is OK. Answer what you can and aim to answer all of them through future observations:

- In general, how strong or weak is the teacher in achieving high levels of rigor/relevance/learner engagement in the classroom?
- Of the three rigor indicators/relevance indicators/learner engagement indicators, where is the teacher strongest? Where could the teacher benefit from receiving support?
- What do you see as the teacher's instructional improvement needs for rigor/relevance/learner engagement?

- Of the three RRE categories, in which one is the teacher strongest? In which area would he/she most benefit from receiving support?
- In terms of the teacher's greatest improvement needs, which category would come first? In that category, which indicator would come first?
- What does the teacher see as his/her current strengths? Is there alignment between this and improvement needs such that you can start from strength?
- In terms of the improvement need where it would be easiest to achieve quick gains, which category would come first? In that category, which indicator would come first?
- Are there needs that also align to school-wide improvement goals that can be prioritized? (More on this in later in the chapter.)
- How open is the teacher to change? How receptive does the teacher appear to the coaching process?

Turning Improvement Needs into Goals

Be sure to leave this meeting with at least one goal ready to go. This is all you need to get started. For maximal impact, it's best practice to focus on leading the teacher to meet only one goal at a time. In my experience, working to achieve many goals at once weighs down and slows the process and teacher growth.

Share with the teacher what you see as a good, initial improvement opportunity that can, of course, start from strength. Explain your rationale to the teacher and get her buy-in. If she objects, offer another improvement need that can also start from strength.

Once you and the teacher agree on the first improvement need you will tackle, turn this into a goal. I suggest using the SMART goal method; that is, building a goal that is specific, measurable, attainable relevant, and time-based.

Please visit www.leadered.com/coachingredefined to download the Coaching Goal Tracker chart.

Together, you and your teacher will fill out the "goal" section of the following chart (or a similar one, if you prefer) to ensure that everyone is on the same page, and that expectations and accountability for everyone are clear. Once you begin the coaching cycle for this goal, you will progress through completing this chart with your teacher. I've included an annotated version, where each section is described:

Coaching Goal Tracker	
Teacher Name	
Goal:	*Make sure that you co-create a SMART goal. Describe the goal here with specificity, including how progress will be measured and in what time frame you and the teacher agree the goal will be met.*
Coaching cycle # _____ for goal	*You will sometimes need to use multiple full coaching cycles to guide your teacher to meet the goal. Keep track of them by logging the number in this chart.*
Step 1: Design Date of this meeting:	*Record what you and your teacher discuss in step 1. Note here any and all plans made pertaining to the modality you've chosen for this cycle.*
Step 2: Develop Date of this meeting:	*The modality that will be used to help the teacher develop skills related to the goal. As needed and where appropriate, note here what you and the teacher will reflect upon after step 2 has been completed to discuss in step 3.*
Step 3: Discuss Date of this meeting:	*Note what you and the teacher discussed pertinent to step 2 and progress toward meeting the goal. If the goal was not met, identify tools or measures that can or must be taken to keep the teacher progressing and growing.*
Resources shared:	*Every time you suggest a resource to the teacher, list it here so that the teacher can easily reference each one in their ongoing learning. (It also helps you remember what the resources you suggested.)*
Action steps:	*List follow-up action steps you and/or the teacher agree to take to continue to make progress toward this goal. Make it clear what is expected by you and the teacher, and by when.*
Date for next meeting:	*With the teacher, set a date for your next meeting/ coaching cycle and list it here.*

You might need more than one coaching cycle for a goal. Repeat this chart as many times as needed to meet one goal. Track the succession of cycles by notating in the chart the coaching cycle number for the goal of your current focus.

Before You Start the Coaching Cycle: Determining GRC Spectrum Placement and the Best Modality

Before you start the coaching cycle with your teacher, you have to plan for it. Doing so means taking some time to reflect on where on the GRC rubric the teacher presently sits relative to the goal. This will be a factor in determining the most appropriate coaching modality to use first, and how you will coach in the coaching cycle, based on the teacher's spectrum placement. Refer back to the sections in this chapter where the GRC spectrum and modalities are explained. Use the rubric to place your teacher on the spectrum. Reflect on which modality would be most appropriate given the goal at hand and spectrum placement. From there, begin planning your first coaching cycle. (Don't worry—the next three chapters provide a range of coaching cycle scenarios to show you how to do this and get you comfortable with the process.)

Prioritizing Future Improvement Goals

A few final thoughts on planning goals the teacher and you might tackle in the future. Where possible, consider how your teacher's improvement goals align with those of the school's defined in the school-wide improvement plan. Is it possible to use any coaching cycles to lead her toward personal growth that can also drive school-wide growth? Where there's alignment around leading growth on the two levels of coaching *redefined*, seize this opportunity. If there isn't, that is OK. You are there to serve the teacher's needs, and that sometimes means prioritizing things that diverge from overall school goals.

Bear in mind, though, that anytime you and your teacher decide on a next goal to achieve, there is some nugget of strength in there from which you can launch the coaching cycle. By keeping your relationship with the teacher built on the positive, you will gain more and more of her trust.

And, in turn, she will grow ever more skilled and adept at serving her students' needs and goals. That's what a great servant leader does.

PONDER & POST

The Gradual Release Coaching rubric has helped me realize _____.

#coachingredefined

Chapter 8

Coaching for Rigor

Why Rigor Matters

In his 2010 book, *The Global Achievement Gap*, Tony Wagner diagnoses the primary deficit of our public schools in the twenty-first century as a design flaw. Our public schools, built for an industrial economy, were not designed to teach students to think. In an economy where most jobs required people to work with their hands, the concept of thinking was reserved for the very few who were set on the college preparatory track.

Wagner doesn't see our schools as "failing," per se. Rather, he sees them as outdated and by and large still working from the old industrial model. We all know that our economy today, which is global and based on complex technologies, is far from industrial. It requires critical thinking, creativity, and the ability to solve problems, often with and around several countries, cultures, and conflicting considerations.

Rigor is what allows people to access the capacity to think critically and on many levels of complexity. Rigor is bedrock to evolving our schools into institutions of deep thinking. Deep thinking is foundational to the career skills all our students need to thrive and prosper in this century. Rigor is where we start if we are to transform our schools to fit the needs of this century.

Defining Rigor

At its core, rigor simply refers to the deeper levels of thinking a person can do. In education, we look to Bloom's Revised Taxonomy for these levels of thinking, from the most basic to the most complex: Remembering, Understanding, Applying, Analyzing, Evaluating, and Creating. Remembering is nothing more than the acquisition of knowledge—a skill, in the internet age, that has become distinctly unremarkable and usually takes little more than a Google search. At the top is the capacity to use multiple kinds of complex thought to create new ideas or concepts. In between are increasingly more cognitively demanding ways of thinking that require varying levels of sub-skills, like synthesis, discernment, judgment, reasoning, and justification, to name some.

Rigorous levels of thinking are accessed through questions and learning tasks that demand it. When we intentionally design rigorous learning tasks for our students, we evolve our schools into institutions of deep thinking. When we don't, we perpetuate the deficient status quo.

When we ask students to think and learn with rigor, we coach them to mold their brains into flexible, adaptable assets that will align them to twenty-first-century careers. We also provide for them foundational career skills such as complex thinking, and skills that stem from it, such as in the social-emotional arena. To relate to people competently, we must be able to think deeply about and reflect deeply upon them—and ourselves.

What Rigor Is *Not*

Rigor is commonly misunderstood. I often see educators confuse it for more work. Or they believe that rigor is only possible with older students. If we are to increase the levels of rigor in our classrooms and schools, we have to begin by clarifying what rigor *is* so that we can avoid mistaking it for what it is *not*.

As I coach educators, I keep this little chart in mind, sharing it with them as needed so that they, too, can see clearly what rigor is—and is not—from the teacher's perspective.

Rigor is	Rigor is not
• Scaffolding thinking • Planning for thinking	• More or harder worksheets • AP or honors courses

Rigor is	Rigor is not
• Assessing the level of thinking about content • Recognizing the level of thinking students demonstrate • Managing the teaching/learning level for the desired thinking level • Possible for learners of all ages	• A higher Lexile level book • More work • More homework • Dependent on the age of child

How to Spot Rigor in Instruction and Learning

As a quick reference, I'm including the rigor portion of the RRE rubrics here. For the full rubrics, please see Appendix 3 or visit www.leadered.com /coachingredefined.

Rigor Rubric

Support teachers in building effective instruction based on rigorous expectations. The three indicators for rigor are: thoughtful work, high-level questioning, and academic discussion.

Thoughtful Work	1 – Beginning	2 – Emerging	3 – Developed	4 – Well Developed
Student Learning	• Students demonstrate their learning by completing recall and retell tasks. Most tasks draw on memorization and focus on answering recall-type questions.	• Students demonstrate their learning by completing tasks that require comprehension. • There are opportunities for students to demonstrate mastery through learning tasks that require them to apply knowledge and comprehend content.	• Students demonstrate their learning by completing tasks that validate their ability to analyze, synthesize, and/or evaluate new instructional content. • Tasks include the opportunity for students to respond to content through inquiry and interpretation.	• Students develop their own learning tasks that stretch their creativity, originality, design, or adaptation. • Tasks include the opportunity for students to assess their own learning and move forward to adapt their knowledge to new activities.
Instructional Design	• Learning tasks include one assigned way for students to demonstrate their thinking.	• Learning tasks include one or more assigned ways for students to demonstrate their thinking.	• Learning tasks allow students to self-select options to best represent their thinking.	• Learning tasks extend students' learning, inspiring them to pursue self-discovery.
High-Level Questioning	**1 – Beginning**	**2 – Emerging**	**3 – Developed**	**4 – Well Developed**
Student Learning	• Students respond to questions that mainly focus on basic recall and retell. • Few students ask questions, and most questions asked focus on basic recall or retelling of content.	• Students respond to questions that demonstrate a comprehension of content. • Students have opportunities to ask questions during the lesson and most questions focus on comparing and contrasting information.	• Students fully explain and justify their thinking when responding to questions that demonstrate different levels of thinking, including questions that require analysis, synthesis, and evaluation of information. • During the lesson, students generate questions about content that demonstrate rigorous independent thinking.	• Students actively engage in developing rigorous questions to challenge the thinking of their peers. • Students are able to respond to rigorous questions generated by peers with little guidance from the teacher.
Instructional Design	• Lesson mainly includes questions at the recall and retell level, and/or not all students are required to respond to each question.	• Lesson includes questions at a range of levels, but not all students are required to respond to each question.	• Lesson uses questioning to carefully support students in moving to higher levels of thinking, ensuring that all students have an opportunity to respond.	• Lesson is designed to inspire all students to engage in high-level questioning around the learning task with their teachers and peers.
Academic Discussion	**1 – Beginning**	**2 – Emerging**	**3 – Developed**	**4 – Well Developed**
Student Learning	• Student discussion is driven by the teacher and mainly remains at the retell level, mostly using everyday language, with little to no evidence of academic or domain-specific vocabulary. • Student discussion focuses on a variety of topics with each student offering his/her own thinking without using ideas from peers.	• Student discussion, structured by prompts from the teacher, includes a combination of retelling, analysis, and/ or stating a claim and defending it with evidence. • Students provide explanations or evidence of their thinking and respond to their peers' comments.	• Students engage with peers in teacher-guided academic discussions focused on analysis, synthesis, and evaluation of content-driven topics, using academic language to express their thinking regarding the major concepts studied. • Students support their ideas with concrete explanations and evidence, paraphrasing as appropriate, and build on or challenge the ideas of others.	• Students primarily drive the discussion, consistently adding value to the dialogue with their peers and teacher, and respecting the opinion and thoughts of both; the lesson shifts to conversation rather than a Q&A session regarding the major concepts studied. • Students are able to stay focused on the activities of inquiry and engage in dialogue, using content-rich vocabulary with their peers.
Instructional Design	• Lesson mostly structures discussion as teacher-led, with the majority of interactions as teacher to student.	• Lesson structures discussion as a mix of teacher-led and peer-to-peer with the teacher facilitating the majority of discussions.	• Lesson mostly structures discussion as independent peer-to-peer. The teacher facilitates and redirects the discussion as needed, while evaluating the quality.	• Lesson is designed to inspire students to independently engage in dialogue and add valuable academic content around the learning tasks.

Please visit www.leadered/coachingredefined to download the following rigor reflection questions.

The following questions can guide you as you look for evidence of rigor in lesson design and learning—across the three RRE indicators of thoughtful work, high-level questioning, and academic discussion—in teachers' classrooms. Remember: take notes objectively and specifically.

I often share these questions with teachers when I ask them to watch me model rigor in their classrooms or to observe a colleague's classroom. Keep in mind that if your teacher is on the guided discovery or self-directed point on the GRC spectrum, you might ask them to come up with their own questions to spot rigor as they observe. As needed, refer back to the questions here to ensure that all major points are covered.

Coaching & Observing Rigor: Reflection Questions

Thoughtful Work	• What level of thinking is required for the work? • To what degree do students participate in learning tasks that require them to analyze, synthesize, evaluate, and/or create information? • How do the learning tasks give students the opportunity to adapt their knowledge to new activities? • What evidence demonstrates that students take responsibility for extending their learning beyond the task assigned? • How do students demonstrate an ability to pursue self-discovery? • To what extent do students take risks and self-select avenues to best represent their own thinking? • Specifically, how is the thoughtful work incorporating today's careers skills, and which ones?
High-Level Questioning	• To what extent are students exposed to questions that ascertain their ability to analyze, synthesize, evaluate, and/or create information? • What evidence do you find that students can create and respond to questions in ways that demonstrate their ability to analyze, synthesize, and/or evaluate information? • What evidence demonstrates that students are able to ask the teacher questions that show they are analyzing, synthesizing and/or evaluating information? • To what extent do students demonstrate independent thinking?

High-Level Questioning	• What evidence demonstrates that students are able to challenge the thinking of their peers? • What evidence demonstrates that students are able to ask classmates questions that probe for analysis, synthesis, and/or information evaluation? • To what degree do students respond to their classmates' rigorous questions without guidance from the teacher? • How do students explain their answers, using credible sources and reasoning, when responding to questions that require them to analyze, synthesize, and/or evaluate information? • How are high-rigor questions creating opportunities for students to apply today's career skills, and which ones?
Academic Discussion	• To what degree do students verbalize learned content through the correct use of content-rich academic vocabulary? • To what degree do students primarily drive the discussion? • What evidence demonstrates that students add value to the thoughts their classmates share? • How do students stay engaged in academic conversations with their peers? • What evidence demonstrates that students are able to justify their thinking with evidence? • How are students taking responsibility to make unsolicited contributions to class discussions? • To what degree do students make an effort to hear from all other students? • What evidence demonstrates that students' thoughts matter to and are respected by all in the room? • How do students ask for clarification when needed? • How are academic discussions creating opportunities for students to apply today's career skills, and which ones?

How to Use the Coaching Scenarios

The majority of this chapter, and chapters 9 and 10, are coaching scenarios. They provide examples of how to coach for rigor—and relevance and learner engagement in the following chapters—based on a range of circumstances and grade levels.

All scenarios in this chapter and the next two will follow the same format, which I'll share in this section with a brief description of all components. A note before we get started: for each scenario to work, it must reflect reality. Before you begin any coaching cycle, recall that you will have done at least one classroom observation of a teacher and met with her at least once to listen to learn about her. We will assume certain insights from these interactions with the teacher in each scenario.

I will include four scenarios in this chapter. Across them, we will see examples of all four coaching modalities, all four Gradual Release Coaching points and their corresponding types of coaching, and all three of the RRE indicators that pertain to rigor. This range of scenario details will also be included in the next two chapters about relevance and learner engagement.

A note on coaching content: teaching and coaching the right content are important. However, even if you teach and coach the right content, if you don't also work toward high levels of rigor, relevance, and engagement, students will still only be consuming knowledge. For the sake of time, we will only address best practices that go across all content areas—which are rigor, relevance, and engagement—in the scenarios. Please do engage in PLNs and other ongoing learning opportunities to maintain fresh content-coaching skills.

Lastly, keep in mind that as you coach, you will be filling out the Coaching Goal Tracker sheet we discussed at the end of chapter 7. As you read through these scenarios, imagine filling out that chart as the coach and teacher progress through the coaching cycle.

Scenario Format

Each scenario will follow this format:

Context: Details to establish the scenario.

Insights from Observation: Points you, the coach, noted while observing the teacher in her classroom that pertain to the scenario.

Insights from Conversation: Points you noted while conversing with and listening to learn from the teacher about her practice, her strengths, her areas for improvement, and her goals that pertain to the scenario.

Your Analysis: Analyzing all the information you've gathered, your determination of the most immediate needs for growth (based on the

RRE rubric indicators) for the teacher that also allow you to start from strength.

The Goal You Co-Create: The goal you and the teacher create together to improve some aspect of the teacher's instruction and learning outcomes. As needed, use vision casting with a teacher when setting a goal, especially when the teacher believes a goal is out of reach. Refer back to chapter 2 to review how to vision cast.

When you do co-create these goals, I suggest making SMART goals—goals that are specific, measurable, achievable, relevant, and time-bound. Surrounding circumstances will inform many details of your SMART goal, e.g., the data-measurement tools in place, how frequently you can meet with a teacher, and other goals you and the teacher might be working on. For our purposes in the scenarios, we will not spell out all five components of a SMART goal, as doing so would require imagining a host of circumstances; omitting some of these details won't take away from the most important points of the scenarios.

GRC Spectrum Point: The point, of the four points along the Gradual Release Coaching Spectrum, on which you determine the teacher currently sits; this will dictate which of the four kinds of coaching is most appropriate for this coaching cycle.

Coaching Modality: The coaching modality you determine will be most effective in supporting the teacher to meet the co-created goal.

Resource(s) Used: Any and all resources used to support the teacher to meet the goal.

Coaching Cycle

1. *Design:* The planning necessary prior to moving to step 2.
2. *Develop:* The work that will help the teacher develop skills pertinent to the goal.
3. *Discuss:* You and the teacher meet to discuss progress toward the goal and any additional support that might be needed.

High Effect-Size Instructional Strategy Alignment: The high effect-size strategies (from Professor John Hattie) that are or can be used in this scenario to fortify teaching and validate the coach's suggestions. In some scenarios, I will spell out how to use a strategy. In others, doing so might not be necessary to complete the coaching cycle (i.e., for a self-directed learner, she would learn on her own, as opposed to the coach explicitly walking her through it).

For the purposes of space, I will not explain in detail how to apply the strategies. Please keep in mind that to get the greatest potential effect size out of any strategy, they need to be applied according to Hattie's research and directives. As needed, please visit one of the many resources online, or one of John Hattie's books, to learn how to apply a strategy for maximum benefit.

Career Skills Used: The career-relevant skills that students will use once the teacher applies insights from the coaching cycle to instruction. For our purposes, we'll use the career skills I mentioned in the introduction to this part of the book, on which I have expanded in Appendix 5.

Scenarios: Coaching Educators to Increase Rigor

RIGOR SCENARIO 1

Context: Mr. Simmons is a fourth-grade teacher whose class is always active. He loves to integrate movement into his lessons, and students love being in his classroom.

Insights from Observation: You observed students are working on multiplication using the following times tables worksheet:

1. $32 \times 9 =$	6. $31 \times 4 =$
2. $6 \times 14 =$	7. $1 \times 22 =$
3. $7 \times 19 =$	8. $37 \times 8 =$
4. $17 \times 5 =$	9. $6 \times 54 =$
5. $8 \times 24 =$	10. $79 \times 0 =$

Students worked with a partner to calculate the answers. As is typical in Mr. Simmons's class, you observed students engaged in academic conversation and collaboration as they solved the times table. As the coach, you are thinking about the learning tasks currently given to students and what they are required to do in these tasks. You understand that such straightforward multiplication tables are very low rigor. You also recognize that how students think will need to change for them to complete higher rigor learning tasks.

Insights from Conversation: Because students are constantly discussing their work with each other, the teacher believes his instruction promotes high rigor. Mr. Simmons demonstrated a reluctance to change his instruction because he's shared that his students' parents are pleased with his teaching and that his students are getting good grades. He fears that if he incorporates more rigorous questions, grades would deflate, and then parents would be upset with him.

Your Analysis: Based on your conversations with and observations of Mr. Simmons's instruction and the work tasks he gives, you can see that rigor needs improvement—and that Mr. Simmons's understanding of rigor is in need of clarification, as he is confusing engagement with rigor. Because you see that his learning tasks are engaging, you suggest starting growth with **thoughtful work**, as you can fold thoughtful work tasks into his current, admirable use of student collaboration.

The Goal You Co-Create: Deepen understanding of rigor and what it looks like at high levels in instruction and learning. Increase rigor through higher levels of thoughtful work. Skillfully scaffold work so that students are eased into increased rigor in their learning tasks. (And: come to see that parents will remain happy, and even, potentially, grow happier, when their children are thinking about math more rigorously and completing more rigorous learning tasks.)

GRC Spectrum Point: **Instructive coaching** because Mr. Simmons is in need of improved clarity around rigor defined and rigor in practice.

Coaching Modality: **Modeling.** Since Mr. Simmons is confusing rigor with engagement and mistaking low-rigor learning tasks for high-rigor tasks, you determine that it would benefit him to see what high-rigor math questions can look like, without sacrificing the engagement his students and their parents so appreciate. You also see that he would benefit from seeing math problems scaffolded to ease students into higher rigor and different kinds of thinking.

Resource(s) Used: Scenario-based math problems designed to scaffold

- **Math problem #1: Lower rigor:**
  Tony wants to make 3 cookies for each of his 6 friends. How many cookies will he have to make?
- **Math problem #2: Higher rigor:**
  Andrea needs to buy 5 pencils and 3 notebooks for her class. She goes to the store and notices the store sells ink pens for $1.00 each, pencils for $0.25, pencil boxes for $3.00 each, and notebooks for $0.75 each. How much does Andrea need to spend to buy what she needs?
- Coaching & Observing Rigor: Reflection Questions for thoughtful work.

Coaching Cycle

1. *Design:* To respect Mr. Simmons's plans for his students, ask him the content he intends to use and the skills he wants students to practice in the next class. Then plan the class you will model accordingly.

Meet with Mr. Simmons to provide context on step 2 and prepare him for observing as you model different levels of rigor in his next class. Begin by praising Mr. Simmons for caring deeply about creating an engaging, active learning environment where students have opportunities to practice collaboration skills. Explain that the active learning environment provides students a great opportunity to collaborate on higher rigor learning tasks.

Because you are using instructive coaching, take time to explain to him how rigor is distinct from learner engagement. Define for Mr. Simmons what rigor is and is not; what rigor looks like at high and low levels; and tools and strategies Mr. Simmons can apply to increase rigor in his classroom, including scaffolding.

Talk specifically about what thoughtful work looks like—as instruction and learning—at varying levels of rigor, using the RRE to guide your conversation. Explain to Mr. Simmons that scenario-based math problems require students to think more deeply, so you will be using them to increase rigor in thoughtful work. Explain to him that as you model, you will be using a range of rigor levels to scaffold the thinking students will work up to in a higher-rigor math problem. Ask him to take notes as you model, specifically identifying levels of rigor, the types of thinking used in your thoughtful-work learning tasks, and insights from how you scaffold them. To help him on this front, share with him the Coaching & Observing Rigor: Reflection Questions that appear at the start of the chapter.

2. *Develop:* Model thoughtful work in Mr. Simmons's classroom. You model two scenario-based math problems, beginning with math problem #1 to serve as scaffolded work for math problem #2. (Problem #2 aligns to Hattie's cognitive task analysis—1.29 effect size). Allow students to solve problems in pairs so that Mr. Simmons can see how high rigor (which requires critical thinking and complex problem-solving) is possible in collaboration. As you model, Mr. Simmons takes notes.

3. *Discuss:* Meet with Mr. Simmons to discuss his observations as you modeled thoughtful work. As you discuss, look to see that Mr. Simmons understood that in math problem #1, the level of thinking required was intentionally lower rigor to scaffold in preparation for problem #2. Ensure that he can see that this problem is low rigor, with all the information the students needed provided and only basic multiplication skills required. Look to see that he can recognize why math problem #2 was more complex; students first had to analyze the problem to grasp what is being asked of them. Then they had to evaluate which data they needed and which data they could ignore. To solve the problem, both multiplication and addition skills were needed. Ask Mr. Simmons how he perceived the student response to being faced with more rigor. Talk him through the power of holding and setting high expectations of all students and designing learning tasks accordingly. Ensure that he understands that when he believes in his students' capacity to learn and grow, his students will come to believe in their own capacity to learn and grow (teacher estimate of student achievement—1.62 effect size).

Where Mr. Simmons is missing key points of higher and lower rigor in thoughtful work, explain as needed to fortify his understanding. If he's clear, together discuss a new goal to achieve. If he needs more practice around thoughtful work, set a new goal accordingly for the next coaching cycle, which might naturally flow into the lesson-planning modality so that you can guide Mr. Simmons toward planning higher-rigor questions.

High Effect-Size Instructional Strategy Alignment:
- Cognitive task analysis—1.29 effect size
- Teacher estimates of student achievement—1.62 effect size

Career Skills Used:
- Critical thinking
- Complex problem solving

RIGOR SCENARIO 2

Context: Ms. Garcia is an eighth-grade history teacher who prefers her class to be quiet and orderly. Her primary method of teaching is through lecture, and she typically follows the order of content in the textbook. For homework, she will usually assign the knowledge and comprehension questions found at the end of the chapter.

Insights from Observation: As you observe Ms. Garcia teach, you notice she asks students various levels of questions during her lectures—some of low, moderate, and high rigor. However, when she asks more rigorous questions, you notice that she provides little wait time and typically ends up answering them for the students. In addition, all the questions she's assigning for homework are of low rigor.

Insights from Conversation: Ms. Garcia has shared that she struggles to get students to answer high-rigor questions in homework and has, therefore, quit assigning them. She demonstrates that she knows the difference between high and low rigor.

Your Analysis: You suggest that you begin coaching higher levels of **academic discussion** and **thoughtful work**. Since Ms. Garcia understands what rigor is and can select or ask high-rigor questions (high-rigor questions can align to cognitive task analysis—1.29 effect size), you see an opportunity to start from this strength in these areas. However, her students clearly need scaffolding to answer these questions.

The Goal You Co-Create: Apply strategies to scaffold high-rigor questions asked in class (oral) and on homework assignments (written). Boost the amount of student-to-student academic discussion (classroom discussion—.82 effect size; high-rigor discussion demands judgment and decision making) so that students can routinely achieve high levels of rigor collectively. Support students in successfully completing rigorous, thoughtful work (complex problem-solving).

GRC Spectrum Point: **Illustrative coaching** because Ms. Garcia understands rigor but needs guidance scaffolding students' thinking to answer high-level rigor questions. You determine that using illustrative examples will help show her effective strategies to move students to think at higher levels.

Coaching Modality: **Observation** because you determine that after showing her examples of rigor scaffolding, you will best serve her by observing her as she puts them into practice in her own classroom. After, you can reflect together on areas of growth and areas where more support might be needed.

Resource(s) Used:

- Video examples of successful rigor scaffolding for oral questions. You share a video of a teacher using scaffolded questions to follow a high-rigor question, supporting students to use deeper thinking to answer the question. Such scaffolded instructions include: "What information do you know already?" "Can you explain your thinking?" "Who can add to that thinking?" When no students answer, this teacher prompts students to a resource where they can find the answer, and then she waits for someone to answer, or asks a student if none volunteers.
- Example of written assignments that include prompts to scaffold student thinking (scaffolding—.82 effect size). You share with the teacher an example of high-rigor written questions that also include support questions to scaffold thinking. Such support questions include: "Read the question. What does it ask? What information does it give you? Can you justify your thinking and how?"
- Observing & Coaching Rigor: Reflection Questions for thoughtful work and academic discussion.

Coaching Cycle

1. *Design:* Acknowledge and praise Ms. Garcia for her skilled understanding of low and high rigor, as well as her commitment to asking high-rigor questions in class and on assignments. Show her the video of a teacher scaffolding rigorous questions. Ask Ms. Garcia to analyze and comment on the questions the teacher uses to scaffold rigorous academic discussion. Share with her an example of a rigorous written assignment that includes prompts to guide students' thinking toward answering high-rigor questions.

Since you will be observing Ms. Garcia, discuss with her how she can apply these strategies in her classroom. To familiarize her students with scaffolded prompts in written questions, suggest that she provides an example in class. She can then allow students to discuss the question and its prompts in groups. This will be followed by a class discussion where students are expected to share about this experience, explain what they learned, and ask additional questions so that they are prepared to complete rigorous homework assignments. Use the RRE to frame this conversation and discuss with Ms. Garcia what thoughtful work and academic discussion look like at different levels of instruction and learning.

Let Ms. Garcia know what you will be looking for as you observe her next lesson (refer back to the Observing & Coaching Rigor: Reflection Questions earlier in the chapter to guide your observation).

2. *Develop:* Observe Ms. Garcia's next class session. Watch to what extent she successfully scaffolds high-rigor questions and takes care not to answer questions for students. Where they cannot answer, see if she points students to a resource to find supporting evidence and then waits for them to share insights. In the exercise around the written questions, check whether the question is well scaffolded. As students engage in academic discussion, once again watch whether Ms. Garcia is scaffolding questions as needed and not answering questions for students. Refer back to chapter 5 for classroom observation protocol; most importantly, do not interrupt the class session and be sure to take detailed and objective, not subjective, notes.

3. *Discuss:* Meet with Ms. Garcia to discuss your observation notes. Discuss with her where she showed growth and strength and make suggestions based on areas still in need of improvement. Ask her if she struggled with anything, if she felt the students struggled with anything, and if she feels she needs more support from you on this goal. As needed, provide more scaffolded questions she can apply. If you both feel she's achieved the goal, move onto a new one.

High Effect-Size Instructional Strategy Alignment:
- Cognitive task analysis—1.29 effect size
- Classroom discussion—.82 effect size
- Scaffolding—.82 effect size

Career Skills Used:
- Judgment and decision making
- Complex problem-solving

RIGOR SCENARIO 3

Context: Mr. Whitworth is a tenth-grade building trades (CTE) teacher. He loves to teach through authentic project-based learning (PBL) experiences and enjoys incorporating student feedback into his lessons.

Insights from Observation: When you observe Mr. Whitworth, the majority of students are actively engaged in learning. He is constantly walking around to assist students. You notice he asks students a wide variety of questions, some at high levels of rigor, others at low levels. Students ask him rigorous questions and he proficiently scaffolds his responses to help them find the answers to their questions. However, you noticed that when he assesses students, he asks them only low rigor questions that do little more than invite students to recall content information.

Insights from Conversation: Through conversation, you learn that Mr. Whitworth struggles to write high-level assessment questions; doing so would help him assess if students are developing the skills needed to work through high-rigor PBL tasks on their own. (When PBL incorporates all intended components and is built from rigorous questions, it requires critical thinking, judgment, and decision-making). He shows that he does grasp about assessments what many miss: if you only ask low-rigor questions in assessment, it communicates to students that basic recall is the information and type of learning that matters most. Mr. Whitworth tells you he really wants his assessment questions to match the level of rigor he achieves in classroom instruction. He demonstrates a clear understanding of what rigor is, which aligns to your observation of his skill at asking questions of a range of rigor in class.

Your Analysis: Mr. Whitworth will benefit from tools to help him take his skill at asking high-rigor questions in class and apply it to drafting high-rigor assessment questions. This will allow you to start from strength to transfer these skills to crafting **high-level questions** for written assessment.

The Goal You Co-Create: Create higher-level assessment questions connected to the content and skills of the lesson that can reveal to Mr. Whitworth how each student is progressing.

GRC Spectrum Point: **Guided discovery coaching** because Mr. Whitworth is already adept at scaffolding oral questions in class and has demonstrated an eagerness to improve his assessments, and your perceptions of his instruction align to his.

Coaching Modality: **Lesson planning.** You determine you can best serve Mr. Whitworth by helping him plan high-rigor assessment questions to apply in his next class session.

Resource(s) Used:

- A high-rigor assessment question prompt. As a guided-discovery prompt (see below), you will share with Mr. Whitworth an example of a high-rigor assessment question, inspired by a *Popular Mechanics* article (Truini, 2017).

Guided-Discovery Prompt for Mr. Whitworth:
Read the following scenario and answer the questions below.

We built a shed on a foundation of 12 solid-concrete blocks. The 4" × 8" × 16" blocks are arranged in three rows spaced 59" apart. These blocks are typically set directly on the ground, but we put down a 4" bed of sand first because our site occasionally receives groundwater. The sand will keep the soil beneath the shed from eroding or becoming soggy.

We eyed the blocks to see if they seemed level. We shimmed up any blocks that seemed low with strips of asphalt roofing, cedar shingles, or 2"-thick concrete patio blocks. Next, we formed each front and rear band joist by nailing a 2" × 6" to a 2" × 8" mudsill. Then we set the mudsills on top of the blocks running across the front and rear of the shed. Finally, we cut a third 2" × 8" mudsill to fit along the tops of the center row of foundation blocks.

Questions:

1. Evaluate the steps the builders followed. What did they do wrong?

2. Based on what we have learned in class, what would happen if these steps were followed?

3. How would you redesign this plan to address these issues?

Coaching Cycle

1. *Design:* As you begin your meeting with Mr. Whitworth, praise him for routinely using authentic PBL in his classroom, which takes advanced skills. Acknowledge his ease at scaffolding rigorous questions in class. Before sharing the guided discovery prompt with him, engage in a brief conversation about rigor and assessment questions. Explain that just as not all questions need to be high rigor in classroom discussion, not all questions need to be high rigor in assessments. Also point out that to suddenly ask students only high-rigor assessment questions would be too dramatic a change; instead, he should plan to fold in more high-rigor questions in the coming weeks, taking care to include some opportunities for students to use graphic organizers and/or journals to transfer skills and reflect on some of their rigorous learning (transfer strategies—.86 effect size).

Share with him the prompt and ask him to dissect it; ask him to consider its components, how it connects to content, and what about it makes it high rigor (i.e., the skills required to answer it). Then ask him to take all these pieces of what goes into a rigorous assessment question to create one of his own. Prompt him to consider what he really wants the children to know for this lesson (i.e., the knowledge they'll need to answer the assessment question) and the skills he wants them to apply in doing so (e.g., critical thinking, judgment and decision making, etc.) prior to creating a high-rigor assessment question. Remind him to reference the RRE to frame his thinking and analysis of questions.

Remain by his side—literally or available to him via email, whatever makes sense given the circumstances—to offer guidance or answer questions. Once he's come up with an assessment of his own, discuss it with him. Offer strategies for improvement as needed.

2. *Develop:* Mr. Whitworth teaches the class and gives the high-level assessment he created.

3. *Discuss:* You meet with Mr. Whitworth to discuss how it went when he gave the students a high-level assessment. Ask him what he thought went well and if he thought he or the students struggled in any way. Ask him if he'd like more guided discovery prompts to improve his skill in drafting high-rigor assessments or if he needs tools to ensure his students are prepared for them. If you both feel he's met this goal, move onto a new one and a new coaching cycle.

High Effect-Size Instructional Strategy Alignment:
- Transfer strategies—.86 effect size

Career Skills Used:
- Critical thinking
- Judgment and decision making

RIGOR SCENARIO 4

Context: You have coached all six middle-school math teachers for a couple of years.

Insights from Observation: You have observed that all six math teachers are asking high-level written and oral questions (which require of students complex problem solving). However, you notice that two of the teachers are leading academic discussion around high-level questions, and the other four teachers allow their students to lead academic discussion (which aligns to seeking help from peers—.85 effect size). In the classes where students are collaborating with each other to ask and answer rigorous questions, you notice that students are growing in their ability to have deeper academic discussions and adapt their thinking based on the thinking of their peers (cognitive flexibility).

Insights from Conversation: Over the years, you have watched all of these eager and motivated teachers grow into self-directed learners. They frequently collaborate and enjoy learning from each other. Each of them knows that what's best for students is what matters most and therefore are always seeking professional learning to improve their teaching practice to this end. They each have a firm grasp on what rigor is and is not.

Your Analysis: Since these teachers have a proven track record of collaborative learning and skill sharing, you see an opportunity for the four teachers still leading **academic discussion** to observe the other two who've turned it over to students. Since the teachers in need of improvement in academic discussion already have a solid grasp of what high rigor is, any of the rigor indicators is an opportunity to start from strength.

The Goal You Co-Create: Apply observed strategies to raise the level of rigor in student-to-student academic discussions.

GRC Spectrum Point: **Self-directed coaching**, as the teachers have for some time now shown eagerness to learn on their own and success with it. They all habitually reflect on their practice and are always working to improve.

Coaching Modality: **Guided observation** because they have historically worked well together, and two of the teachers are skilled in the area where the other two teachers want to improve.

Resource(s) Used:

- Other teachers and their skill in their own classrooms
- Reflection questions for the observation (to be drawn up by the teachers as a group in step one of the coaching cycle). Refer back to the Coaching & Observing Rigor: Reflection Questions as needed to ensure teachers aren't missing major points.

Coaching Cycle

1. *Design:* Praise the teachers for their ongoing commitment to doing whatever they can to do what's best for students. Ask that the group

of all six teachers meet to discuss the goals at hand. Ask them to come up with reflection questions to consider and answer (by taking notes) as they observe their colleagues. If they are stuck, suggest they refer to RRE to frame their thinking. As needed, guide teachers to learn or review an observation protocol (which you can provide from chapter 5, or they can find a resource on their own) in advance of doing their observation.

2. *Develop:* Have two teachers observe one of the teachers having success with academic discussion, and the other two observe the other teacher who is having success. (By sending teachers in at least pairs to observe, it allows for a common observation, which facilitates discussion in step 3.) As they observe, they keep in mind the questions from step 1 and take notes on the questions they hear.

3. *Discuss:* Teachers regroup and discuss what they observed. As needed, they include you for feedback or additional support. Or, if you and they are comfortable with them meeting without you at this step, simply ask them to commit to each other to adapt at least one strategy they observed into their classrooms by a certain date. Ask them to share this commitment with you for added accountability.

High Effect-Size Instructional Strategy Alignment:
- Seeking help from peers—.85 effect size

Career Skills Used:
- Complex problem solving
- Cognitive flexibility

Strategies & Tools for Elevating Rigor in Instruction and Learning

What follows are strategies and tools, with brief descriptions, that are effective in incorporating higher levels of rigor into instruction and learning. This is a starting point and by no means a complete list. In your own ongoing commitment to shoring up your coaching and instructional skills, you will surely come across other strategies and tools you can use to improve rigor. Use your judgment.

Note that a rigor strategy or tool could also support relevance and engagement—and vice versa. While it happens, it is rare that a strategy or tool will strictly support only rigor, only relevance, or only engagement. It is typical that a strategy or tool will be capable of driving the largest impact in one area (e.g., rigor) and drive smaller impacts in others (e.g., relevance and/or engagement).

When I coach for rigor, I will often suggest to teachers that they apply these strategies/tools, as they are strong drivers of rigor. Depending on where a teacher is on the GRC spectrum will inform how explicit I am in how to use a strategy/tool expertly. For example, if the teacher would benefit from instructive coaching, I will outline in detail how to use the strategy/tool. If he is at the point of self-directed coaching, I will leave that learning to him.

Academic Vocabulary Cards: To promote academic discussion, the teacher provides students with an index list of academic vocabulary words that correlate with the topic they will be discussing in groups. The teacher places the index card in the middle of each of the groups. As groups engage in discussion, they are expected to accurately use as many vocabulary words on the index card as they can. As the teacher circulates the room to listen to all group conversations, she makes note of the terms she hears students use correctly.

Agree/Disagree: To promote academic discussion, the teacher asks all students if they agree or disagree with a student when an answer is given to the teacher's question. Students can give a thumbs up if they agree or a thumbs down if they disagree. To start a dialogue, the teacher follows-up with, "Why do you disagree/agree?" and "What evidence can you provide to support your answer?"

I Know, You Know: This strategy allows students to recall what they know about a topic and build on that knowledge through small group academic conversation. The teacher gives students a text and the I Know, You Know graphic organizer, which you can find in Appendix 6. Students are asked to skim the text. They silently record what they already know about the text's topic in the numbered rows on the graphic organizer. Next, they have a conversation with group members to discuss what each knows at this point. Then, students silently read the text in full, annotating newly learned information in the text. The group has a conversation about the information they learned from the reading, and each person notes on her graphic organizer what her peers shared. Finally, each person records any questions that come up while discussing the text.

Improve This!: This strategy encourages students to think through different ways to solve a problem. The teacher gives students a text, object, or complete answer to a problem and asks students to enhance or improve it in a specific way. For example, the teacher could give students a published story and ask students to improve the dialogue in the story to show more of the characters' emotions. Or a teacher could give students a car that was designed during a science lab and ask students to make it run faster. Another teacher might give students an answer to a math problem and ask them to explain the steps that went into clearly and specifically.

Jigsaw: This strategy, which has a 1.2 effect size, provides students a structure to assist with meaningful academic conversations based on material they've read. When working in small groups, students are assigned roles. Students will divide a text, read their assigned sections of the text, and make note of any important information on the jigsaw graphic organizer. Once everyone in the group has finished reading his or her section, all group members will use their roles to take turns sharing important information from what they read. Finally, the group collaboratively writes a summary of the text and records it on the graphic organizer. See Appendix 7 for an example of the jigsaw graphic organizer.

Not Quite, But Close: To promote the idea of growth mindset, a teacher selects a student answer to share that isn't one hundred percent correct but has many correct qualities. The teacher first asks and gains permission from the student to use his work-product, without his name attached. Then the teacher displays the work without the student's name on it. Students engage in a conversation to discuss what is correct about the answer and what could be corrected to make the answer one hundred percent correct. The teacher takes time to praise the student for sharing his work as a learning opportunity for the whole class.

Rate the Work: A teacher gives students several samples of completed work from their peers and ask students to have an academic discussion about the work samples. Students are expected to ask their peers rigorous questions about the completed work and provide their classmates ideas for improvement. Then, time is given to their classmates to use the feedback to improve their work.

Reciprocal Teaching: This strategy gives roles to team members, typically around the cognitive strategies of predicting, summarizing, questioning, and clarifying. As a group, students read a text and then record their thoughts in a graphic organizer about it based on their role (summarizing it, making a prediction about it, etc.). Group members then take turns sharing what they wrote on the graphic organizer and discussing everyone's contributions. Note that this strategy can also be carried out by individual students. Please see Appendix 8 for the reciprocal teaching graphic organizer.

Socratic Smackdown: The Socratic Smackdown uses research to promote academic debate. During this game, which mimics a Socratic Seminar, students are divided into teams. Each team is given time to research a topic related to an essential question. Then all teams participate in an academic debate on the topic. Points are given when students make valid arguments based on evidence, and points are subtracted if students interrupt each other. (The full Socratic Smackdown teaching guide can be found at www.instituteofplay.org/learning-games.)

Student Conversation Starters: The teacher provides students with conversation-starter questions to assist them in learning how to have more meaningful and rigorous student-to-student conversations and academic discussions. Please see Appendix 9 for a list of conversation starters.

Technology Integration: Teachers can integrate technology into instruction to promote rigorous learning. Various interactive learning technologies—such as EDpuzzle, PlayPosit, and Nearpod—help a teacher to embed rigorous questions into PowerPoints, videos, or gifs.

Visit www.leadered.com/coachingredefined for an evolving and updated list of strategies and tools to elevate rigor in instruction and learning.

Teachers, then, can pause instruction at intentional learning moments to ask rigorous questions, giving students opportunities to think critically about content and teachers opportunities to assess their understanding. Always keep in mind that technology is only as strong as the pedagogy behind it. Take care to consider the levels of rigor in the questions and learning tasks that are incorporated into any tech tools.

Trade-a-Thought: This activity is meant to help students reflect on their own thoughts, share those thoughts with others, and actively listen to their classmates as they share their thoughts with them. On a graphic organizer, students will write their responses to a prompt given by the teacher. Students in grades K–2 may draw a picture and write a sentence under the picture. They will trade papers with one partner and each will take turns sharing and listening to thoughts. After, the teacher will lead an academic discussion where students explain to the class what their partners shared with them. For students in grades 3 and up, they will write their thoughts as complete sentences. Students will then join groups of three students, where each student will ask the other two to share their thoughts while recording both classmates' responses on their own graphic organizer. After group work is complete, the teacher may choose to lead a whole-class academic discussion where students are asked to share and reflect on the thoughts they gathered from their classmates. See Appendix 10 for an example of the graphic organizer for students in grades K–2 and for students in grades 3 and up.

PONDER & POST

To coach toward more rigorous instruction, it's important to remember _____.

#coachingredefined

Chapter 9

Coaching for Relevance

Why Relevance Matters

Relevance matters in our schools and to our students for two primary reasons. The first, and more straightforward, reason comes down to the fact that you wouldn't teach someone to play basketball simply by having them read a book about it. You'd get them on the court, have them run drills, practice dribbling, practice shooting, and practice playing the game both defensively and offensively on a team. Or, you wouldn't teach someone to make beef bourguignon—perhaps the crown achievement of Julia Childs' *Mastering the Art of French Cooking*—simply by telling them to read the recipe. You'd have them *make* the recipe while you guide them through the hows, whys, science, and mechanics of each ingredient and step.

The same must become true of career skills. It's not enough to tell students that lawyers use analysis, judgment and decision making, negotiation, and evaluation in their work. It's not enough to tell students that electricians must be dependable, honest, patient, and capable of reacting to different circumstances and making quick, but thoughtful, decisions. It's far more powerful to create learning tasks that, as closely as possible, replicate these scenarios so that students can *use* these skills.

This is relevant learning. It is what allows our students to put skills to use, to practice them, hone them, improve them, and—in time—adapt them flexibly and confidently to different scenarios. It's what helps take instruction and learning from the abstract to the concrete, from the strictly academic to the real world.

The more real-world relevant learning is, the more it can help students discover and grow familiar with different career paths and the skills required of them. It can also begin to help students envision themselves as capable, competent, confident assets in their eventual careers. It is here where relevance matters for a second reason.

Career and college ready—*in that order*. As I've said, every student needs a career; not every student will need a college degree—especially one that could saddle them with debt for decades to come.

Defining Relevance

Always aiming to weave relevance into instruction is how we evolve our schools into institutions that help students make the most sensible, sound, responsible, and realistic decision for themselves after high school gradu-ation. By exposing students—from an early age—to a range of careers and career skills, we help them begin to recognize their natural aptitudes. We help them discover career interests. We help them grow confident in their skills. We help them consider which careers match those skills they have honed well and enjoy using and which do not. By intentionally bring-ing relevant learning into our classrooms and engaging students in con-versations about the skills that go into these scenarios, we are laying the groundwork for students to think deeply about possible careers and, in time, make informed decisions about them, including any additional edu-cation that might be necessary to pursue them.

Three Channels of Relevance

The most common misunderstanding I see in schools is that people believe relevance can only be accessed through circumstances happening in the real world. This is a fair misunderstanding as we hear the term "real-world relevance" again and again. We've heard it here in this chapter.

However, relevance is more nuanced than that. There are three chan-nels of relevance, which means there are three ways we can help students access relevant learning. They are:

1. Personal Relevance: Learning that addresses an individual's aspi-rations, interests, and experiences (Glossary of Education Reform, 2013). It is through this channel that we help students explore careers through the lens of their natural skills and interests.

2. Cultural Relevance: Learning that incorporates cultures and students' backgrounds. It is through this channel that we teach our students that their culture and heritage are valuable, valued, and provide them unique perspectives and insights into the world they can apply to enrich a range of circumstances. Cultural relevance is a profound and accessible way to promote equity, which in turn instills confidence in our students (Ladson-Billings, 1995).

3. Global Relevance: Learning that incorporates real-world challenges, problems, and circumstances. It is through this channel that we show how knowledge and skills connect to the broader world.

We must seek to use all three channels evenly in our instructional design. I think part of the reason that schools tend to over-emphasize global or real-world evidence is because ten years ago, it might have been enough to do so. Today, it's not.

As I mentioned, relevance is also about guiding students to see themselves as having natural gifts and value. Only in accessing personal and cultural relevance, in addition to and equal to global relevance, can we help make relevant learning feel personal to them.

Furthermore, we are all reading more and more stark, alarming headlines about the mental health crisis our students and children are facing. It's not the purpose of this book—nor is it within my professional grasp—to diagnose what's shifted in our culture or values to cause so much emotional distress among our students. But my experience has made me confident that teaching the whole child is one way we as educators can begin to counter our students' emotional and mental distress.

Whole, human children—with lives, stressors, and challenges at home—walk into our schools every day. We as educators must acknowledge this. Yes, we call them "students," but they are so much more than that. They are innocent, impressionable children under our care for several hours a day. We must see them, treat them with care, listen to them, learn from them, and show a sincere interest in them and their wellbeing.

Personal relevance and cultural relevance are the channels through which we can show we care about *knowing*, not just teaching, our students. It is through these channels that we build relationships with them,

Relevance Rubric

Support teachers in building effective instruction based on relevance of experiences to learners. The three indicators for relevance are: meaningful work, authentic resources, and learning connections.

Meaningful Work	1 – Beginning	2 – Emerging	3 – Developed	4 – Well Developed
Student Learning	• Student work is procedural and structured, reflecting a basic understanding of information learned during the lesson/unit. • Student work focuses on class-specific content, with an emphasis on building skills, developing comprehension, or other foundational skills.	• Students think critically about content and apply information learned to address a specific task. Student work demonstrates originality. • Student work requires application of knowledge learned during the lesson/unit.	• Students think critically about content and apply information learned to address a range of cross-disciplinary tasks. Student work demonstrates creativity and originality. • Student work requires real-world predictable and/or unpredictable application that has a direct connection to a career in the related field of study.	• Students think and act critically to curate content and apply information learned to address a range of cross-disciplinary tasks which are both creative and original. • Student work requires the ability to select, organize, and present content through relevant products with multiple solutions.
Instructional Design	• Lesson provides students an opportunity to demonstrate foundational understanding of content.	• Lesson provides students an opportunity to complete a specific task that requires application of knowledge.	• Lesson provides students an opportunity to select from a range of real-world, relevant tasks, using critical thinking about new learning to complete the task.	• Lesson inspires students with an opportunity to think critically about new learning to create their own real-world, relevant tasks.

Authentic Resources	1 – Beginning	2 – Emerging	3 – Developed	4 – Well Developed
Student Learning	• Students mainly engage with one source of information for the lesson and/or unit. • Students use one source to complete simple tasks focused on making simple connections to content.	• Students engage with one primary source of information for the lesson and/or unit, and use secondary resources to support it. • Students use one or more sources to complete real-world tasks focused on making simple connections to content.	• Students engage with multiple sources of information, both primary and secondary, during a lesson/unit. • Students use multiple sources of information to complete real-world tasks involving comparisons, analysis, argument, and research.	• Students engage with multiple sources of information, both primary and secondary, during a lesson/unit, including multi-format resources. • Students select and use a variety of resources to solve predictable or unpredictable real-world scenarios.
Instructional Design	• Lesson relies on one source of information. The unit/lesson is organized around the structure of the content-specific text.	• Lesson is structured around an essential understanding/question, uses primary and secondary sources, and includes opportunities for students to connect content to a content-specific text and an additional resource.	• Lesson is structured around an essential understanding/question and relies on multiple authentic texts and resources to conduct comparisons, analysis, arguments, research, and other relevant, real-world tasks.	• Lesson is structured around an essential understanding/question and relies on students to select multiple authentic texts and resources to engage in real-world problem solving.

Learning Connections	1 – Beginning	2 – Emerging	3 – Developed	4 – Well Developed
Student Learning	• Students seldom have the opportunity to engage in content that has explicit connection to real-world application. • Some students may attempt to make connections between content learned and real-world application, but these connections are volunteered rather than included as part of the lesson.	• Students occasionally engage in content that has explicit connection to real-world application. • Some students begin to articulate the connections between content learned and real-world application.	• Students engage in content that has explicit connections to real-world applications. • Students clearly articulate the connections between content learned and real-world application.	• Students discover opportunities to apply content to their lives as well as real-world application. • Students independently make thoughtful connections between content learned and real-world unpredictable situations.
Instructional Design	• Lesson provides appropriate content, but without explicit connections to real-world application.	• Lesson provides some opportunities to connect content learned to real-world application.	• Lesson provides multiple explicit opportunities for students to connect content learned to real-world applications.	• Lesson inspires students to create their own opportunities to connect content learned to their lives, as well as real-world applications.

make them feel seen and valued, and that they come to see us as adults they can trust. And when they trust us, they will listen to us. When they listen to us, they will believe us when we tell every single one of them that they *all* have gifts and are capable of achieving at high levels. When they trust us, they will take leaps of faith in their learning with us.

Global relevance is vital in our classrooms. But it is no longer enough for preparing our students to thrive in the real world. To help our students nurture the social-emotional skills that will fortify their resilience, confidence, and capacity to persevere through life's challenges, we must intentionally and evenly incorporate all three channels of relevance in our classrooms.

How to Spot Relevance in Instruction and Learning

As a quick reference, I'm including the relevance section of the RRE rubrics here. For the full rubrics, please see Appendix 3.

The following questions can guide you as you look for evidence of relevance in lesson design and learning—across the three RRE indicators of meaningful work, authentic resources, and learning connections—in teachers' classrooms. Share these questions with your teachers as appropriate, or ask them to come up with their own when they observe you model relevance or observe relevance in a colleague's classroom.

Visit www.leadered.com/coachingredefined to download the Coaching & Observing Relevance: Reflection Questions

Coaching & Observing Relevance: Reflection Questions

Meaningful Work	• To what degree are students engaged in tasks that require them to apply learned information in interdisciplinary tasks?
	• How do students create original content while engaged in interdisciplinary tasks?
	• How do students demonstrate cognitive flexibility when completing learning tasks?
	• To what degree do students exhibit the ability to select, organize, and present content through relevant products?
	• What evidence shows that there are multiple possible solutions to the task students are assigned?

Meaningful Work	• How does the lesson encourage students to create their own relevant, real-world tasks? • Specifically, how is meaningful work incorporating today's careers skills, and which ones?
Authentic Resources	• What evidence demonstrates that students are engaging with multiple sources of information? • To what degree do students use a variety of sources of information, both primary and secondary? • What evidence demonstrates that students utilize real-world tools to complete the learning task? • What evidence demonstrates that students utilize digital tools to complete the learning task? • To what degree are multi-format resources utilized during the lesson? • What evidence demonstrates that students are able to select and use a variety of resources? • What evidence shows that students have an opportunity to solve both predictable and unpredictable real-world problems? • How is the lesson structured around an essential question that relies on students selecting multiple authentic texts and resources to engage in real-world problem solving? • How is the use of authentic resources creating opportunities for students to apply today's career skills, and which ones?
Learning Connections	• How do students demonstrate an ability to apply learned content to their lives? • How do students demonstrate an ability to apply content to real-world applications? • How do students demonstrate the ability to connect learned content to real-world, unpredictable situations? • How is the lesson designed to give students an opportunity to create connections between the learned content and the real world? • What evidence demonstrates that time has been allotted for students to make personal connections as part of the lesson? • How are learning connections being used to create opportunities for students to apply today's career skills, and which ones?

Scenarios: Coaching Educators to Increase Relevance

RELEVANCE SCENARIO 1

Context: Ms. Rose is a third-grade teacher currently completing a unit on money.

Insights from Observation: When you observed her classroom, Ms. Rose had given students a matching game to play. They were to match a picture of a coin or paper money to a card that matches its monetary value.

Insights from Conversation: Ms. Rose has expressed to you that she cannot see how third graders are old enough to handle relevance in the classroom. She does want to incorporate more meaningful work but is struggling to imagine what this could look like for students so young.

Your Analysis: You determine that Ms. Rose doesn't have a strong enough understanding of relevance, as a strong understanding of relevance allows a teacher to imagine its application at any grade level. Because of Ms. Rose's desire to improve in the area of **meaningful work**, coupled with her current use of the real-world concept of money, you believe meaningful work is a place to start from strength.

The Goal You Co-Create: Focus on meaningful work as a means to bring relevance, and higher levels of it, into the classroom wherever possible, so that students can begin to see how the concepts they're learning directly relate to life beyond school.

GRC Spectrum Point: **Instructive coaching** because Ms. Rose needs to broaden her definition and deepen her understanding of relevance.

Coaching Modality: **Modeling** because Ms. Rose, who struggles to imagine relevant learning for third graders, would benefit from seeing it in practice.

Resource(s) Used:

- Canned foods, boxed foods, and fake play foods
- Coaching & Observing Relevance: Reflection Questions for meaningful work

Coaching Cycle

1. *Design:* Praise Ms. Rose for having the courage to admit that she struggles to see how third-grade learning can be real-world relevant while acknowledging how important it is that she knows it must be. Also praise her desire to seek help and to improve.

Prior to designing the lesson, you will model and as a sign of respect, ask Ms. Rose what skills she wants to focus on in the next class session; be sure to design a lesson based around them. Ms. Rose says she wants students to use judgment. You design a lesson where students have to make a judgment about when and how to use their money. You take care to include time for students to engage in academic discussion around money, as you are aware—and want to make her aware—that increased academic discussion (rigor) and increased meaningful work tend to go hand in hand.

You meet with Ms. Rose to explain to her what relevance is, using examples of what it can look like in classrooms of students at any grade level. Explain to her why relevance matters, even among young students. Check for clarity, and further elucidate relevance as needed, using the RRE as needed to frame the conversation.

Share with her what you will be modeling and why. Provide for her the meaningful work questions from the Coaching & Observing Relevance: Reflection Questions for her to think through as she watches you model in her next class session.

2. *Develop:* You model the class while Ms. Rose observes. She takes notes, using the questions you provided for her. For the class, you've set up a fake grocery store with different canned foods, boxed foods, and fake play foods. You've assigned costs to all items. Students will take time playing the role of shopper and cashier (being a cashier requires using a service orientation). Each student is given a different budget and the same amount of fake money and is then asked to "go shopping" accordingly (which requires judgment and decision making). The shopper then engages with a cashier, who must calculate all costs and request payment (which requires coordinating with others). The shopper pays the cashier, and the cashier must give accurate change (which aligns with problem-solving teaching—.61 effect size).

While students shop, ask them to write a log of what they buy and write down their calculations. Ask cashiers to write down all the calculations of their customers' purchases as well. After all students have played both roles, ask students to work in pairs to have an academic discussion about their math (and if it stuck to the customer's budget) as they check it together. At the end of class, ask them—as a class—to reflect on and discuss their performance, and to assess how comfortable they would be shopping in a store and paying for their items (which aligns to self-verbalization and self-questioning—.64 effect size). They should also turn in their calculations so that you can check their math.

3. *Discuss:* You meet with Ms. Rose to discuss her insights from when she observed you model a relevant lesson. Ask her what she observed in terms of relevant learning in unpredictable scenarios, and if students were struggling with any of the math skills required in their roles. Ask Ms. Rose to consider and explain how she plans to adapt the strategies you modeled in designing her next class session. Create a plan for you to follow-up with her once she has done this, in order to ascertain how much support she might still need toward meeting this goal.

High Effect-Size Instructional Strategy Alignment:
- Problem-solving teaching—.61 effect size
- Self-verbalization and self-questioning—.64 effect size

Career Skills Used:
- Coordinating with others
- Judgment and decision making
- Service orientation

RELEVANCE SCENARIO 2

Context: Mr. Harvey is a high school English teacher whose instruction rests primarily on a study of fictional stories or books. Discussion and learning tasks usually remain focused solely on the story/book at hand.

Insights from Observation: When you observe his classroom, you see that students are currently working from an excerpt from *The Hunger Games*.

Mr. Harvey will frequently ask students to analyze characters in the stories, make predictions about what will happen next in a story, and to answer inference questions during class discussion. You observe that Mr. Harvey has a solid understanding of rigor and can use it skillfully in the classroom.

Insights from Conversation: When you meet with Mr. Harvey, you can tell he loves his content and really wants students to see the value of learning from it. He has shared with you that he struggles to understand how to make English more relevant to students, because having the ability to read is relevant to all people in most scenarios. Put another way, he sees the mere act of reading and comprehension as sufficiently relevant.

Your Analysis: You can see moderate levels of relevance in how Mr. Harvey uses fictional stories, in that he's asking his students to take the information they've gathered and apply it to imagining or predicting different possible outcomes, which relies on showing some originality. While these predictions remain focused only on the story, you do see a deepened focus on **meaningful work** as an opportunity to start from strength. You also see incorporation of **authentic resources** as low-hanging fruit to increase relevance, as authentic resources often make it easier for teachers new to relevance improvement to see obvious connections to the real world. Of significance, you ascertain that part of why Mr. Harvey struggles is that he's unclear on what "unpredictable scenarios from the real-world" means when translated into classroom learning.

The Goal You Co-Create: Connect multi-format, authentic resources to fictional texts so that students can analyze the fictional text and apply it to solving unpredictable, real-world scenarios.

GRC Spectrum Point: **Illustrative coaching** because Mr. Harvey's understanding of relevance is somewhat constrained when it comes to English; he's only focusing on its most basic skill of reading (which he sees as a relevant to every human in every scenario). He does recognize he has an understanding gap, though, that is thwarting his growth in relevant instruction, and he sees the need for improvement.

Coaching Modality: **Lesson planning**, as you believe that Mr. Harvey would benefit from seeing a lesson planned specifically to connect a fictional text to real-world-relevant learning tasks.

Resource(s) Used:

- Videos to show examples of relevance in English
- Socratic Smackdown (see detail about this strategy in the "Strategies & Tools for Elevating Rigor in Instruction and Learning" at the end of chapter 8)

Coaching Cycle

1. *Design:* Commend Mr. Harvey for routinely achieving high levels of rigor in his classroom and for striving to improve relevance, even though he struggles with it as a concept in English. Praise him for making bold content decisions and prioritizing learning.

With Mr. Harvey, design a lesson around the essential question, "How should people stand up to corrupt government?" Clarify to Mr. Harvey that he can use ideas and concepts from *The Hunger Games* as launching points for students to work collaboratively on meaningful work and discuss different ways people can stand up to corruption in their government. As foundational learning, you discuss with Mr. Harvey what the term *unpredictable scenarios* means in the classroom. You explain that these are scenarios that have no black-and-white solution, no one concrete answer. When dealing with the unpredictable, you can teach students how to think through an answer, but you cannot provide one concrete answer, nor are you directing them to one answer. Ensure that Mr. Harvey sees why the idea of standing up to corrupt government is such a strong question for relevance, as it has numerous valid and possible answers.

Suggest to Mr. Harvey that the class be built from the jigsaw teaching method (1.2 effect size; jigsaw also uses students seeking help from peers—.83 effect size), where teams use authentic resources to research and discuss various ways people have successfully and unsuccessfully stood up to governments throughout history. This can be followed by a Socratic Smackdown, where students debate their ideas as a class (which requires cognitive flexibility).

As you guide Mr. Harvey through planning this lesson, visit websites where students could find authentic resources to research. Ask him to comment on the strength and relevance of different resources so that he can hone his skill of identifying high-relevance authentic resources. Refer to the RRE as needed to frame the conversation. Discuss how students will work in groups (which requires cognitive flexibility and negotiation skills). Show videos of Socratic Smackdown (which uses classroom discussion—.82 effect size, and transfer strategies—.86 effect size). Use examples that show a Socratic Smackdown of low and high relevance. Ask Mr. Harvey to comment on what made the learning in one video low in relevance and what made the learning in the other high in relevance. Support his thinking and understanding as needed.

2. *Develop:* Mr. Harvey completes the lesson per the plan you designed together.

3. *Discuss:* Meet with Mr. Harvey to ask him how well he thought the lesson went. Ask him to provide evidence of his assertions (e.g., student work, examples of authentic resources some used, etc.). Ask Mr. Harvey if he feels he needs more opportunities to improve his meaningful work and authentic resources skills, and provide them accordingly. Check to make sure Mr. Harvey now clearly sees how English can be made real-world relevant. If he appears to need more assistance in this area, make a plan for the next coaching cycle. Create a new goal if you both agree he's ready to move on.

High Effect-Size Instructional Strategy Alignment:
- Transfer strategies—.86 effect size
- Students seeking help from peers—.83 effect size
- Classroom discussion—.82 effect size
- Jigsaw—1.2 effect size

Career Skills Used:
- Cognitive flexibility
- Negotiation

RELEVANCE SCENARIO 3

Context: Ms. Florence is a 15-year veteran eighth-grade science teacher. She likes her classrooms to be quiet and orderly.

Insights from Observation: When you observe Ms. Florence's eighth-grade classroom, you notice that she has a learning objective on the board stating that students would be writing a research paper in today's class. Ms. Florence hands out an article titled, "Should Bottled Water Be Banned? Top 4 Pros and Cons." She instructs students to read the article before writing their research paper in their composition notebooks. A student raises his hand to ask if he can use his phone to research other resources. Ms. Florence answers that she prefers they stick to the article she provided. You notice all students quietly follow her direction, reading the article and writing a research paper in their composition notebooks.

Insights from Conversation: When you conversed with Ms. Florence, she remarks with enthusiasm how much she loves to research online to find ways to help her students deepen their learning. She comments that she's really excited about getting students involved in more research-based learning tasks.

Your Analysis: You see that Ms. Florence is confusing reading and summarizing with research. She is also limiting her students' practice of real-world relevant skills by providing them an article to read and discouraging them from doing their own research. While her use of authentic resources is of low relevance, she is trying; you see expanding upon her current **authentic resources** skills as an opportunity to start from strength. You also see that she would benefit from coupling higher-level authentic resource use with higher level **meaningful work** tasks to further elevate relevance.

The Goal You Co-Create: Evolve and improve authentic, research-based learning opportunities so that students engage in work of higher relevance to the real world.

GRC Spectrum Point: **Guided discovery coaching** because Ms. Florence is already accustomed to doing her own research and learning. You would serve her well by providing her research and learning prompts so that her own professional learning can become effective at increasing relevance in her classroom.

Coaching Modality: **Guided observation** because you see that Ms. Florence would benefit from seeing how research can be used at higher levels of relevance in the classroom. Importantly, Ms. Florence is in a school where teachers respect each other and often collaborate, making her a good candidate for guided observation. An observation of a teacher who is skilled in this area will help evolve Ms. Florence's understanding of highly relevant, research-based learning tasks. In this scenario example, we will walk Ms. Florence through two classrooms whose teachers use research at high levels of relevance.

Resource(s) Used:

- Other teachers and their skill in their own classrooms
- Coaching & Observing Relevance: Reflection Questions for meaningful work and authentic resources

Coaching Cycle

1. *Design:* Begin by praising Ms. Florence for her passion for research-based learning tasks, as they have the potential to be highly rigorous, relevant, and engaging. Share with Ms. Florence lesson plans or lesson summaries from various teachers who help students work together to conduct research in classes (which aligns with seeking help from peers— .83 effect size). Be sure to select a range of relevance levels in these examples. Provide prompts for Ms. Florence to consider as she reviews these lessons, such as:

- What do you see in each example?
- What levels of relevance do you see and why?
- What makes a lesson low vs. high relevance?
- How does this lesson compare to what you do?
- How do teachers include classroom discussion to ensure students are learning from the research of others (which aligns to classroom discussion—.82 effect size), and what features of the classroom discussion make it highly relevant?

Because Ms. Florence's understanding of relevance could use some clarification, walk with her through one of the examples you provided, asking her to answer each reflection question. Discuss how various teachers provide strategies to help students make choices about the quality of articles they find while researching a topic (which aligns to metacognitive strategies—.69 effect size). Then ask Ms. Florence to complete, on her own, her reflections for the remaining questions, which you will discuss when you meet at a later date.

2. *Develop:* Meet with Ms. Florence for a few minutes before you walk with her to observe two predetermined classrooms. Ask her to share with you some of her thoughts based on the reflection questions from the examples you provided. Make sure that she is clear on the hallmarks of high levels of relevance around authentic resources and meaningful work. Share with her the questions for these indicators in the Coaching & Observing Relevance: Reflection Questions.

Walk with Ms. Florence to both classrooms so that you can, upon exiting them, discuss in real time how she might be able to use pieces of the lessons to enhance her own. Ensure that she sees students should be expected to conduct their own research around relevant topics, use multiple resources, and have an opportunity to process through their research in groups, as they try to answer the learning task's essential question (which requires critical thinking, judgment and decision making, and negotiation).

3. *Discuss:* Meet again to discuss further what Ms. Florence observed in her colleagues' classrooms and how she plans to apply new strategies in her own classroom, and why. Use RRE to frame the conversation and ensure that her plans will achieve higher levels of relevance. Make plans for another coaching cycle so that you can discuss how it goes in her classroom when she applies these strategies with her students.

High Effect-Size Instructional Strategy Alignment:
- Seeking help from peers—.83 effect size
- Classroom discussion—.82 effect size
- Metacognitive strategies—.69 effect size

Career Skills Used:
- Critical thinking
- Judgment and decision making
- Negotiation

RELEVANCE SCENARIO 4

Context: Mr. Carter is an enthusiastic seventh-grade math teacher who is constantly seeking better ways to reach his students. He frequently utilizes small PBL tasks to engage students in learning that requires them to connect math to the real world. To prepare for these, he conducts his own research and builds projects that align to best practices of PBL.

Insights from Observation: When you observed Mr. Carter's classroom, students were doing a PBL math task. Each student was asked to plan a family holiday-dinner celebration. They were to plan the menu based on the number of guests; determine how much food would need to be purchased; calculate how much all the food would cost; and multiply all recipes so that there would be enough food for all guests. At the end of the project, each student would contribute one recipe to a class cultural recipe book for each to take home.

Insights from Conversation: Mr. Carter has said that he loves teaching math through PBL. He understands that it has the potential to be of high relevance to real-world scenarios, but shared that he too often has to tell students how the math connects to the real world, what math to use, and sometimes even show the steps of that math. He expressed frustration that when he does this, he feels he's doing most of the work. He would like to see more evidence that students are starting to make learning connections on their own, and he wants *them* to do the work.

Your Analysis: Mr. Carter understands learning connections but is struggling to help his students understand what it means in their own learning to make connections between classroom content and the real world. He's capable of making the **learning connections** for them but needs support in guiding them to do so on their own. Because he has a clear grasp of relevance, any relevance indicator is an opportunity to start from strength.

The Goal You Co-Create: Gain and improve strategies that guide students to make learning connections between content and the real world and unpredictable scenarios.

GRC Spectrum Point: **Self-directed coaching** because Mr. Carter understands relevance and learning connections. He's also very accustomed to doing his own research and conducting his own professional learning.

Coaching Modality: **Observation** because Mr. Carter is a strong self-learner. You see value in suggesting tools for his research into supporting students to make learning connections. You'll observe how he puts the results of his research into practice.

Resource(s) Used:

- Websites to look up the cost of food
- Math organizer to determine how much food is needed, and all costs

Coaching Cycle

1. *Design:* Commend Mr. Carter on his commitment to PBL, which is a challenging and high-skill form of instruction. Also praise his ability to reflect on his practice and identify his improvement needs. Meet briefly so that Mr. Carter can explain the lesson plan to you that you will be observing.

In advance of the class, and as his self-directed coaching assignment, suggest that Mr. Carter research reflection questions that can help students identify what they have learned, and connect this learned content to the real world. Also ask him to research any instructional strategies or learning tools he could use in his next class that would help students connect learning to the outside world. Remind him to consider how to fold in career skills. Lastly, explain to him what you will be looking for as you observe, using the RRE to frame the conversation.

2. *Develop:* Observe the lesson, noting the strategies and tools that Mr. Carter ended up using based on his research to boost learning connections, as well as how effectively he used them. Note evidence of students making their own learning connections and of the career skills involved. Using objective evidence, note his areas of growth and where there might still be improvement needed.

3. *Discuss:* Meet to discuss with Mr. Carter how he thought the lesson went and your observations of it. Ask him if he thought the strategy/strategies he used helped students make more learning connections on their own, and why or why not. Together, determine whether he could benefit from more coaching in this area or is ready to move onto a new goal.

If you feel that Mr. Carter could have benefited from using more effective instructional strategies or learning tools, make specific suggestions to him. Explain that thoughtful reflection questions for students to connect learning to the real world are also a means of incorporating creativity and critical thinking into learning. Encourage Mr. Carter to build questions that make use of high effect-size learning strategies wherever possible. Examples include:

- What math have we studied that might help me answer these questions? (organizing conceptual knowledge—.85 effect size)
- Why might I use that math in this place? (transfer strategies—.86 effect size)
- In what scenarios, in or outside of school, have I used similar math, and why? (transfer strategies—.86 effect size)
- What is a scenario outside of school that I could imagine using this math, and why? (organizing conceptual knowledge—.85 effect size; creativity and critical thinking)

Next time, Mr. Carter could put these reflection questions in a graphic organizer so that students have a tool to help frame their thinking and prompt learning connections. He could also benefit from pre-planning when in the lesson students would answer the reflection questions, using stop-and-reflect moments to pause instruction, and give students dedicated, periodic opportunities to fill in the graphic organizer. In these moments, students could discuss what they have written with a partner, giving them an opportunity to think metacognitively about their answers (metacognitive strategies—.69 effect size).

High Effect-Size Instructional Strategy Alignment:
- Organizing conceptual knowledge—.85 effect size
- Transfer strategies—.86 effect size
- Metacognitive strategies—.69 effect size

Career Skills Used:
- Creativity
- Critical thinking

Strategies & Tools for Elevating Relevance in Instruction and Learning

What follows are strategies and tools, with brief descriptions, that are effective in incorporating higher levels of relevance into instruction and learning. Where on the GRC spectrum a teacher is will inform how I recommend to teachers to research and apply any of these strategies/tools.

As with the rigor strategies/tools, please continue to seek and research additional ones that you can guide teachers to use to increase relevance. This list is simply to get you started. It is not complete.

Career Connections: Teachers can increase relevance by helping students connect content and skills to careers. The Occupational Outlook Handbook found on the U.S. Bureau of Labor Statistics website, CareerOneStop.org, and Salary.com can help students learn about various career paths. Students can watch videos of people in specific careers, research salary and education requirements associated with careers, research skills required for different jobs, and explore the demand for jobs connected to careers.

Community Service Projects: After studying a unit, students apply the information they just learned to a community service project. Some ideas include writing notes to residents in a nursing home, painting a mural in a hospital, designing advertisements for a local nonprofit business, etc. Students can also participate in longer-term community service projects. I have seen students build a marketing campaign to help raise awareness for a cause on behalf of a local nonprofit organization. Students manage the campaign's implementation for a predetermined number of weeks and, where possible, track results. At another school, students built a "community kitchen" on their campus to provide food donations to school families in need. Students launched and managed a campaign for ongoing food donations from community members and local businesses. They built a schedule for the kitchen's open hours (two days a week after school), and students signed up to volunteer throughout the school year. As a final idea, students could build a website for a nonprofit or cause-driven startup.

Current Events: Teachers use current events to help students make learning connections. The teacher explains a current event and then asks her students how the content they are learning is connected to the current event. Though there are numerous places to obtain current events, some reliable places to pull quality current event articles are Newsela, TweenTribune, and Student News Daily.

Guest Speakers: Inviting guest speakers into the classroom is a great way for students to gain a different and real-world perspective on a topic they are studying. If speakers can't come to the class, teachers may consider using a video conference technology (Skype, Facebook Live, etc.) to broadcast an interview or discussion into the classroom.

Primary Sources: Instead of simply reading about a topic in a textbook or from a worksheet, students use direct sources, or primary sources, of information. This may include a magazine cover, photograph, diary entry, newspaper article, video recording, etc.

Project Based Learning: During this type of learning, students are immersed in authentic learning experiences. Students experiment, grapple with authentic issues, and work collaboratively with classmates and community members to pursue knowledge. Teachers begin with a real-world problem and design learning tasks that help guide students as they research solutions to the problem. For PBL to elicit highest possible levels of learning, it should follow a certain protocol. Visit the "Resources" tab on my website to access various resources connected to the implementation of successful PBL: www .reflecttolearn.com/resources. Career and technical education teachers may find the resources at CTEonline.org helpful.

Quick Career Reflection: Teachers designate time in all or some classes (less than five minutes) to pause instruction and ask students to conduct a quick online search for ways the content they are studying can be used in various careers. As a group, the class then discusses what they found during their research time.

RAFT: This literacy strategy allows students the opportunity to demonstrate the ability to see a subject or idea from various real-world viewpoints. Along with a text related to the subject or idea, teachers give students a copy of the RAFT worksheet, which you can find in Appendix 11. The teacher will explain each section of the worksheet:

1. **R**ole of the Writer: Who are you? For example, a consumer, buyer, student, company president, etc.
2. **A**udience: To whom are you writing?
3. **F**ormat: What is the format of your writing? For example, a speech, letter, memo, etc.
4. **T**opic: What is the subject and purpose of your writing? Examples might include to educate the audience, persuade the audience to change their minds, to present a new argument on a known subject or idea, etc.

For each of these sections, the teacher can assign roles, audiences, formats, and topics if she wants students to think about the topic through a specific lens. Or the teacher can let students choose all parts. Learning goals will likely dictate which approach a teacher takes.

Students will use the information in the text to write about the topic from different viewpoints and fill out answers in the worksheet.

Real-Life Submissions: Students submit their work (articles, essays, artwork, etc.) to outside publications or organizations to see how the content at hand and their work can connect to the real world. Teachers are advised to do an online search to determine where students could submit works and how she can assist them to that end. Depending on the grade level of the students, the teacher will calibrate her level of assistance as students complete submissions, i.e., more support for younger students and less for older students. Ideas for outlets to which students can submit work include a local magazine or newspaper, Cicada Magazine, Stone Soup (a magazine for creative children), Celebrating Art, and the Real World Design Challenge (a competition of students' STEM-based designs), to name some.

Real-Life Tools: Real-life tools used in careers are a form of authentic resources. They can include rulers, protractors, maps, scales, microscopes, hammers, etc. By incorporating these into instruction, students can broaden the kinds of learning connections they make between the content at hand and certain careers.

Visit www.leadered.com/coachingredefined for an evolving and updated list of strategies and tools to elevate relevance in instruction and learning.

Simulations: Students can use simulations that replicate real-life situations. Some examples include conducting virtual lab experiments, utilizing flight simulators, exploring various simulations on CK12.org, participating in the Stock Market Game, etc.

Technology Integration: Teachers can integrate technology into instruction to enhance relevant learning opportunities. As with any and all technology used in learning, the instructional tasks must be designed with high levels of relevance (or rigor and engagement) in mind. From there, technology can enhance and facilitate learning. But without strong pedagogy undergirding its use, technology does little to boost learning.

When students are asked to sift through and curate multiple sources of information to support their original ideas and conclusions, Popplet is a great tool to help keep information and ideas organized. When students are doing group research projects aimed at solving a real-world problem, Padlet facilitates collaboration and content organization from multiple resources. Also in such group work, Google Classroom enables virtual collaboration.

You're Important to Me: To build personal relevance, teachers benefit from knowing students. At the beginning of the school year, teachers can provide students with the You're Important to Me handout, which can be found in Appendix 12. The answers to these questions, followed by a supportive conversation, can help teachers build relationships and tailor their teaching to the learning preferences of their students.

PONDER & POST

To enhance personal, cultural, and global relevance, I will _____.

#coachingredefined

Chapter 10

Coaching for Learner Engagement

Why Learner Engagement Matters

We all intuitively know why learner engagement matters. We've all experienced learning that is exhilarating and exciting and learning that is boring and underwhelming. When learning is exhilarating, we *want* to learn. We are interested in the content, curious about its meaning and relevance, and view ourselves as capable of growth around the content. When we're bored, we cannot see the value of the content, cannot see how it relates to us, and lack any desire to show up fully for learning about it.

Engaging learning captures the attentions and imaginations of our students. It's how we make them feel they are a part of learning, and when they feel that, they also view themselves as having the power to impact and own how they learn and how much they learn. In other words, they have a growth mindset. They see themselves as capable and full of potential to work, persevere, and productively struggle to meet learning goals.

Often, the disengaged learner feels disempowered and can easily default into a fixed mindset. They see themselves as the recipients of learning rather than the drivers of it. Disengaged learners, without intervention or guidance to grasp their empowerment, will be unlikely to grow into curious, lifelong learners. This is problematic because the curious, lifelong learners are the ones who will continue to gain new skills, keep pace amid rapid, constant economic change, and maintain relevance in a shifting career landscape.

We engage students by thoughtfully creating an engaging learning environment where they feel safe and encouraged to participate actively and where they feel ownership over their ability to master content and skills. By intentionally creating an engaging classroom, we enable higher levels of rigor and relevance; if rigor and relevance are roots, then an engaging classroom is the fertile soil.

Defining Learner Engagement

Per research, there are three types of learner engagement:

1. Emotional engagement: How a student feels about the learning and herself in it. When a child is emotionally engaged, she feels safe in the environment, comfortable taking risks, and believes in the purpose and value of the learning.
2. Cognitive engagement: What the student is thinking about while in the classroom. When the student is thinking about the content, he is cognitively engaged; when he's thinking about something that someone said earlier in the day or what happened last night at home, he is not. Cognitive engagement is accessible through emotional engagement and is dependent on the learning task or instructional strategy the teacher is using.
3. Behavioral engagement: What the student is doing. Behavioral engagement is the most observable type of engagement, as the teacher can see if a student is doing the work as intended or is off task or distracted. (Almarode, 2018)

The research shows that emotional engagement is what unlocks the most meaningful cognitive and behavioral engagement. The emotionally engaged child is the child who feels like an active agent in her learning. She is the empowered learner. She is confident grappling deeply with content, and she is more likely to be moving through the task with attention and intention and as designed.

The emotionally engaged learner is also the encouraged learner. We know this from our own experience: when we are encouraged, we try;

when we are not, we don't. It's a simple formula and makes clear that we as educators must encourage students. Doing so is the low hanging fruit of helping them grow more emotionally engaged in their learning, more willing to struggle productively, and more comfortable taking learning risks.

In his important book, *Engaging Students with Poverty in Mind*, Eric Jensen wrote: "In poor homes, the ratio of positives (affirmations) to negatives (reprimands) is typically a 1-to-2 ratio. Contrast this to the 6-to-1 positives-to-negatives ratio in the homes of higher-income families" (p. 15, 2018).

Professor Hattie gives emphasizing positive behavior a .65 effect size. We have to prioritize encouragement and reinforcement of students' skills, strengths, and behaviors in our classrooms. We have to do this for every student—especially those in poverty, as the effects of discouragement on these students can slip-slide into an even deeper lack of confidence and belief in their own empowerment. To miss any opportunity to encourage them is to perpetuate or exacerbate the wealth and achievement gap.

How to Spot Learner Engagement in Instruction and Learning

As a quick reference, I'm including the learner engagement portion of the RRE rubrics here. For the full rubrics, please see Appendix 3.

The following questions can guide you as you look for evidence of relevance in lesson design and learning—across the three RRE indicators of active participation, learning environment, and formative processes and tools—in teachers' classrooms.

Share these questions with your teachers as appropriate, or ask them to come up with their own, when they will observe you model relevance or observe relevance in a colleague's classroom.

Learner Engagement Rubric

Support teachers in creating and implementing an effective learner environment that is engaging and aligned to learner needs. The three indicators for learner engagement are: active participation, learning environment, and formative processes and tools.

Active Participation	1 – Beginning	2 – Emerging	3 – Developed	4 – Well Developed
Student Learning	• Limited student engagement, with the exception of hand-raising. Some students are off-task or have disengaged from the lesson and are not redirected. • Lesson is teacher led and students progress through new learning with some challenges with productivity.	• Most students remain focused and on-task during the lesson. Students answer questions when asked, but not all students have the opportunity to actively respond. • Lesson is led by the teacher, and students productively progress through new learning.	• All students remain on-task, responding to frequent opportunities for active engagement throughout the lesson. • Lesson is led by both teacher and students, and students productively progress through new learning.	• All students remain on-task and proactively engaged throughout the lesson. • Students take ownership of learning new content, actively seeking ways to improve their own performance.
Instructional Design	• Lesson relies mainly on direct instruction with few opportunities for student engagement through application.	• Lesson relies on one or two strategies designed to engage students, with the lesson focused more on direct instruction than on student engagement through application.	• Lesson provides multiple strategies designed to maximize student engagement, and contribution is monitored to ensure full participation.	• Lesson achieves a focus on student-centered engagement where the students monitor and adjust their own participation.

Learning Environment	1 – Beginning	2 – Emerging	3 – Developed	4 – Well Developed
Student Learning	• Students rely on peers or teacher for answers to questions. There is a lack of evidence of students being required to persevere in responding to rigorous tasks or questions. • Students demonstrate a lack of respect for peers, teacher, and/or learning environment.	• Students exhibit some evidence that they are beginning to take risks and persevere in learning rigorous content. Students demonstrate respect for the learning environment, but challenges exist in demonstrating respect for peers.	• Students are encouraged to take risks and persevere through productive struggle. Students are praised for demonstrating commitment to learning. • Students demonstrate respect for peers, teacher, and the learning environment.	• Students are encouraged to take risks and persevere through productive struggle. Students are provided with effective feedback to guide them in their learning. • Students demonstrate respect for peers, teacher, and the learning environment.
Instructional Design	• Classroom learning procedures and routines are inconsistently communicated and/or implemented.	• Classroom learning procedures and routines are visible, but are not consistently implemented.	• Clear classroom learning procedures and routines are visible and are consistently implemented.	• Classroom learning procedures and routines are clearly established, but remain flexible and fluid to adapt to the learning task as needed.

Formative Processes and Tools	1 – Beginning	2 – Emerging	3 – Developed	4 – Well Developed
Student Learning	• Lesson includes few instances of formative assessment to evaluate students' mastery of content. Assessment results indicate that student growth is minimal. • Students are partnered or grouped, but all students receive the same lesson content, process, and product.	• Students demonstrate mastery of content by engaging in formative assessments that allow for reciprocal feedback. Assessment results indicate that student growth is progressing. • Students are partnered or grouped and receive some opportunities for differentiated learning based on adjusting content, process, and/or product.	• Students demonstrate mastery of content by completing a variety of formative assessments that allow for reciprocal feedback. Assessment results indicate that students are meeting expectations. • Students are strategically partnered or grouped based on data. Lesson content, process, and/or product is clearly differentiated to support varying and specific student needs.	• Students demonstrate mastery of content through opportunities to self-reflect, set learning goals, and share responsibility for their learning. Assessment results indicate that students are exceeding expected outcomes.
Instructional Design	• Results from formative processes and tools are used to monitor progress.	• Results from formative processes and tools are used to plan and implement aspects of differentiated instruction and monitor progress.	• Results from formative processes and tools are used to strategically adjust instructional pacing, plan differentiated instruction, and monitor progress.	• Results from formative processes and tools, along with effective feedback, are used to immediately adjust instructional pacing, plan differentiated instruction, and monitor progress.

Coaching & Observing Learner Engagement: Reflection Questions

Visit www.leadered.com/ coachingredefined to download the following Learner Engagement Reflection Questions.

Active Participation	• What evidence demonstrates that students stay on task and actively engaged during the entire lesson? • How do students take ownership of learning new content? • How do students demonstrate active listening during the lesson? • How do students exhibit respect for their classmates? • To what extent is class time utilized wisely with minimal disruptions or lost instructional time? • How do students seek to improve their own performance? • What evidence demonstrates that students monitor and adjust their own participation? • What evidence demonstrates that students collaborate with others to accomplish assignments? • What evidence demonstrates that students corrected each other respectfully when off task? • To what extent do students exhibit signs of valuing the content taught? • What evidence demonstrates that students are given opportunities to interact and collaborate with their peers? • In what ways is active participation creating opportunities for use of today's career skills, and which ones?
Learning Environment	• To what degree are the classroom learning procedures and routines well established yet remain flexible to adapt to the learning task as needed? • How are students participating in the development of classroom expectations? • What evidence demonstrates that students are provided with timely and effective feedback to help them guide their learning? • What evidence demonstrates that students persevere through productive struggle? • To what extent do students exhibit signs of feeling safe to make mistakes? • To what extent do students demonstrate care and respect for peers, the teacher, and the learning environment?

Learning Environment	• How effectively do students transition from one learning task to another?
	• To what extent do students pay attention to the details of their learning tasks?
	• What evidence demonstrates that high expectations are set for all students?
	• What evidence demonstrates that students exhibit pride in high-quality work?
	• How is the learning environment promoting use of today's career skills, and which ones?
Formative Processes and Tools	• What evidence indicates that students demonstrate mastery of content through opportunities to self-reflect and set goals?
	• To what degree do students demonstrate the ability to share responsibility for their learning?
	• What evidence demonstrates that students understand and can articulate how their work is assessed?
	• How do assessment results indicate that students are exceeding expected outcomes?
	• To what extent are formative assessment results used to adjust instruction immediately?
	• How is differentiation utilized in the classroom and to what impact?
	• Are students aware of the criteria that will be used to assess their learning?
	• To what extent are students engaged in self-reflection?
	• How are formative processes and tools contributing to the use of today's career skills, and which ones?

Scenarios: Coaching Educators to Increase Learner Engagement

LEARNER ENGAGEMENT SCENARIO 1

Context: Mrs. Norder is a middle school health & PE teacher enthusiastic about diet and fitness. She knows her content really well and enjoys sharing it with students.

Insights from Observation: On the day you observe Mrs. Norder, she is walking sixth graders through a PowerPoint presentation listing the reasons people gain and lose weight. She has given students a copy of the slides with select words left out, words that students have been asked to fill in during the lecture. As Mrs. Norder scrolls through the slides, you notice that the words omitted in the printed copy are underlined on the screen. Throughout the lecture, you observed Mrs. Norder ask only one question, albeit three different times: "Are there any questions?" After she did this, she provided barely any wait time, and no students asked any questions. In fact, you notice that not one student spoke during the entire observed lesson.

Insights from Conversation: When meeting with Mrs. Norder after this observed lesson, she shares her excitement over the level of active engagement she felt students showed. Because all students filled in the blanks on their printed slides and because they were quiet the whole time, she believed they were actively engaged in the task at hand.

Your Analysis: You can see that Mrs. Norder's understanding of learner engagement is in need of clarifying. She appears to be confusing engagement with compliance and quietness with being deeply engrossed. Mrs. Norder has been successful in getting her students focused on and participating in one learning task, which means **active participation** provides an opportunity to start from strength. You recognize that she is in need of strategies to make learning tasks far more engaging and to put students in charge of their own learning.

The Goal You Co-Create: Gain and apply a broader range of strategies to increase the level of engagement through active participation, such that students demonstrate more ownership over and focus in their learning.

GRC Spectrum Point: **Instructive coaching** because Mrs. Norder's understanding of learner engagement is misguided and in need of clarification. Her perceptions of the engagement in her classroom are vastly different from yours.

Coaching Modality: **Lesson planning**, as you recognize that Mrs. Norder could greatly benefit from assistance in planning a lesson specifically to achieve high levels of engagement.

Resource(s) Used:

- Reciprocal teaching graphic organizer (see Appendix 8)
- Reflective questions
- Bloom's questioning strategies

Coaching Cycle

1. *Design:* Praise Mrs. Norder for caring so deeply that her students are engaged in their learning and her desire to share with them her passion for health and fitness. Before you guide her through highly engaging lesson planning, explain to her the difference between active learner engagement and compliance. Ask her to consider who's doing the work, who's doing the thinking, the level of the work, and the level of the thinking in a compliance-based learning task and in a highly engaging learning task. Guide her to see that when a learning task is compliance based, the teacher is doing the work and thinking, and that work and thinking are often low level.

Ensure she comes to understand the difference between cognitive and behavioral engagement, clarifying that her students were merely behaviorally engaged. Point out that when cognitive engagement (rigor) goes up, overall engagement goes up meaningfully. Therefore, successful learner-engagement strategies often include high-rigor strategies.

Suggest that together you plan a lesson around reciprocal teaching, as it is a high effect-size strategy (reciprocal teaching—.74 effect size) that is highly cognitively and emotionally engaging and relatively easy for teachers to apply. It also allows a teacher to observe how readily engaged students are in the task and how complex their thinking and work is. Ask Mrs. Norder to select a text that the reciprocal teaching will be based upon; ensure that it connects with the learning goals she has for her students. Together, design a lesson that puts nearly all the onus on students to think and work at high levels. Use the RRE to guide conversation and Mrs. Norder's thinking as you plan.

Select a reciprocal teaching graphic organizer that addresses the strategy's four points: questioning the text, clarifying understanding, summarizing, and predicting. Make sure that the lesson is designed so that students apply what they've learned in the reading to the graphic organizer. Suggest to Mrs. Norder that she put students in groups to complete the graphic organizer; this way, she can walk around and assess their thinking as they collaborate (which, in the reciprocal teaching strategy, requires judgment, decision making, and coordinating with others).

Listing reflective questions, guide Mrs. Norder through what to look for as she walks around the room observing how students are filling out the graphic organizer:

- Are students correctly summarizing the text?
- Are students able to help each other clarify any misconceptions regarding the text's content?
- Are students coming up with meaningful questions about the content in the text?

Explain to her that her role in this scenario is to let students do as much of the work and thinking as possible; as needed, she can scaffold to support rigorous thinking (which aligns to scaffolding—.82 effect size) or guide students toward clarity when something is misunderstood. Encourage Mrs. Norder to move away from asking, "Are there any questions?" Instead, help her develop a habit of using questions from Bloom's question starters (which can be found with a Google search); this way, she is helping her students process information at a higher level of rigor, which elicits deeper engagement.

2. *Develop:* The teacher conducts the lesson according to the plans you drafted together. Given that you are currently using instructive coaching, you might decide it's best to observe the lesson.

3. *Discuss:* After Mrs. Norder teaches the lesson, meet to ask her how it went, or discuss together if you observed the class. Ask her how she felt using reciprocal teaching, where she felt she was successful with it, and where she might have struggled. Offer strategies for improvement next time, as needed. If you did not observe the class, ask for evidence that her students were engaged at higher levels, including how they might have been engaged emotionally, cognitively, and behaviorally. Ask Mrs. Norder where she believes she could benefit from additional support and make a plan for the next coaching cycle to provide it. Try to hand over more of the thinking and planning work to her in the next cycle.

High Effect-Size Instructional Strategy Alignment:
- Scaffolding—.82 effect size
- Reciprocal teaching—.74 effect size

Career Skills Used:
- Judgment and decision making
- Coordinating with others

LEARNER ENGAGEMENT SCENARIO 2

Context: Mr. Schmidt is an elementary school teacher who takes pride in designing mini project-based learning (PBL) tasks for his students. He builds them to be challenging so that students can work through higher-level tasks and achieve at greater levels.

Insights from Observation: When you observe Mr. Schmidt's elementary school class, students are working in small groups to design an advertisement for a local business in the community. He is circling the room to answer numerous questions. When students struggle with something, you observe that they almost immediately raise their hands to ask for Mr. Schmidt's help. You do not observe students asking each other for assistance. While they wait for Mr. Schmidt to get to them, most students stop engaging in the learning task, even though he's asked them to complete it. Yet, you do notice that students don't talk or disrupt the class or other students as they wait for Mr. Schmidt's attention and assistance.

Additionally, Mr. Schmidt talks into a microphone. He sets it aside but leaves it on when he's giving assistance to groups of or individual students. Students can then hear these private conversations, which distracts them (at best) and makes them nervous or embarrassed by the idea of speaking directly with him and having their conversations audible to the rest of the class (at worst).

Insights from Conversation: Mr. Schmidt shares that he's frustrated that his students won't take more risks in their learning. He has spent a great deal of time developing wonderful PBL experiences and feels this time has been wasted because students "refuse to work through rigorous tasks."

Your Analysis: Mr. Schmidt is aware that students need to take risks in their learning and struggle productively through rigorous, cognitively engaging tasks. He needs assistance in applying simple strategies to create the kind of **learning environment** where students feel safe and emotionally engaged in persevering through productive struggle. He also needs to be made aware of the small and subtle ways he's precluding this kind of learning environment from taking shape, and thwarting his students' sense of safety in taking risks, particularly in front of their peers. Because students show respect for Mr. Schmidt and their peers by not interrupting him or each other when they are waiting for or getting his assistance, you do see **learning environment** as an opportunity to start from strength.

The Goal You Co-Create: Apply strategies to transform the learning environment such that students feel safe and encouraged to take risks, productively struggle, and persevere through high levels of work.

GRC Spectrum Point: **Illustrative coaching** because while Mr. Schmidt has a reasonably solid understanding of engagement, he would benefit from assistance reflecting productively on how his own practice improves or impedes an engaging learning environment. To achieve this, you determine that he would be well served by seeing examples of an engaging learning environment and then reflecting upon them.

Coaching Modality: **Observation** because after studying and reflecting on illustrative examples, you determine that Mr. Schmidt would benefit from applying new strategies while you observe, such that afterwards you can offer praise to reinforce improvement and feedback for continued growth.

Resource(s) Used:

- Teaching Channel videos on student collaboration, perseverance while problem-solving, and group roles and responsibilities
- Coaching & Observing Learner Engagement: Reflection Questions for learning environment
- Group roles and responsibilities (see Appendix 14)

Coaching Cycle

1. *Design:* Commend Mr. Schmidt on his commitment to PBL (which uses critical thinking and judgment and decision making), especially for

elementary-aged students. Acknowledge that planning effective PBL takes a skilled teacher, and you respect his efforts to teach in this way so that students can have significant opportunities for rigorous, relevant, and engaging learning.

Together, watch select Teaching Channel videos on collaborative work, perseverance while problem-solving, and group roles and responsibilities. Ask Mr. Schmidt to look for ways the teacher does or does not encourage risk-taking and perseverance and how group roles and responsibilities support productive collaboration and engagement. Then discuss his thoughts. Use questions and the RRE to guide your discussion with him, e.g.:

- How did the teacher in the video get students to work on more rigorous tasks without relying on the teacher to walk them through each step?
- How did the teacher coach students to work together and persevere? (which aligns to seeking help from peers—.83 effect size)
- What strategies or tools did you observe to promote an engaging learning environment?
- How did the teacher use positive reinforcement to help the students find the confidence to persevere through the task? (which aligns with positive behavior—.65 effect size).
- How did the teacher use group roles and responsibilities to help students manage their own behavior?

Ask him what his plans are for the lesson you will observe, and then guide him to consider how he can adapt some of the strategies observed in the videos into his class session. This might include using mini-lessons, should multiple students end up struggling with the same content (which aligns with micro-teaching—.88 effect size). Or it might be assigning roles to students to bring cognitive and behavioral structure and engagement to their collaboration. Share with Mr. Schmidt an example of group roles and responsibilities, and explain how they promote people management and emotional intelligence.

Let Mr. Schmidt know what you will be looking for as you observe, sharing with him the Coaching & Observing Learner Engagement: Reflection Questions for learning environment.

Prior to observing the lesson, ask Mr. Schmidt if he'd like you to record portions of it that you can discuss with him in step 3. (Note: only do this if you can first confirm that videoing teachers is allowed in the school. If so, and if the teacher agrees, take care to have any and all necessary permissions in place prior to recording.)

2. *Develop:* Mr. Schmidt conducts the lesson while you observe. Take objective notes, looking for evidence that Mr. Schmidt applied strategies you discussed together in step 1 and to what effect. Note objectively how the students reacted to these strategies, including evidence of improved emotional, cognitive, or behavioral engagement.

3. *Discuss:* Meet to discuss with Mr. Schmidt how he thought the lesson went. Ask him how he felt as he applied new strategies and his sense of how his students responded to it. If you recorded some of his class, watch portions and talk through your feedback, praise, and ideas for improvement. If you did not, simply share with him your feedback based on the objective notes you took. If needed, refer back to the Teaching Channel videos to clarify points or, where applicable, compare it to the video you took of Mr. Schmidt. Together, discuss if he could benefit from further coaching and plan a follow-up coaching cycle accordingly or one based on a new goal as appropriate.

High Effect-Size Instructional Strategy Alignment:
- Seeking help from peers—.83 effect size
- Positive behavior—.65 effect size
- Micro-teaching—.88 effect size

Career Skills Used:
- Critical thinking
- Judgment and decision making
- People management
- Emotional intelligence

LEARNER ENGAGEMENT SCENARIO 3

Context: At the beginning of the year, Mrs. Cook, a CTE/business high school teacher, expressed an interest in utilizing more group work in her classroom. At the time, she was mainly teaching through lecture; but after professional learning on workforce skills, she realized the value of collaborative skills. You have provided for her some instructive coaching about group work; as a result, Mrs. Cook recently began using small group learning tasks.

Insights from Observation: When you observed Mrs. Cook's class, you noticed many students were off-task in their groups. Some students were on task, but you saw others arguing about what to do first, ultimately accomplishing very little. You saw a handful of students playing on their phones. And you noticed that a couple of students had completely tuned out the group and were trying to accomplish the task on their own.

Insights from Conversation: Mrs. Cook expresses her frustration. She's extremely knowledgeable about her content and has put time into designing high-level group-learning tasks. She is passionate about helping her students foster collaborative skills, as she knows these skills are directly tied to their future careers.

Your Analysis: Mrs. Cook feels, and you agree, that in terms of learning-task design, everything is in order for high levels of learning. Mrs. Cook needs assistance in evolving the **learning environment** so that students stay on task. Specifically, she will benefit from tools to create and apply clear learning guidelines and procedures so students have a better grasp of what's expected of them in her classroom. For a teacher who's spent most of her career relying on lectures to teach, designing high-level group work is no small task. You believe that Mrs. Cook has built so much positive momentum through this impressive achievement that there will be strength in moving onto the new task of improving her learning environment.

The Goal You Co-Create: Grow adept at using a range of strategies to establish, clarify, and enforce a clear set of learning guidelines and procedures to help students remain on task.

GRC Spectrum Point: **Guided discovery coaching.** You have been coaching Mrs. Cook this school year. She has recently taken more and more initiative in researching, learning, and practicing the fundamentals of rigorous and relevant instructional design on her own. Now she needs to research, learn, and practice the fundamentals of engaging instructional design but with some structure from you.

Coaching Modality: **Modeling.** You determine that after conducting some guided research about how to improve the learning environment, this concept will quickly become clear to her upon seeing you model strategies to improve the learning environment.

Resource(s) Used:

- Stop-and-reflect moments
- Group guidelines (see Appendix 13)
- Group roles and responsibilities (see Appendix 14)
- Coaching & Observing Learner Engagement: Reflection Questions for learning environment

Coaching Cycle

1. *Design:* Prior to meeting Mrs. Cook, email her select links about group roles and responsibilities and group guidelines. Ask her to research these concepts and come to your meeting with ideas for the roles her students can assume and to what end, as well as some group-guidelines ideas and rationale. In your meeting, ask Mrs. Cook to share with you what she's come up with, as you will use these in the class session you model. Check to see that her thinking is sound and her planning matches the intent. Where needed, discuss with her tools for improvement and adjust her ideas accordingly. See Appendix 13 for an example of group guidelines and Appendix 14 for an example of group roles and responsibilities.

Out of respect, ask Mrs. Cook her instructional intentions, the content of the class, and the goals she has for students during the lesson in which you will model using group roles and responsibilities and guidelines.

Prior to the class session you will model, ask Mrs. Cook to email you, at least one day in advance, a list of questions to guide her observation of your modeling. Share that you will provide feedback as needed so that her observation of your modeling will be most instructive. (Make sure questions seek to observe evidence that shows how well students are responding to learning environment tools and touch on all the important points in the Coaching & Observing Learner Engagement: Reflection Questions for learning environment. Where she might be missing points, include them for her in an emailed reply.)

2. *Develop:* Model the class. Begin by explaining to students their roles, responsibilities, and guidelines for group work (which promotes cognitive flexibility, emotional intelligence, and people management). Because you had observed the class arguing about what to do first in their groups, ensure you detail for students the steps they must follow to accomplish their work in their group time (which promotes clarity—.75 effect size). Since group work is still new to the class, be mindful to scaffold instruction through small mini-lessons, giving them opportunities to accomplish small parts of the task prior to giving them additional material to complete (which aligns to scaffolding—.82 effect size and micro-teaching—.88 effect size).

Throughout the class session, use strategies to ensure that students are on task or redirect them when they are not. As an example, you could model stop-and-reflect moments on seven-minute intervals. To apply this strategy, stop the class and ask students questions based on the learning goal and learning task, e.g., "How well are we working in groups?" "Are we on task?" "Are we minding the noise level?" (which aligns with evaluation and reflection—.75 effect size).

Meanwhile, the teacher observes as you model, taking objective notes based on the questions she drafted to guide her observation.

3. *Discuss:* Meet to discuss Mrs. Cook's observation notes of your modeling, using RRE to frame the conversation. Ask her which strategies and tools she found most and least effective and to give evidence for both. Ask her how she plans to adapt the more effective group roles and responsibilities and group guidelines into her next class session. Make sure her thinking is sound and her instructional planning is intentional. Set a plan for the next coaching cycle so that you can ensure she applies these tools effectively.

High Effect-Size Instructional Strategy Alignment:
- Clarity—.75 effect size
- Scaffolding—.82 effect size
- Micro-teaching—.88 effect size
- Evaluation and reflection—.75 effect size

Career Skills Used:
- Cognitive flexibility
- Emotional intelligence
- People management

LEARNER ENGAGEMENT SCENARIO 4

Context: Mr. Holmes is a motivated middle-school social studies teacher. He is constantly seeking opportunities to improve his teaching. Presently, he is seeking ways to use formative assessment tools to see if students are making adequate progress toward learning goals.

Insights from Observation: When you observe Mr. Holmes's classroom, you notice that he asks lots of really good, high-rigor questions, though typically, only the same three students answer the questions.

Insights from Conversation: Mr. Holmes mentioned to you that he needs more ways than just asking questions to assess students, so that he can check all students for understanding, not just the ones who answer his questions. He would also like students to gauge their own progress.

Your Analysis: It's clear to you that Mr. Holmes is a motivated, eager learner who understands rigor. He's also making use of a solid formative assessment tool—asking questions to check for comprehension. Because he's having moderate success on this front, you see **formative processes and tools** as not only an area for growth for Mr. Holmes, but also an area where you can start from strength.

The Goal You Co-Create: Use **formative processes and tools** to ensure all students are making adequate progress toward learning goals.

GRC Spectrum Point: **Self-directed coaching** because Mr. Holmes is highly motivated and has a track record of conducting independent professional learning. He's already seeking ways to use formative assessments and tools on his own. You see that, by simply nudging his research into a more specific direction, he can learn on his own with even greater success.

Coaching Modality: **Guided observation** because you have observed Mr. Holmes's peers using technologies such as ClassFlow and Quizlet to deliver quick, robust formative assessments, and that the teachers in his school have strong, respectful relationships. You see that Mr. Holmes could benefit from observing his colleagues and learning from their successful use of formative processes and tools.

Resource(s) Used:
- Other teachers' classrooms and application of formative assessments and tools

- Coaching & Observing Learner Engagement: Reflection Questions for formative processes and tools

Coaching Cycle

1. *Design:* Provide for Mr. Holmes a list of teachers using different technology-based formative processes with success. Ask him to research the tools they use to determine which ones are most appealing to him, as this can help inform which classrooms he chooses to observe. Suggest that he reach out to at least three teachers so that he can observe a range of technologies.

Ask Mr. Holmes what he plans to look for when observing. Make sure his answers include: how the teacher seamlessly incorporates the technology as an assessment tool into instruction and learning; how students are able to demonstrate mastery of content through these tools; how teachers give students feedback based on their assessment results (which aligns with feedback—.70 effect size when following the Hattie model of feedback, which is outlined at the end of the chapter); how rigorous the questions are that are fed into the tool (which, when rigorous, promotes critical thinking); and if the teacher allows students access to the technology tools outside of class so they can continue practicing (which aligns with students self-regulating learning—.75 effect size). If he doesn't mention all of these points, briefly talk through the importance of each with him, referring to the Coaching & Observing Learner Engagement: Reflection Question for formative processes and tools as needed.

2. *Develop:* Mr. Holmes observes the classrooms of the teachers to whom he reached out. He takes objective notes, specifically writing down how teachers use each technology tool and how students demonstrate mastery per each tool.

3. *Discuss:* Meet with Mr. Holmes so he can walk you through what he noted and learned in the classes he observed. Ask him to share his plans to adapt one of these formative processes and tools into his own classroom such that every student has the chance to demonstrate mastery. Where helpful to Mr. Holmes, refer to RRE to offer guidance or clarification for how the chosen technology tools work and how to incorporate high-rigor questions into them. As needed, plan another coaching cycle so that you can ascertain how successfully he applied these tools and if additional support is needed.

High Effect-Size Instructional Strategy Alignment:
- Feedback—.70 effect size
- Students' self-regulating learning—.75 effect size

Career Skills Used:
- Critical thinking

Strategies & Tools for Elevating Learner Engagement in Instruction and Learning

What follows are strategies and tools, with a brief description, that are effective in incorporating higher levels of learner engagement into instruction and learning. Of course, let where a teacher is on the GRC spectrum inform how you suggest and explain these strategies to her. As with the strategies and tools for rigor and relevance, this list is here to launch your ongoing search for additional engagement strategies and tools you can suggest to teachers.

> **Accountable Talk:** Accountable talk strategies create opportunities for all students to stay engaged during classroom activities. One such strategy is Numbered Heads, where students are placed in groups and then assigned a number, such that each assigned number occurs once in each group. The teacher calls on different numbers to share the group's response to different questions. A different take on this strategy is using a Talking Clip (aka a paper clip). Only the student with the paper clip is allowed to answer. The Talking Clip is moved from student to student in the group until all students have had an opportunity to share their thoughts. A third strategy is the use of playing cards. Each student in a group is given a different card and categories of cards can align to certain responsibilities (this requires you taking from a deck of cards only those cards you need in advance of distributing them). For example, the "diamonds" are responsible for

gathering supplies for the group, while those with "clubs" are responsible for being the group reporter. Take care to ensure each group receives the same card distribution.

Feedback: Student feedback can be written or oral and should always be delivered with compassion and respect toward the student. Feedback should be timely, in that it should help students deepen learning about the content currently being taught. Teachers should not shy away from discussing errors with students in feedback, as guiding students to work through errors promotes resilience, perseverance, and a growth mindset.

Hattie assigns feedback, when used expertly and strategically, a .70 effect size. According to an article on the Visible Learning website, there are nine guidelines to using feedback to elicit its maximal effect size (2018). An adapted version of them follow:

1. Keep feedback's focus on the task, not the student.
2. Provide detailed feedback that uses content-specific language.
3. Present detailed feedback in manageable chunks; calibrate feedback chunks to a student's age.
4. Be specific and clear in your feedback.
5. Take care to ensure that feedback is unbiased and objective.
6. Keep feedback as simple as possible but not overly simplified.
7. Use feedback to help the student cultivate a learning-goal orientation.
8. Ensure that the student clearly grasps the goals and how her performance can help her meet goals.
9. Give feedback after students have attempted a solution or completion of a learning task.

Group Guidelines: A Group Guidelines sheet outlines the expectations of groups as they collaborate on learning tasks. Prior to assigning any type of group work to the class, the teacher provides this sheet to all groups and goes over the rules with them to ensure understanding. During group work, each group of students displays the Group Guidelines sheet. As the teacher circulates to offer assistance to groups, students make notes on the sheet to indicate how well they are abiding by the guidelines and staying on task. At the end of the group work, the students also assess their individual behavior on the same sheet and then turn it into the teacher. Please find an example Group Guidelines sheet in Appendix 13.

Group Roles and Responsibilities: Assigning roles and corresponding responsibilities to students doing group work helps keep students on task and coordinated toward meeting learning goals. The roles also help students feel accountable for their learning and to each other, which deepens emotional engagement. In Appendix 14, see an example of a Group Roles and Responsibilities sheet I use, which includes roles and explanations of responsibilities for leader, manager, recorder, and spokesperson.

Leadership Development: Leadership skills are those that enable a person to work positively and productively with others and earn their respect and trust. When students struggle with leadership, they often struggle with self-responsibility and self-awareness; the ability to set goals and commit to reaching them; the ability to communicate clearly and effectively; perseverance and remaining positive, especially in the face of setbacks, to name some. When you see students struggle in some or all of these ways, they will benefit from applying leadership to their own lives and learning. When one can lead one's own learning productively, then her skills are developing to the point where they can be used to motivate and inspire others to do the same, i.e., where she demonstrates strong leadership potential.

Teachers have several tools they can apply in their classrooms to promote leadership skills. To begin, the teacher can make a point to acknowledge, praise, and explain when a student exhibits leadership skills. The explaining point is key; the teacher will name the skill and explain to students its importance in one's own life and the impact on others. As an example: "Pedro, thanks for helping Samantha learn that content instead of telling her the answer. You showed real leadership by helping her think through the problem, as this helps her take responsibility and leadership for her own learning. This helps her become a leader, too."

More formally, the teacher can intentionally assign reading materials that portray leadership skills and their impacts. A learning task or discussion time should be attached to the reading. The teacher can also create leadership opportunities in her classroom and assign roles to students to practice leadership skills. Roles can include:

- Greeter: greets guests as they come into class.
- Teaching Assistant: often, teachers will use the "ask three and then ask me" rule, where students must ask at least three students a question before going to the teacher if the question has not been answered. Teachers can assign the "teaching assistant" role to three students, and students know to go to them to ask questions before turning to the teacher. The role can also be assigned to one student in the absence of the rule.
- Praise Leader: offers praise to students when they achieve goals and have success; encourages other students to do the same.
- Goal Leader: helps remind students to track their learning goals and set new ones.
- Effort Leader: encourages students in class to persevere when they begin to struggle.

Teachers can incorporate journal writing into learning so that students can reflect on their leadership skills. Journal prompts can include:

- Do you consider yourself a leader or a follower, and why?
- What qualities make someone a good leader?
- How are you working to develop your own leadership skills?
- Why are leadership skills important in today's world?
- Who is a leader you admire, and why do you admire them?

For students who really struggle with leadership, the teacher can look for ways to increase these students' ownership over their own learning. Personalized instruction is one of the strongest ways to do this. Specifically, teachers routinely should set clear learning goals with these students. Formative processes and data should be used and discussed regularly with students so that they know exactly where they are in progress toward goals. These students and the teacher should have an ongoing dialogue about what the students say they need to meet goals—which puts them in the driver's seat, with the teacher always there to guide and support. Throughout these conversations, the teacher should make a point to name and discuss leadership skills and—importantly—never miss an opportunity to praise these students when they exhibit them.

My Goals: Students use a goal-setting worksheet to record content standards and/or behavior goals and to track their progress toward reaching them. As they track their progress, they should reflect on actions needed to reach their goals. For an example of a "My Goals" goal-setting worksheet, see Appendix 15.

My Vocabulary Progress: This strategy helps students track mastery toward learning new vocabulary terms. Students are provided with a text and a copy of the worksheet found in Appendix 16. The teacher provides students with a list of academic vocabulary words from the text, and each student chooses unfamiliar words to study. While reading the text, students record where the word is located in the text and its meaning. Then, on the graphic organizer, students draw a picture, write a synonym, and/or use the word in a sentence. When students feel they have mastered the meaning of the vocabulary words, they check it off on the worksheet.

Quick-Write: Quick-Write is a short response to a prompt used to assess student thinking. The teacher typically gives students less than five minutes to quickly and quietly respond to a provided prompt. As the students write their responses, the teacher circulates the room to evaluate their thinking and assess the need for clarification on certain points.

Reflection Time: Incorporating reflection time at the end of class helps students assess their behavior and set goals for the following day. At the end of the class, the teacher asks all students to assess their level of engagement throughout the lesson. Students can rate themselves on a scale of 1 to 5 and justify their answer with evidence from the class.

The teacher should then share her assessment of the degree of engagement at the class level, providing evidence for her rating. Finally, the class should set goals for the upcoming class.

Stop-and-Reflect Moments: Stop-and-reflect moments can have many purposes, including aiding in self-assessment, deepening understanding, and regrouping when off task. If the teacher sees a need for some kind of pause to ensure everyone is on the same page, she can incorporate short periods of time (one to five minutes) into the class for whole-class reflection. For example, if students are off task, the teacher can stop instruction, thank those specifically staying on task, and then ask students to reflect on their current level of engagement and progress toward completing learning task goals. A brief discussion of students' assessments can help them regroup and focus on the task at hand. Or if many students are struggling with the same content, the teacher can pause instruction and ask students to take a moment to reflect on what they're learning and share their thoughts. This will help the teacher determine why students are struggling. She can then conduct a quick mini-lesson to support understanding accordingly.

Student Learning Rubrics: Student learning rubrics are a great way for students to assess their own learning and set learning goals. There are many tools available online to help teachers create rubrics specific to their classes and students. Some general rubric makers include Teacher Rubric, Rubric Maker, Rubi Star and EssayTagger. For assessing career competencies such as leadership, problem-solving, collaboration, and creativity, a helpful Life/Career Skills rubric builder can be found at www.nyctecenter.org under the Instruction Tab (2016).

Technology to Enhance Engaged Learning: There are several great technology tools available today that can ensure all students are answering questions and that offer students opportunities to give immediate feedback to the teacher or ask questions in real time. In turn, the teacher can alter or adapt instruction in real time based on the changing needs of the students. Such current technology tools include Class Flow, Formative, Quizizz, Kahoot!, Nearpod, and Quizlet, to name a few. Flipgrid is a technology where students can upload videos of themselves presenting on a topic or answering a question. Students then view classmates' videos and provide the presenter with feedback and ideas for improvement.

Visit www.leadered.com/coachingredefined for an evolving and updated list of strategies and tools to elevate learner engagement in instruction and learning.

Write-Pair-Share: This strategy builds upon Quick-Write and is also used to assess student thinking. The teacher gives students less than five minutes to respond to a question. Students write their responses. Once everyone is finished, the teacher asks them to share their responses with a neighbor. After students are done sharing, each pair selects the best from their two responses to share with the class.

PONDER & POST

Of the learner engagement strategies discussed in *Coaching Redefined*, I am most excited about utilizing _____.

#coachingredefined

Chapter 11

Building a Sustainable System of Learning and Growth

"What I have learned is that people become motivated when you guide them to the source of their own power and when you make heroes out of employees who personify what you want to see in the organization."

Anita Roddick, founder of The Body Shop

On February 9, 2001, Jack Welch, outgoing CEO of General Electric (GE), issued his final letter to shareholders. In it, he outlined what he believed had allowed the company to achieve enormous success and international renown—not just in the year prior, but under Welch's twenty-year tenure as CEO.

GE dates back to Thomas Edison who, in 1879, created the longest lasting light bulb the world had ever seen. This single-handedly changed the way the world would be able to use nighttime hours, and far more safely than afforded by candlelight. In the 1880s, Edison was invested in a handful of electricity companies and working with them to harness the power of electricity and, eventually, distribute it across the world. American financier and titan of industry, J.P. Morgan, funded Edison's research; in 1889, Morgan helped merge Edison's interests into one company, which would be called Edison General Electric Company. Three years later, that company would merge with another electric company in Massachusetts under the new banner of General Electric (General Electric, 2018).

GE's history is long, storied, and truly American. It was one of the original twelve companies on the Dow Jones Industrial Average. Both RCA, the Radio Corporation of America, and NBC, the National Broadcasting Corporation, were born under GE. Thanks to GE, radio and television, and the content they could deliver, would become staples in nearly every American home. The company would go on to play a pivotal role in aviation and jet engine technologies, computing, software, healthcare, and wind turbines, to name some.

Jack Welch joined GE in 1960 as a junior chemical engineer. A year later, he intended to quit; he was frustrated by the meager raise offered to him and the bureaucracy he believed slowed down processes and growth across the company (Byrne, 1998). An executive, who clearly saw talent in Welch, convinced Welch to stay and promised to help him create a more informal, small business-like environment. Over the years, Welch rose the ranks, steadily dismantling bureaucracies where he could. In 1981, he was named the youngest CEO in GE's history. His objective was to continue to unburden the company of the layers of management he perceived as stifling the company's growth, potential, and efficiency (CNBC, 2014).

In 1980, the year before Welch assumed the CEO position, GE recorded $26.8 billion in revenue. By 2000, Welch's last full year at the company's helm, it earned $130 billion in revenue (General Electric, nd). *Fortune* magazine named Welch "Manager of the Century" in 1999. The magazine also featured GE as "Most Admired Company in America" for the fourth year in a row in 2000, and the *Financial Times* named it "The World's Most Respected Company" for the third time (Welch, 2000).

To say that Welch went out on top is an understatement. Under his leadership, he successfully transitioned GE into a lean, efficient, extensively international company well positioned for the digital, globalized age. By 2000, as many companies struggled to understand, navigate, and adapt to the internet era and a newly globalized marketplace, GE stayed ahead of the curve and developed a shrewd and productive online business strategy.

In that last shareholder letter, Welch listed GE's goal-oriented initiatives that allowed the company to generate its highest ever revenues in one year and at the fastest rate ever. Those included initiatives around growing global sales; expanding the company's services, as opposed to product offerings; ongoing Six Sigma training, a company-wide program of process and quality improvement; and moving more sales online. Through dedicated focus on these initiatives, the company achieved goals across the board that had a direct and very big impact on the bottom line.

Yet, it wasn't the achieved goals that Welch credited above all for the company's success. Above all, he wrote that the most important initiative had been the company's commitment to evolving into a true learning organization. Specifically, Welch wrote:

> The (aforementioned) initiatives are playing a critical role in changing GE, but the most significant change in GE has been its transformation into a **Learning Company**. Our true "core competency" today is not manufacturing or services, but the global recruiting and nurturing of the world's best people and the cultivation in them of an insatiable desire to learn, to stretch and to do things better every day. By finding, challenging and rewarding these people, by freeing them from bureaucracy, by giving them all the resources they need—and by simply getting out of their way—we have seen them make us better and better every year . . . We have a company more agile than others a fraction of our size, a high-spirited company where people are free to dream and encouraged to act and to take risks. (Welch, 2000)

Far more than any goal, any initiative, any product, any milestone, any next billion earned, Welch credited GE's team of insatiably curious learners for the company's success.

But that wouldn't have been possible without a company-wide system of learning.

A Learning Organization

So, what is a learning organization, why does it matter, and how can we turn our schools into them? In the history of business-management theory, the idea of a learning organization is relatively new.

In 1990, Peter Senge—founder and chair of the Society for Organizational Learning and a senior lecturer at MIT—brought the idea of a learning organization to the mainstream with the publication of his book *The Fifth Discipline: The Art & Practice of the Learning Organization*. In the book, Senge describes a learning organization as place "where people continually expand their capacity to create the results they truly desire, where new and expansive patterns of thinking are nurtured, where collective aspiration is set free, and where people are continually learning how to learn together" (Senge, 1990).

Creating a learning organization was originally seen as a way to gain a competitive advantage. If your leaders, managers, and employees were constantly given opportunities to learn, grow, and gain new information and skills that all point toward specific goals, the entire company would reorient itself to staying agile and ahead of the curve. If the environment around us is always changing, we, too, must always change. A learning organization provides and fosters the systems and programs that support constant change through constant learning.

If we confront new problems, we cannot remain competitive if we apply old, outdated solutions. We cannot create new products for a new market environment and new customer needs if we are using old information. We cannot remain agile and capable of responding to change if we use only old ideas.

The same is true of schools. We are confronting very new problems: The ever-rising costs of college are changing the way students must consider post-high school options and the way schools must counsel them. The pace of technology development and evolution is rapidly changing the career skills our students need. The global marketplace has cracked wide open the pool of candidates our students will compete with for high-paying careers. Constant access to social media is changing how students engage with peers and strangers, which is changing their social skills and impacting emotional health and wellbeing. The ubiquity of information—real and otherwise—is changing how we must teach students to consider, vet, and consume it. To name just some.

Like any business that cares to continue to meet customer needs, stay relevant, and survive in a globalized, always fluctuating marketplace, schools must take measures to meet students' needs, stay relevant, and survive. Like any savvy business converting into a learning organization to remain productive, savvy schools must do the same.

After all, we coaches *redefined* know something not everyone does: the school system and the individual educators within it must work together to unlock the greatest growth potential for both. You have put so much time, energy, and good faith into building a school-wide instructional plan—despite the fact that you might have been surprised to see this step as the purview of a great instructional coach. You have taken so much care to nurture relationships, meet each teacher you coach where she is, and treat each as the humans they are. It is in this chapter where we will learn to sustain this incredible momentum and capture the exponential potential that is unleashed when the two levels of coaching *redefined* come together. This truly is a situation where the whole is greater than the sum of its parts. Like GE under Welch's leadership, we will use a learning organization model to support ongoing growth and constantly unlock new growth in new ways so that we—as educators and schools—may remain valuable and relevant in an always changing environment.

The Conjoining Pieces of a Learning Organization

Fortunately for us, Peter Senge put forth a roadmap to becoming a learning organization. I will share it here as guidance to building within your school a sustainable system of learning and growth.

According to Senge's research, growing into a learning organization rests on five disciplines:

1. **Personal mastery:** "A discipline of continually clarifying and deepening our personal vision, of focusing our energies, of developing patience, and of seeing reality objectively."
2. **Mental models:** "Deeply ingrained assumptions, generalizations, or even pictures of images that influence how we understand the world and how we take action."
3. **Building shared vision:** The practice of "unearthing 'shared pictures of the future' that foster genuine commitment and enrollment rather than compliance."

4. **Team learning:** "Starts with 'dialogue,' the capacity of members of a team to suspend assumptions and enter into genuine 'thinking together.'"

5. **Systems thinking:** This is the fifth discipline—the discipline that "integrates the disciplines, fusing them into a coherent body of theory and practice" (Senge, 1990).

In the next section, we'll inspect all five principles more closely to unpack what they mean for our schools, our educators, our coaching, and ourselves. I will also provide you tools to bring each principle into your coaching and leadership, so that you can lead your school's transition into a learning organization.

Bringing It All Together: Turning Your School into a Learning Organization

As we walk through how to bring Senge's five disciplines to your school, we will see that coaching *redefined* has allowed us to put many wheels into motion already. In following the steps and processes laid out in parts 2 and 3 of this book, you have been laying the groundwork of the learning model and a sustainable system around it. At this point, our focus will shift largely to maintenance and motivation, so that growth momentum is harnessed and used to its fullest capacity.

First and foremost: the ultimate goal of turning your school into a learning organization—of creating this sustainable system of growth—is to wean teachers off of your coaching. Hence, the idea of the gradual release coaching model is to coach teachers to lead their own lifelong learning. You can be far more useful to more people when you can coach more people! In most cases, it is impossible for one coach to coach all teachers at once. Therefore, in an ideal situation, the coach can cycle through teachers, gradually releasing more of them to lead their own learning so that the coach can move onto new teachers in need of one-on-one support.

Guiding people toward leading their own learning is a matter of accessing the right tools and having a certain confidence in one's potential. Put another way, it's a matter of a growth mindset. We have focused in this book on how vital keeping the human element front and center is to coaching *redefined*. We do this to make our educators feel safe, valued, seen, heard, ever more comfortable with being vulnerable, and—with time—at ease with constant change, confident in their capacity to thrive amid it. These are the roots of lifelong learning. These are the things that allow us to believe in ourselves and in our limitless growth potential.

Using Senge's five disciplines, we will now merge this human element with a system of growth that capitalizes on the intersection of the school system and individual teachers. Steadily, this learning system will position everyone in it to lead his or her own learning for life. As a general rule, I suggest applying what is laid out here around the same time that you begin your one-on-one coaching.

Before we get started, recall the tribe you began building in chapter 3? Those people you noticed as potential leaders and partners in spreading the message of growth and the vision for the school? Keep those people in mind as you begin to build and maintain a sustainable system of learning and growth. They will be a wonderful resource to you in supporting growth and helping you help the school realize all and future school-wide improvement goals.

The First Discipline: Personal Mastery

Personal mastery is a matter of self-awareness and our willingness to be vulnerable. It speaks to how our behaviors and actions impact ourselves and others, and how aware we are of the impact. Personal mastery allows us to recognize and consider others' perspectives, viewpoints, and experiences. It uses self-improvement, authenticity, and principled behaviors to foster better relationships. Embedded into personal mastery is the reality that when the environment is always changing, learning can never stop.

Personal mastery, of course, applies to your teachers; you are trying to coach them toward it. But it also applies to you. Since the lion's share of this part of the book focuses on helping teachers achieve personal mastery, here will focus on helping *you* to do so—keeping in mind that everything laid out here is transferable to your teachers to further guide them toward their own personal mastery.

By now, I hope I have you are well convinced that you are a leader—and a crucial one at that. As a leader, you cannot lead if you aren't a little bit ahead of the curve. This means learning to anticipate student and teacher needs and having the tools, ideas, resources, and skills on hand to meet them at their place of need and guide them to fulfillment.

To be able to see what's ahead of the curve, you, too, must develop a practice of lifelong learning. As an instructional leader, in particular, you will benefit from ongoing learning in two main categories:

1. Instructional skills: strategies, technology tools, evolving career skills, social-emotional learning tools, content skills—anything and everything that must be in your toolkit of effective, future-focused instruction to suggest to teachers as you lead school-wide improvement and manage one-on-one coaching.
2. Business skills: particularly leadership and management skills, in addition to other business skills, to convince people—as individuals and as teams—to trust you, share your vision, follow your lead, and take a leap of faith with you.

A Simple Framework for Personal Mastery

In their *Harvard Business Review* blog article "The Best Leaders Are Constant Learners," leadership and learning consultants Kenneth Mikkelsen and Harold Jarche set forth their "personal knowledge mastery" process. This is a simple tool they've designed to create a framework for constant learning. It is: seek, sense, share (2015).

To **seek** is to search out information to grow your knowledge base in a relevant way. Meaning, seeking requires that we use smart filters to avoid as much time as possible wasted on the wrong paths. Smart seeking means developing a sense of which knowledge to pursue and which to disregard. This requires knowing trustworthy resources of information, including people. Smart seeking also asks us that we reevaluate our resources with regularity to ensure they've maintained integrity, relevance, and a future-focus.

To **sense** is to reflect on information we've gathered and think deeply about what to use and how to use it. Smart sensing leans on our experiences and feelings to contextualize new information and learning.

To **share** is to exchange new knowledge, ideas, and resources with our networks. Doing so allows us to earn trust and relevance in our networks so that those in them also openly exchange ideas and collaborate with us.

Seek: Gathering Information from Resources Familiar and Unfamiliar

How you seek (and sense and share) is up to you and how you like to learn. Keep in mind that there are scores of great professional learning resources and communities available to you as an educator. What matters is that you gain new knowledge and practice new skills in all the areas of coaching *redefined*. Seek content and instructional knowledge and skills. Seek business knowledge and skills. Seek interpersonal knowledge and skills. Doing so might mean broadening your typical networks and go-to resources. Growth sits just beyond your comfort zone.

It is my sincere hope and intention that peppering mini business case studies throughout this book has not only shown you the value of learning about business skills; I also hope that it has piqued your interest in developing your own practice of seeking business knowledge and skills. As you delve deeper into this world, you will discover the thought leaders, podcasts, blogs, and books that speak to you best. To help get you started on that end, please see Appendix 1 for my go-to business and leadership learning resources.

Please also revisit chapter 2, The Instructional Coach's *Real* Values, as often as necessary. In addition to helping create a foundation of values as you coach, I provided these to help you have a framework for growing all the skills pertinent to being a coach *redefined*. Develop a practice of reflecting on how you are growing relative to all of the coach's real values. This will show you where you need to direct new seeking.

Sense: Reflecting on Your Coaching Practice*

Included in personal mastery is always striving to improve your interactions with and your service to the teachers you lead and coach. It is in sensing that you reflect on your interactions. If you are to grow into a coach *redefined*, you must create and prioritize time for reflecting on how you think you are doing as a coach. For me, sensing is a three-part practice; I reflect on how my teachers are progressing, on my actions after each coaching session, and on my coaching practice at large.

How your teachers are progressing is an indicator of how effectively you are coaching them. You will quickly see that once you start coaching, especially once you start coaching many teachers at once, it's easy to lose track of each teacher's progress. You must keep tabs on exactly where each teacher is relative to goals and why for their sake—and also for yours. To help to this end, develop a practice of taking notes after each meeting with a teacher, notes that will be only for you. As you reflect, consider:

- How and where is the teacher growing? How and where is she not?
- What challenges do I have when helping her grow?
- Where should the teacher grow next?
- What has worked and not worked with the teacher?
- What should I do during my next meeting with the teacher to better meet her needs?

The second part of assessing your effectiveness and how teachers are responding to your coaching is reflecting on your own behaviors and actions. After each meeting, reflect on your performance in the coaching session:

- What did I do well today?
- What could I have done better?
- Where did I have any knowledge gaps that prevented me from providing the teacher what she needed?

The third and final part of this self-assessment is to make a habit of periodically stepping back to reflect on your coaching practice at large. To do this, I like to journal. I find the act of writing clarifying. In re-reading what I've written, I can often see myself with a bit more objectivity and see things I'd been missing. That said, this is a personal process. Find what works for you and what allows you to be as objective as possible about yourself.

When I reflect on my coaching practice holistically, I consider:

- What have I learned about myself through coaching?
- In what areas am I growing? What is the evidence of this growth?
- What am I struggling with, and where can I turn for help?
- Of the coach's real values, where do I feel that I am strong, and what is the evidence?
- Of the coach's real values, where do I feel a need for growth? Where can I go for help?
- How can I expand my coaching skill set? What am I doing to ensure that my coaching toolkit remains relevant and future-focused?
- What am I doing to expand my academic content skills?
- What am I doing to expand my business, strategic planning, and leadership skills?
- Am I connecting with new leaders who can help me grow and enhance my practice? If not, why not?
- What does the data say about my effectiveness as a coach? What does it say about where I might need to focus improvement efforts as a coach?
- What does data not tell me? And where can I go to get information where there might be data gaps?
- How are my relationships with my colleagues? Where might some be in need of improvement, and what can I do to nurture them?
- For coaches who have moved from teachers to coaches in the same school: What do I need to do to maintain my friendly relationships with teachers while also ensuring the level of professionalism required between teacher and coach?
- Am I sufficiently visible in the school and to all teachers so that they are always reminded that I am a resource there to support all of their ongoing learning?

The Typical Coaching Calendar of the Highly Visible Coach On that last point, I will share a typical coaching calendar for the week. Once the school-wide improvement plan is well underway, you will be spending more time with teachers one-on-one. This means that if you don't build in visibility to all teachers, at best they might think you're too busy with the teachers you coach to help them. Or at worst, they might think you're not working. For a coach *redefined*, mastery must include visibility.

An example of a typical weekly coaching schedule follows. In addition to coaching cycle time and professional learning sessions, it's wise to do some classroom walkthroughs every week. They will typically fall into one of three categories:

1. Walkthroughs with an administrator: you should strive to join an administrator on her walkthroughs once a month. Together, you will spend around ten minutes in a class to get an overall view of what's taking place in the school or in a grade and to ensure you both are on the same page in terms of expectations and learning goals.

2. Walkthroughs on your own: you spend around ten minutes in the class to get an overall view of what's taking place in the school or in a grade. Aim to get into all classrooms at least once a month at a minimum and more often if you are in a small school.

3. Quick, casual pop-ins: Throughout the week, pop into classrooms to see if teachers need support and to remind them you are there to be a support. Strive to pop into all classrooms at least once a month at a minimum and more often if you are in a small school.

Share: Creating a Habit of Exchanging Wisdom

The most effective way to network and create success is to give. Psychologist and professor at the Wharton School of the University of Pennsylvania, Adam Grant, wrote an entire book about this. In *Give and Take: A Revolutionary Approach to Success*, Grant challenges the reader to assess if she is a giver or a taker. Takers are self-serving in their interactions (2014). They are people who go into most interactions thinking, *What can I get from this person?* A giver, on the other hand, does the opposite. A giver goes into most interactions thinking, *What can I give to this person?*

Sample Weekly Coaching Schedule

	Monday	Tuesday	Wednesday	Thursday	Friday
7:45 am–8:45 am	Design observation plans with Teacher 1	Walkthroughs with school administrators	Lead team professional learning	Conduct walkthroughs of various classes	Facilitate professional learning meeting
8:45 am–9:45 am	Observe planned lesson with Teacher 8 (designed the previous week)	Model lesson for Teacher 2	Observe Teacher 1 (discussion of observation will take place next week)	Complete research to answer teacher questions that have come up in coaching	Weekly debrief with school administrators
9:45 am–10:45 am	Observe planned lesson with Teacher 9 (designed the previous week)	Observe Teacher 3	Discuss modeled lesson with Teacher 4	Lead professional learning meeting	Complete research to answer teacher questions
10:45 am–11:45 am	Assist guided observations with Group 5	Facilitate professional learning meeting	Observe Teacher 10	Prepare and research for upcoming professional learning	Discuss observation with Teacher 3
11:45 am–12:15 pm	Lunch	Lunch	Lunch	Lunch	Lunch
12:15 pm–1:15 pm	Lead team professional learning	Study student learning data	Facilitate professional learning meeting	Discuss guided observations with Group 5	Review research to use during upcoming professional learning session
1:15 pm–2:15 pm	Model lesson for Teacher 4	Conduct walkthroughs of various classes	Prepare and research for upcoming professional learning	Discuss observation with Teacher 10	Design lesson plans with Teacher 6 (observe planned lesson next week)
2:15 pm–3:15 pm	Conduct walkthroughs of various classes	Pop-ins for Grades 9 and 10	Discuss modeled lesson with Teacher 2	Review instructional data/progress toward goals and plan how to communicate progress with teachers	Design lesson plans with Teacher 7 (observe planned lesson next week)
3:15 pm–4:15 pm	Plan for upcoming professional learning	Journal coaching self-reflection (successes, struggles, opportunities for improvement)	Pop-ins for Grades 11 and 12	Review feedback from professional learning sessions and make plans for upcoming sessions	Self-reflect and journal about struggles/successes of coaching for the week; set goals for upcoming week

Excluded from the book's title are matchers. Matchers are those who try to keep a balance in their level of giving and taking. They tend to operate on a quid pro quo. Most people, Grant found, are matchers.

He was curious to learn who excels most in organizations—givers, takers, or matchers. Per every success metric Grant could track, givers are consistently at the top and bottom of performance. Meaning, givers will either be your top performers or your bottom performers. When they are at the top, it means not only that the organization creates an environment where they can excel; it also means they can perform at higher levels than takers or matchers are capable of. When givers are the bottom performers, it means the system is not designed to give them what they need to excel, and they burn out as a result.

What givers need to excel, Grant found, is an environment where asking for help is normalized. It's often not natural for givers to ask for help. But it is only giving and never taking that burns them out—and squanders their superior performance potential.

To be a coach *redefined* is to be a giver. To avoid burning out, we must also learn to take from people we trust. The way to encourage people to give to you is, perhaps a bit ironically, to give to them. When you share your knowledge and wisdom in your networks, people in them will see you as valuable. They will be grateful for your generosity. They will remember you. This will achieve two things. It will make them more likely to be generous with you. And when you ask for help, they will be more likely to return the favor happily.

To ask for help is to be vulnerable. It is also to be confident. Which—we know from our real values and from the value we place on making our teachers feel comfortable being vulnerable with us—is to be a coach *redefined*. Hopefully help-seeking is the norm in your school or in your personal learning networks. If not, you can play your role in changing that by giving often and asking for help openly. Put another way: when you help people succeed, they will help you succeed in return.

The Second Discipline: Mental Models

Mental models refer to the beliefs held by the individuals that make up a system and the beliefs that dominate at the level of the system. They are the set of assumptions that drive people's thinking, behaviors, and actions. They matter because if we are to change behavior, we must change the mental models behind that behavior. For mental models to align with effective practices, they must be seen honestly and be available to be questioned and challenged. As a leader, you must reflect on the mental models in your school and understand those that are favorable to growth and those that aren't. As a leader in quest of personal mastery, you must also reflect on your own mental models—which the seek, sense, share approach is designed to help you do.

As a coach *redefined*, you have already gone to great measures to grasp the mental models shaping actions and attitudes in your school. The listening tour is a discovery process of mental models. In chapter 4, you reflected deeply on the mental models behind your school's readiness for change. You got to the root of your school's attitudes around change and have a set of tools to help change those attitudes so that the school can begin to rethink and, in time, embrace change. You've also put enormous and admirable effort into getting to know each of your teachers personally. In doing so, you establish the trust needed for them to open up to you and reveal their mental models, especially those that are standing in the way of their growth. Once you know those mental models, you can work with teachers to dismantle and rebuild models that have lost their relevance and unlock their limitless growth potential.

On that front, perhaps the most important mental model is a growth mindset. When it comes to understanding and working with mental models to create a sustainable system of growth and learning, always keep an eye on who has a growth mindset in the school and who doesn't. Make sure your vigilance on this front is ongoing. Refer back to chapter 4 as needed for tools to encourage those still stuck in a fixed mindset. Use the Five Whys to get to the root cause of their fixed mindsets or resistance to change. Spend personal time with these educators. Vision cast with them. Encourage them. And always, always remind them they have limitless growth potential— and it's up to them to see this, believe it, and move toward it.

Finally, as a coach, help your teams stay anchored by a very practical mental model—best practices, as they are best practices for a reason. Stay focused on what works. Global skills will change. Technology will change. Silver bullets and the latest, greatest tools will come and go. Let best practices merge with a growth mindset to be the dominant mental models that drive attitudes, behaviors, and actions at your school.

The Third Discipline: Building a Shared Vision

This idea of building a shared vision is not new to you as a coach *redefined*. You've been doing this since beginning the work of building a school-wide improvement plan. You know what matters most—student learning and success. And you've methodically done the work to determine what must be changed and achieved in your school to create the most fertile ground for student learning and success. You have a map for winning buy-in of your vision and steps to share it with enthusiasm and optimism. You have become ever more practiced at the art of vision casting to help every person in your school visualize success at the school level and see their personal roles in it.

Yet building and communicating a shared vision does not start and end with the school-wide improvement plan or the first meeting you have with the teachers you coach. It never ends. It must be maintained. Teachers must always be reminded of why they're doing this and why the goals you've co-created matter. Especially when other priorities and urgent matters crop up—and they always will. It's your job to ensure that surrounding circumstances do not cause teachers to lose sight of the long-term, data-validated, and student-focused goals you have co-created. In taking every opportunity to remind people of the shared vision, you remind them of what matters most and keep them motivated to that end.

Finally, constant reminders of the shared vision also have a practical purpose, which is that teachers come and go. New teachers must be brought into the shared vision and must be made to feel valuable, needed players in its realization.

Vision as Motivation

In his book *Drive: The Surprising Truth About What Motivates Us*, author Daniel Pink—who's written and spoken extensively about business, work, and behavioral science—explains that when it comes to motivation, there's a gap between what science knows and what most businesses do.

Most businesses use a carrot-and-stick model, where they dangle certain external rewards (usually financial) in front of people to motivate them to do something specific. This worked well in the typically compliance-based, rote jobs of the twentieth century. But for the twenty-first century, Pink found that research shows that such finite, external rewards don't work and can even backfire (2011).

Instead, Pink explains that when it comes to the complicated, problem-based, unpredictable work of this century, workers will excel only when intrinsically motivated. Specifically, Pink learned that there are three drivers of intrinsic motivation that compel people toward lifelong learning, growth, and great performance over the long term:

1. Autonomy: the natural desire to direct our own lives, meaning control what we do, when we do it, and with whom. Autonomy unlocks creativity, which in turns deepens engagement and counteracts mere compliance.
2. Mastery: the desire to get better at the things that matter to us. The concept of mastery is what makes a growth mindset possible. When one seeks mastery, they seek constant improvement of skills and a hunger to gain new ones.
3. Purpose: the inherent desire toward making meaning and doing work that is in service of something larger than ourselves. Motivation is lost when someone cannot grasp the greater purpose of their efforts, which over time will feel like wasted time.

No educator believes that her job is simple or straightforward. To be an educator today is to grapple with complex problems and situations and then think critically through them to decide on one of many possible solutions. It is to adapt quickly to ever-evolving content and technology tools. And it absolutely demands that we use emotional intelligence every day to personalize our instruction to the many unique students who pass through our schools. Our work is the work of the twenty-first century, and there is nothing rote about it. Our work, then, requires autonomy, mastery, and purpose if we are going to remain engaged in it for the long term.

As coaches *redefined*, we naturally allow for this model of intrinsic motivation to materialize and drive teachers. The co-creation process and the

GRC model leave room for autonomy, with data-driven goals serving as guardrails. To coach *redefined* is to meet teachers exactly where they are and co-create their journey toward mastery of the skills they want to develop to be better teachers. And to build a shared vision and systematize its ongoing reiteration is to create purpose and remind educators of it all the time.

Practice What You Preach

If you speak often of the shared vision, yet don't back up your words with actions, you will lose credibility and no one will buy into the vision. Remember that, as more of your time is spent doing one-on-one coaching, you might become less visible. Yet because you are a coach *redefined* and because you play a pivotal role in leading school-wide improvement, you must remain visible to all teachers, not just the ones you coach.

Keep your door open—literally and metaphorically. Remain available and accessible to any teacher in the school who might seek your insights or help. Make it clear that you are a growth resource for everyone, whether you are currently coaching them or not.

Get out of your office. Pop into classrooms routinely every week (refer back to the typical weekly coaching schedule in the personal mastery section). For best effect, these should be brief and for the express purpose of showing all teachers you are there for and available to them. Another purpose of these pop-ins is to, over time, make the pop-in a non-event. You want to get all teachers and students used to your presence so that they grow comfortable with you in their classrooms. When they—teachers and students—become comfortable with you, they grow more honest. And we know how important honesty and vulnerability are to growth potential.

Use Communication Channels to Market and Advertise the Shared Vision with Regularity

This is an excellent opportunity to lean on your tribe. Help them get and keep the word out about the shared vision. With members of your tribe, devise a plan to broadcast the vision through available channels and delegate responsibilities accordingly. This could be writing regular updates on progress toward goals in a newsletter. It could entail celebrating when the school and individuals achieve milestones that relate to the vision. It could be putting vision-related slogans on banners and signs throughout the school. Give voice to your tribe as you come up with ideas to broadcast the vision on a schedule. Be creative and have fun.

A while back, I worked with a school that had a practice they called "Name It, Claim It, Explain It." It worked like this. While doing a walkthrough, the principal would take a picture of any great practice she saw that supported school-wide goals. In the next staff meeting, she would put the picture on the screen. The teacher whose classroom was in the picture would "claim it" and then explain to colleagues what was going on in the image and make it clear how it related to school-wide goals.

Ultimately, when you design a process for reiterating the shared vision, you are constantly reiterating the need for ongoing learning. A shared vision cannot be realized without ongoing learning, progress, and growth. Thereby, keeping the shared vision front and center is vital for establishing an encouraging a learning organization.

The Fourth Discipline: Team Learning

Team learning is more than just people learning in teams. According to Senge, it's what happens when teams start *thinking together*—that is, the multiplied learning when we are learning from our own research and reflection (seeking and sensing) and also from the wisdom of others (sharing). When learning includes reflection time and is pinned to strategic goals, we can learn more together than we ever could learn alone. Team learning allows a natural circumstance for more givers to take and takers to give. In time, more givers will avoid burnout and more takers will evolve into givers.

We cannot talk about team learning without talking about professional learning. This is because professional learning is the strongest place to start building up team learning in a school. It provides the most natural opportunity. It is not the only place, but it is low-hanging-fruit to begin encouraging collaboration and team learning.

Anyone who's been in education for at least ten years or so knows how much the general view of professional learning has changed, and mostly for the better. For starters, there's been a move away from the term "professional development" (PD) and toward "professional learning" (PL) to emphasize the ongoing nature of growth. PL is less often seen as an event and more of a process—as it should be. In the past, we'd have professional development days, where learning on the topic would start and end on that day. Now, more schools spread PL out over an extended period of time, building in time for reflection and review, and providing opportunities to practice applying the skills or content at hand, with the hope that all involved will achieve mastery. In the strongest schools, PL is highly team-based and collaborative for the reason that thinking together multiplies learning. PL, then, respects and supports the realities of how adults learn best and most effectively far more than PD ever did.

As a coach *redefined*, it is my belief—and hopefully the belief of your colleagues—that you must play a role in shaping your school's PL process. Coaching *redefined* exists because of your unique perch at the intersection of the school system and the teachers. You gain insights into how the system is or is not supporting growth on both the school and individual levels. You also gain insight into teachers' changing needs. Not to lend—or not to be invited to lend—these insights to building the strongest and most tailored PL process in your school is to have your wealth of valuable knowledge squandered.

To those of you reading this who have not been included in crafting PL, an honest conversation where you share your insights with a school administrator could have great value in the quality of PL at your school. A PL process designed with your input will without a doubt help better serve the needs of your teachers—and in a way that is customized to the moment.

In many schools, the coach will lead some or many PL sessions. In others, the coach will not. Regardless of how hands-on you are with the actual PL sessions, know that you can and should attend them whenever possible. This will allow you to assess their efficacy, how aligned they are to goals, how interactive they are, how they stretch out over time into true learning processes, and how much collaboration and team learning they encourage. As you will see in this section and the next—systems thinking—PL will create several opportunities for you to enhance the function and success of the system as a whole.

Checking for and Generating Indicators of Successful Team Learning

In addition to sharing what you're seeing in classrooms and among teachers, be sure that your input into PL includes the hallmarks of effective team learning. In doing so, you will help ensure that the PL process can contribute to turning the school into a full-scale learning organization.

When team learning is happening at its greatest potential, you will see evidence of it around you. As a coach, regularly check for evidence of successful team learning. What follows are indicators of successful team learning, reflection questions for how to identify them, and what to do if you are not seeing them. Use these insights to influence, adapt, and improve your school's PL program and team dynamics.

A few notes before we outline indicators of successful team learning. First, in this section, we will discuss only those team-related components of PL. When PL follows the standards of best practice, it is ongoing with structured time set aside for teams to learn, reflect, and think together. It is here we will focus in this section. Indicators of successful PL will also show up in the next section, but they will speak to whether PL is contributing to the establishment of an overall learning organization.

Second, in closely following the processes set forth in this book, you will be setting up PL, and the teams used in it, for success. Sometimes, the tool or process for doing the work to generate evidence of this indicator can be found in another part of this book. In such cases, I will remind you of where in the book to look for ways to ensure an indicator of team learning is being realized. When we're talking about an indicator we haven't delved deeply into yet, I'll lay out steps and share tools to make sure it is realized.

Third, when you do see evidence of these indicators, always thank teachers and celebrate their growth and successes.

Team Learning Indicator 1: PL teams meet on a fixed schedule to stay engaged in PL and promote accountability and growth.

Reflection questions:

- Are meetings—and all teachers in it—focused on current PL goals and accountability measures?

- In meetings, do teachers show evidence that they have been applying strategies and tools learned in PL sessions in their classrooms? And are all discussing these experiences in meetings?
- Are teachers comfortable sharing in meetings what went well and what did not go well as they've attempted to try new PL strategies and tools in their classrooms, such that meetings promote a growth mindset and enable shared growth from individual setbacks?

Generating evidence of this indicator: Since we are aiming for a PL process that supports a learning organization, PL must include dedicated time for teams of teachers to meet and discuss what they're learning. Where a team is in their collective growth, what they are currently focusing on in PL, and the size and scope of current PL goals, will dictate how often teachers should gather for these PL meetings.

When I'm coaching in a school, at the beginning, I will attend and lead these meetings. When I see enough evidence that teams are progressing in their ability to meet PL milestones, and demonstrate consistent progress toward PL goals, I will ask a teacher who demonstrates leadership potential to co-lead meetings with me. (We will go into detail about meeting leadership roles in Systems Thinking Indicator 10.) Steadily, I will hand over the reins to her, but I will remain in attendance so that I can answer questions as needed. With more evidence of productive meetings, I will begin to pop in only for a few minutes. I strive to get to a point where I pop in less often. But I will never stop popping into these meetings now and then, as I will never stop wanting to remind teachers I'm available to support them.

Team Learning Indicator 2: Teachers exhibit healthy conflict-management skills in all PL sessions and meetings.

Reflection questions:

- Do teachers routinely argue in PL and struggle to find common ground and resolution?
- Can teachers resolve inevitable disagreements and conflict that come up in PL?
- In the face of conflict, do teachers know how to regroup by finding common ground and reminding each other of what really

matters—students and realizing the shared vision of school-wide improvement?

Generating evidence of this indicator: Conflict on any team is inevitable. As a first step, remind teachers of this—that conflict isn't necessarily a sign of dysfunction. What *is* a sign of dysfunction is when a team refuses to learn conflict-resolution skills. When a team is driven by a set of healthy norms, then conflict is healthy. Healthy conflict is the natural byproduct of a team that is honest with themselves and each other, that will challenge each other's assumptions and ideas, and that understands that creative friction can produce even better results and ideas.

I always make sure that all teams have a set of group norms, or standards, for how every team member is expected to behave and conduct themselves. I find it a useful exercise for teams to come up with their own norms. It gives each member the chance to ensure that her voice and perspectives are included, which naturally makes it feel collaborative and fair. As the coach, it's your responsibility to be sure that no major points are missed. To that end, see Appendix 17 for an example of group norms.

Team Learning Indicator 3: Teachers are voluntarily collaborating more—within PL processes and on their own.

Reflection questions:

- Are teachers working together?
- Do teachers appear comfortable working together? Why or why not?
- Are teachers leaving their doors open? Or are most teachers' doors shut most of the time?

Generating evidence of this indicator: Part of fostering more voluntary collaboration is through the prior indicators. Yet, sometimes there are schools where teachers are highly reluctant to collaborate. This could be because teachers don't know each other, they feel they don't have time to share strategies or ideas, or they simply don't have opportunities to do so. If you are in a school where teachers aren't eager to collaborate, do a Five Whys analysis to get at the root cause. This will, as we know, help you suggest the most fitting solutions.

Beginning to foster collaboration can be very simple. First, if team PL meetings are already in place, attend all of them. You can keep an eye on what they're working on and begin to understand team dynamics and potential productive partnerships. At the end of meetings, you can suggest that pairs of teachers meet to practice a strategy together or exchange information.

You can do this outside of team meetings as well. You can lean on your coaching to identify pairs of teachers you can connect to grow together.

When I do this, particularly in schools where the reluctance to collaborate is high, I use a staged approach:

- I begin by mentioning other teachers in a positive light as often as possible. I might refer to the technology one teacher is using or the instructional strategy another teacher is using. The idea is to begin to show teachers that their peers are resources of knowledge and tools.
- Then I will begin to think about whom I can pair up to exchange information. Let's say I see John using a strategy that would really help Karen meet a goal of hers. I ask John if he'd be comfortable with me suggesting to Karen that she come speak to him about the strategy. If he says yes, then later I tell Karen John might have information that could be of help to her. I then ask her if she'd be willing to pop into John's classroom for five minutes this week to pick his brain.
- Then when Karen is beginning to grow more comfortable with collaboration, I might suggest that she observe Hannah's classroom. I, of course, acquired Hannah's permission first.
- Once Karen is showing progress toward her goal, where it makes sense, I will ask her to pop over to a colleague's classroom to share what she's learned.
- Each time I suggest a connection, I always make it clear to the teachers involved that the purpose is to observe and/or discuss a specific practice or strategy, so that collaboration remains intentional and goal oriented.

The point is to ease people into receiving and giving help, and to help teachers see their colleagues as resources. Be sure to mix up the teachers you suggest others tap for help, as you don't want to appear as though you have favorites. Also be sure to make each teacher serve as a resource to another, so that everyone feels valuable to colleagues. When everyone feels they have something to offer, they will feel more confident seeking out teamwork and collaborative learning opportunities. They will also begin to see the multiplying value of the open and regular exchange of ideas.

Team Learning Indicator 4: Weekly team meetings are in place to discuss instructional practices and student learning needs.

Reflection questions:

- When teachers convene for weekly team instructional and student learning meetings, are they also discussing things that don't pertain to instruction and student learning, like upcoming school events, management issues, students, or teachers?
- Is there distinct time for team meetings to focus on instructional improvements and distinct time for management of other issues?
- If not, how can distinct time for team instructional meetings be carved out and systemized?

Generating evidence of this indicator: A weekly team meeting to focus solely on instructional improvements to better meet all student needs is a must in a learning organization. These teams may or may not be the same teams as the PL teams mentioned in the first indicator. What matters for the weekly team meetings is that those in a team teach the same students. The core focus of these meetings will be discussing ways to improve or adapt instruction, as a collective group, to better meet all the needs of the shared students. In doing so, these teams move closer to meeting the full potential of Hattie's highest-rated strategy, collective teacher efficacy, which has a 1.57 effect size.

If no such weekly team meeting is in place, make a point to have conversations with an administrator to stress the importance of ongoing team learning opportunities to improve instruction and student outcomes. Explain that these meetings enhance a team's capacity to personalize learning and support for all students, especially those who are struggling. Scheduling is typically the biggest impediment to putting weekly

Visit www.leadered.com/
coachingredefined to
download the Team Meeting
Agenda sheet.

team meetings in place. The goal is to work with an administrator to get them up and running in the next school year.

I have made a practice of always providing for teams a meeting agenda sheet. It includes space to note discussion about what they want students to learn in the upcoming week; the strategies they will use to boost students' success; how student success will be measured; and how they will better support students who are currently struggling. The agenda also asks teachers to think through plans for the next meeting and what they might need from the coach in advance of it. Please see Appendix 18 for a sample weekly team meeting agenda.

The point of the sheet is to bring structure and a clear focus to meetings. When team meetings are intentional, they are productive. Throughout the meeting, the team learning manager (a role we will discuss in the Systems-Thinking Indicator 10) will take notes. If the coach wasn't in attendance at a meeting, the manager will make sure the agenda is shared with the coach.

In terms of my involvement as the coach, I approach these meetings as I do PL team meetings. I will lead them, as needed, in the beginning and gradually hand them over to a teacher who's demonstrated leadership potential. Once she's ready to fully lead these meetings, I will pop in on occasion to remind the team of my availability and support.

Football coach Tom Coughlin, who has three Super Bowl championships under his belt, said when he announced his retirement: "Championships are won by teams who love one another, who enjoy and respect one another, and play for and support one another." Without team learning, the learning in any organization will remain siloed and limited within individual brains. It is only through collaboration that knowledge can be shared and learning can be multiplied exponentially.

The Fifth Discipline: Systems Thinking

We are, at last, at the "fifth discipline," that part where we bring all prior ones together. When each person has an ongoing learning practice and is working toward mastery; when the mental models all tie back to a growth mindset and best practices; when everyone is united in a shared vision; when teams are high-functioning and able to learn and think together; then all the pieces are in place for a true learning organization.

When it comes to systems thinking, we must step back to see the forest for the trees. We must look to see if all the puzzle pieces are coming together to promote constant learning, in every corner, such that the vision can be realized. And such that new visions can be imagined when the collective is ready for new goals and new growth—and, thus, new learning.

Take time to reflect on how all your incredible effort in leading school-wide improvement and coaching individuals is coming together to create a system of learning. Make a practice of stepping back periodically to attempt to see the whole. In doing so, you will unearth sticking points that might be impeding ongoing learning and growth. You will also ensure that a small detail isn't skewing your perception, that you aren't stuck in the weeds. It's easy to get fixated on a detail, positive or negative, and view it out of proportion to its real impact or importance. Meaning, if this thing over here is going really well, it can be easy to think everything is going really well. Or if that thing over there is not going well, it can be easy to think nothing is going well. In taking the time to reflect on the whole system of learning and growth, you can check your assumptions (those mental models) and best unpack what needs fixing or improvement, so that the full potential of school-wide and individual growth is always accessible.

Stepping Back to Think About the System as a Whole

The process of reflecting on your coaching practice outlined in the Personal Mastery section will help reveal how some puzzle pieces are interacting with and contributing to the whole. To see the system as a whole at work, the best thing to do is get out there and watch it at work.

At different cadences throughout the year, I will aim to complete each of the following practices:

1. Topic-specific mini-observations (approximately once a month): Conduct ten-minute walkthroughs in every classroom (that you coach or all, depending on the circumstances) to analyze system-wide progress on one specific goal or component of a goal. If the

school is currently working to improve relevance, spend a day looking only for the level of learning connections being made in all classrooms. Or pop into all classrooms to get a sense of the level of active participation in all classrooms, if the school is working toward engagement goals.

2. Spend a day with one grade level (approximately once a quarter): Pop into one class (or a portion of one class, as time permits) of every grade-level teacher. The goal is to get a sense of what school and learning are like for students in that grade.

3. Shadow a student (approximately once a quarter): Get a student's schedule for a day, and pop into each of that student's classes for ten or fifteen minutes. The goal is to get a sense of what it's like to be a student in the school, day in and day out.

4. Participate in walk-throughs with other leaders (approximately once a month): Join the principal, another administrator, or district staff on their walk-throughs of classrooms for a day. In between classrooms, have conversations about what you both are observing. You want to get a sense of whether your expectations about teaching and learning are aligned; whether you're on the same page about what you're seeing and not seeing in classrooms; and whether you view progress toward goals similarly.

5. Conduct a one-day, mini listening tour (approximately once a semester): Devote a day to having fifteen-minute conversations with at least one person from every key stakeholder group. Refer back to chapter 3 to refresh on how to go about this process. Be sure to get a sense of whether stakeholders believe that positive changes have been made; what those changes are, if so; why they think positive change has happened; and why they think change isn't happening if they don't see evidence of it. Use the indicators of successful systems, which follow in the next section, to help come up with additional questions to ask that feel relevant to the current circumstances of your school.

After completing each of these practices, take notes and reflect on what you've learned. These processes and their insights will show you gaps in systems that might be thwarting learning and growth. They can reveal where people are aligned or not in their perceptions on teaching, learning, goals, and progress toward them. Often, the root cause will be apparent. When it isn't, use the Five Whys to get to it. Engage others who might hold key insights to help you move through the Five Whys. Only in seeing gaps and misalignments, and in unearthing their root causes, can you come up with the right solutions to repair them.

Checking for and Generating Indicators of Successful Systems

As there is for team learning, there are indicators that your school's systems of learning and growth are aligned and working together or misaligned and impeding each other. When you do your periodic assessment of how the system is working as a whole, look for the indicators that follow in this section.

Many of these indicators overlap and relate to each other. And that's the point! When all your efforts to foster growth and learning at both the school and individual levels come together, they enhance each other. They steadily shift attitudes about ongoing learning and growth potential. This will reap rewards that begin to change other school processes and systems. A true virtuous cycle of growth is unleashed—or *can* be unleashed—by routinely checking for indicators of the system to ensure they are functioning successfully as a whole.

Where you see evidence of any indicator, you have an opportunity to celebrate progress and growth with the school. Use the various channels of communication to champion accomplishments. Give space and time for educators to shine.

Systems-Thinking Indicator 1: A growth mindset has become part of the culture.

Reflection questions:
- Do teachers take risks?
- Are mistakes and failures stigmatized and shamed? Or are they seen as part of growth?
- Do teachers appear to value their own progress and growth?
- Are teachers driving their own learning?
- Do students exhibit a growth mindset?

Generating evidence of this indicator: The internet has no shortage of resources on how to counter a fixed mindset and nurture a growth mindset. One of the most effective ways to do this, in my experience, is to talk about how failure and setbacks are a necessary and inevitable part of growth. Often a fear of failure is the basis of or solidifies a fixed mindset. In normalizing failure and encouraging risk-taking, you help people reframe failure. You help them see that confronting a failure doesn't mean they are inherently incapable, it means they are human. And what they are really confronting is an opportunity to learn, grow, and try again.

A simple way to do this is, in a staff meeting, to share a story of a mistake you made, what you learned from it, and how you overcame it. It's compelling to invite administrators and instructional leaders to do the same. When such conversations are commonplace, the school can put into practice a regular time for groups to discuss mistakes and workshop possible solutions. This is a powerful practice that makes it undeniable that mistakes and setbacks often make for the most fertile ground for learning and growth.

We'll discuss the student growth mindset in the next indicator.

Systems-Thinking Indicator 2: Students demonstrate a growth mindset on a daily basis.

Reflection questions:

- Are teachers giving students opportunities to direct their own learning?
- Do teachers encourage students to take risks in learning? And are students, in turn, taking risks?
- Are students' mistakes and failures stigmatized and shamed? Or are they seen as a vital part of growth?
- Do students appear to value their own progress and growth?
- Are students familiar with the concept of and need for lifelong learning?

When a true growth mindset culture takes hold, it will always extend to everyone in the building, from administrators to students. Thus, these first two indicators tend to correlate, and weakness in one often signals weakness in the other.

The tools to drive a growth mindset in students are similar to ensuring it among educators. However, all educators must remember that they hold enormous power when encouraging (or discouraging) students regarding a growth mindset. I always tell those I coach to talk about the differences—in the immediate and over the course of a life—between fixed and growth mindsets with all students on a regular basis. In simply learning this concept, students will be open to cultivating a growth mindset.

When I don't see frequent growth mindset dialogue happening, I will do a Five Whys analysis. Sometimes, the habit simply hasn't been formed, or the school hasn't thought to use classwork or communication channels to champion a growth mindset.

Perhaps, though, the most worrisome root cause is when teachers— some or all—don't believe that ALL students are capable of limitless growth. The severity and pervasiveness of this belief will inform how I counteract it. When the problem is at its most pervasive and entrenched, I will facilitate PL sessions about the growth mindset and the dangers of a fixed mindset to humans over the course of their lives. I will share data and research that says students often believe in themselves only as much as the adults in their lives do. I will require a study of Carol Dweck's book, *Mindset: The New Psychology of Success*, with discussion meetings and accountability measures throughout. If more learning is needed, I will ask teachers to read articles about the growth mindset or conduct their own research (with accountability built in).

I will also take note of the language teachers are using. When teachers don't believe all students are capable of limitless growth, I will see it manifest in their language. In groups or with individuals as appropriate, we will discuss the kinds of comments and language they must begin using in their classrooms to flip from pushing a fixed mindset to a growth mindset. For example, "You aren't good at this," versus "Maybe you haven't mastered this yet, but you can." Or "Your answer is wrong," versus "It seems like you made a mistake here, let's talk about what you can learn from it so you improve next time." Or "You did your best, which is all we can do," versus "Let's think about some other perspectives or approaches that might help you see the problem differently."

With teachers working toward a belief in all children's potential, I will only and always refer to students as "learners." I try to do this at all times regardless, but it is of particular importance with such teachers. With every opportunity, I will remind them that all children are capable of learning, all children are in their classrooms to learn, all children need to grow into lifelong learners, and all children CAN grow into lifelong learners—so long as they are given the gift of teachers and family who believe in them.

When teachers believe wholeheartedly that all children have limitless growth potential, yet are struggling to get their students to believe the same, I will ask them to incorporate read-alouds of books that support and teach a growth mindset. Depending on the age of the students, either the students or teacher can do the read-alouds. Instructional tasks or academic discussions to promote deep understanding of the growth mindset can follow. See Appendix 19 for a list of books for different grade levels that promote a growth mindset.

I will also remind these teachers that the RRE guides the kind of instruction that gives students agency over their learning and encourages risk-taking. I will also encourage teachers to normalize mistakes and failure in their classrooms, from routinely sharing their own mistakes and failures and encouraging students to do the same, so that together the class can discuss what they can learn and how they all can grow from a given mistake.

When all adults in the building hold the belief that ALL students have unlimited growth potential; when all adults constantly push learners to adopt a growth mindset, the results are powerful. It will naturally align to several high effect-size Hattie strategies, including: collective teacher efficacy—1.57 effect size; student self-efficacy—.92 effect size; and positive behavior—.65 effect size. Simply put, the power of the growth mindset is too great to ignore.

Systems-Thinking Indicator 3: Teachers and administrators habitually and routinely praise each other.

Reflection questions:
- Has staff developed a habit of complimenting each other?
- Does the staff feel uncomfortable or comfortable praising colleagues?
- Are there opportunities and channels for staff to praise each other?

Generating evidence of this indicator: When people freely compliment each other, it says that they view each other as capable resources. When people view their colleagues as resources, one of the most important components of successful team learning is in place. Creating time and opportunities for the exchange of praise is a way to contribute to the foundation of team learning.

In the absence of this indicator, I will create opportunities for it. As an example, I have asked members of a team to come up with a strong or creative instructional practice they've recently witnessed in a colleague's classroom. I ask them to report on this colleague's practice in the next team meeting. This is a simple exercise that prompts people to think about their coworkers in a positive light and go the extra step of praising them publicly. Where people are shy or hesitant, I will rely on members of my tribe to go first.

Another tool I've used is at the end of a PL session, I've asked all participants to write down a compliment to someone they learned something from in the session and hand it to them. Inevitably, the teachers who positively contributed to the PL session get the most notes. Those who did not get none. This practice creates a kind of positive peer pressure, where more and more teachers will want to receive written compliments. There is then a motivator in place to encourage people to contribute in PL sessions.

Systems-Thinking Indicator 4: Teachers are asking you and each other deeper questions.

Reflection questions:
- Are teachers asking you and others deeper questions that convey more complex thinking in one-on-one coaching sessions, staff meetings, and PL sessions?
- Are only some teachers asking deeper questions?
- Are most teachers asking simple questions about simple concepts and topics?

Generating evidence of this indicator: When people begin asking deeper questions, it means they are thinking more deeply. It means they've come to grasp fully the simpler concepts and are ready to move onto more complicated ones. Deeper questions also lead to deeper answers. A practice of deeper questions will, in turn, allow educators to problem solve with more creativity and cognitive flexibility to arrive at stronger, more robust solutions.

John C. Maxwell's book, *Good Leaders Ask Great Questions*, forever changed my perception of—and respect for—questions. In Maxwell's view, questions are the starting point for every problem or challenge. Deep questions spur growth. They forge human connection. They show paths out of problems. They open up minds. They allow us to see the previously unseen and hear the previously unheard.

If your school is to grow into a learning organization, everyone in it must grow into askers of deeper questions. If the level of questions teachers ask in your school isn't budging beyond the simple, look for patterns in their questions. You might begin to see several areas or concepts with which teachers are struggling. Knowing where they struggle will allow you to methodically move through depth of questions, scaffolding learning—in coaching or PL sessions—accordingly.

Systems-Thinking Indicator 5: More and more teachers are moving from instructive to self-directed coaching.

Reflection questions:

- Are the teachers you coach all steadily moving toward consistent self-directed coaching?
- Are too few teachers progressing toward consistent self-directed coaching, and why?
- Are you following the coaching protocols and fulfilling your expectations? If not, why?
- Are teachers following the coaching protocols and fulfilling their expectations? If not, why?

Generating evidence of this indicator: If a meaningful number of teachers are failing to meet their terms of the coaching process, conduct a Five Whys inquiry to understand the root cause. Reach out to administrators to help you make the changes and put the supports in place that will encourage teachers to hold up their end of the bargain. It's important to make sure teachers understand why they are being coached—that it is not punishment or a mark against them and that it is not being used for any evaluative purpose. Rather, it is because everyone has limitless growth potential and everyone can benefit from one-on-one coaching.

If both you and your teachers are all following the protocol, return to the personal mastery section to reflect on your practice. In addition to those questions, ask yourself:

- Am I accurately placing teachers on the GRC spectrum?
- How can I increase my accuracy in placing teachers on the GRC spectrum?
- How can I more effectively meet each teacher where she is and meet her needs at a given moment?
- Am I motivating teachers according to their dominant intrinsic drive?

On that last point, recall Daniel Pink's work around autonomy, mastery, and purpose as the primary intrinsic drivers of motivation. Growing into a self-directed learner takes effort, and effort takes motivation. Through conversation and observation, seek to determine which of the motivators is dominant in each teacher you coach and then create as many opportunities for it as you can.

Systems-Thinking Indicator 6: Teachers reflexively and routinely use data to improve their instruction.

Reflection questions:
- Do teachers voluntarily and regularly review data, analyze it, and apply insights to improving instruction?
- Do teachers review and rely on data for improvement only when reminded?
- Do teachers rely on you or others to review and analyze data for them?
- Are teachers collecting and reviewing the right data?
- Are sufficient data-collection processes in place?

Generating evidence of this indicator: When teachers rely on others for data review and analysis, use a Five Whys analysis to understand why. Often, people fear data; they view it as too complicated to understand or believe that they lack the skills to navigate it. Perhaps, they simply haven't yet developed a data habit, and rearranging a few daily to-dos to create space for it can allow them to do so. Maybe they don't yet understand how crucial data is to setting the right goals and making the right decisions as to how to achieve those goals and track progress.

If the teachers you coach are struggling to create a habit of data review and analysis, plan one or more coaching cycles until whatever has been blocking them is removed and they grow comfortable with data. If the issue extends beyond the teachers you coach, consider a PL session on the topic. Take care to build in follow-through, accountability, and dedicated team learning and practice time.

Systems-Thinking Indicator 7: PL is viewed not as an event but as a process with follow-through and accountability.

Reflection questions:
- Does PL take place over weeks and months, with checkpoints for learning and additional structured opportunities for teachers to ask questions and deepen understanding?
- Does PL have dedicated time for consumption of knowledge (learning); dedicated time for practice (application); and dedicated team-meeting time for teams who share the same students to reflect, discuss the topic together, and share ideas and knowledge (thinking together)?
- Are expectations of teachers relative to PL clear? Has it been confirmed that they understand what's expected of them?

Generating evidence of this indicator: Look back to the school-wide instructional improvement plan. You built into this plan the steps needed to realize the plan, the timeframe for each step, and how you would measure progress toward meeting each step and the goal in general. Let this information and process guide how PL can be broken down into steps, and how indicators of progress can be spaced out to create accountability.

Refer to chapter 6 for how to communicate goals to win buy-in and convince people of the importance of the goal. Use vision casting to keep teachers motivated throughout ongoing PL. Consider how coaching can be integrated into PL to provide for teachers structured practice time.

Systems-Thinking Indicator 8: All PL has an intentional and goal-oriented focus related to the shared vision around school-wide improvement.

Reflection questions:
- Does all PL stem from goals that can be directly tied to the shared vision and school-wide improvement plan?
- Does the topic of PL constantly change, bounce around, and feel unfocused?
- Are PL goals clearly articulated to and understood by all teachers?
- Does everyone understand the expected outcome of PL?

Generating evidence of this indicator: Thanks to part 2 of this book, goal-oriented PL should be happening naturally. If it's not, revisit how you went about determining school-wide improvement needs and turning them into goals. Review how you earned buy-in and brought educators into your shared vision. Inspect and analyze the link between school-wide improvement goals and PL to understand where it might be broken and why.

Consider where improvement efforts on your part might be needed so that school-wide goals are understood and accepted, the vision is clear and inspiring, and everyone feels like a necessary and valued part of realizing the vision—and is aware that collective, ongoing learning is what will realize the vision. As necessary, work with administrators and instructional leaders to recalibrate PL offerings and their processes so that they are supporting, not thwarting, school-wide improvement goals.

Systems-Thinking Indicator 9: PL goals are data driven and data monitored.

Reflection questions:
- Can all goals be explained as stemming from what data reveals?
- Is data routinely being used to measure the success and efficacy of PL?

Generating evidence of this indicator: As you moved through part 2 of the book, did you gather enough data about what is valued, prioritized, and happening in the school? Did you review as much data as possible about student performance? Did you analyze it sufficiently?

As necessary, do the data review and analysis to make sure every goal can be justified against data. Appeal to your tribe to help you review data in a structured and ongoing basis to measure progress toward goals.

Systems-Thinking Indicator 10: Teachers have team roles and responsibilities.

Reflection questions:

- Are teachers given opportunities—if even slowly and steadily, as needed and appropriate—to take leadership roles in their PL teams and weekly team meetings?
- Am I, or is an administrator, handling all instructional leadership and management of learning for teachers?
- Is there an understanding among the administrative team that for teachers to remain motivated to learn, they must have autonomy and a sense of ownership over their learning? (Remember what we learned from *Drive*.)

Generating evidence of this indicator: There are two categories of leadership roles that teachers can assume relative to their teams—both PL teams and the weekly meeting teams. (Recall that sometimes these will be the same teams, sometimes they won't.) They are: team instructional leaders and team learning managers. Instructional leaders are those who've proven ready to lead their team meetings. Team learning managers are those who've proven ready to manage the logistics around the team learning and meetings.

The team instructional leader's role is to ensure that all meetings remain focused and aligned to current learning goals or instructional and student improvement needs. This includes leading discussions as needed that will cover: PL milestones and progress toward goals; team members' experiences in applying newly learned strategies and tools in their classrooms; how to use data for instructional improvement;

different approaches teachers are using to teach standards to boost learning; instructional strategies that can better serve student needs; showcasing or demonstrating technology tools that can ensure equitable learning opportunities; and how to better support struggling students.

The team learning manager's job is to manage communications and logistics in and around meetings. This includes: sending meeting reminders; taking meeting notes and sharing them with the team and with the coach as needed; distributing relevant materials in preparation for meetings; and, after meetings, distributing materials that might have come up in a meeting; etc.

If a team has no teachers in leadership positions, tap those you deem ready to assume them. Because you have identified your tribe, these leaders will likely come from it. Have a private conversation with these people. Explain what it is about them that shows leadership potential and why you believe they'd be an excellent leader or manager for their team. Lay out exactly what the role entails and what would be expected of them, including how much time they can anticipate devoting to this role each month. Be sure also to ask them what they believe they'd need from you to feel supported such that this new role doesn't cause their other work as teachers to suffer. For those teachers who accept these roles, check in with them regularly to see how they're doing and if they need more support.

If there is a team where none of its members is in your tribe, then you will likely have to manage the aforementioned team leadership role responsibilities at the outset. Keep an eye out for those teachers on a team who show early and meaningful growth. Tap them to begin to lead parts of meetings or manage certain areas of team logistics. Gradually release more and more responsibility to them.

System-Thinking Indicator 11: Teachers are key contributors to PL planning.

Reflection questions:

- Do teacher needs drive PL topics and processes?
- Do teachers have an opportunity to voice their needs and request specific PL opportunities and processes?
- Is there a process in place to solicit teacher feedback about PL?

Visit www.leadered.com/
coachingredefined to
download the Reflecting on
the Day worksheet.

Generating evidence of this indicator: If it is not common-place or considered logical and reasonable for teachers to request PL opportunities, I use a simple tool to begin to make this standard protocol. After a PL session, I distribute the Reflecting on the Day worksheet that all participants are expected to fill out. An example of this worksheet is in Appendix 20.

This worksheet has four writing prompts for teachers to address, each of which I purposefully designed to push teachers to think forward and positively and promote a growth mindset. The prompts don't leave room for complaints, but rather constructive thoughts that can inform the next PL session.

The first two prompts ask teachers "What I thought I would learn" and "What I learned." Their answers can help you grasp how effectively expectations were set in advance of learning. This matters because it can frustrate teachers to devote time to something when they thought they were going to get something else. The next prompt says, "What worked best for me." The answers will tell you the learning strategies you used that teachers found most effective so that you can use more of them in their future PL sessions. What they don't mention, particularly as a pattern, will tell you what they didn't like and what should be used less or not at all in future PL. Lastly, teachers are to write a response to the "What I need or need to know now" prompt. Teachers' answers will show you the topics and ideas they want to discuss in future PL sessions. Or it might show you that in order to reinforce learning, they need time to reflect and apply learning in classrooms or they need team practice time.

Systems-Thinking Indicator 12: Teachers are moving from being consumers of information to leaders of learning.

Reflection questions:

- Are more of the teachers you coach growing into self-directed learners?
- Are more teachers being given or taking instructional leadership opportunities?
- Are teachers leading part or all of some PL sessions?

Generating evidence of this indicator: If you don't see teachers beginning to assume instructional leader roles, do a Five Whys analysis. In many cases, there will be aspects of the culture that block opportunities for teachers to take leadership or prevent teachers from stepping forward to do so. I will often consider the following questions to help find the right Five Whys path or paths to go down:

- Does the culture encourage teacher leadership?
- Does the school have pathways for teacher leaders, i.e., specific and known opportunities for teachers to take on leadership roles?
- Are teachers mocked for stepping forward to take on leadership or to volunteer?
- Are teachers punished if they try something new and it doesn't work?

As coaches, we must accept that we cannot control everything. Sometimes there are pieces of the culture that really are a big block on the road to nurturing teacher leaders. Sometimes we alone cannot change this part of the culture quickly. Instead, focus on how you can make small changes on the individual level to chip away at it. Where possible, give opportunities to teachers to lead portions of any PL sessions you might be in charge of. Help create opportunities for them to take leadership in their team meetings. And where even these ideas are difficult to pull off, provide for teachers ideas or materials for PL outside of school where they might be able to show leadership and grow their confidence as future leaders.

Systems-Thinking Indicator 13: Students are demonstrating more excitement about learning and school.

Reflection questions:
- Has there been a noticeable change in student attitudes about being at school?
- Do students appear to understand how school directly links to their future opportunities and careers?
- Do students believe in their own limitless growth and see the value of rigorous work?

- Do students engage with each other in and out of class?
- Do students appear comfortable engaging with teachers?
- Do students appear excited to be at school? If not, why?

Generating evidence of this indicator: Last, but certainly not least, is perhaps the most important indicator—the one we've been working to realize in this whole process of coaching *redefined*. Students will let you know if the changes and improvements put into place are working. They will let you know in quantitative data, like scores and grades. And they will let you know in qualitative data, like enthusiasm in classrooms, interactions with teachers, interactions with each other, and through the general feeling of morale in the building.

In addition to reviewing quantitative data, take the time to talk to students. Refer back to chapter 3 for guidelines. Also remember to review artifacts around the building. Revisit the part of the listening tour guidelines in chapter 3 that outline how to study the learning environment for clues about student attitudes. Look for evidence of changes to create a more encouraging, supportive, and celebratory learning environment.

Sometimes you will find there simply aren't enough opportunities to assess qualitative evidence of student attitudes. In this case, put them into place. As an example, put a "favorite lesson of the month" box in the cafeteria or a common area. Invite students to write on a form their favorite lesson in the past month, why they loved it, and the teacher who led it. The participation rate alone will show a level of student enthusiasm and engagement. The submissions will begin to reveal patterns in what is driving student engagement; for example, students are feeling encouraged to try, even if they "fail"; students are being trusted with more rigorous learning; students are excited to see how learning connects to the real world; etc. When those submitted lessons align to school-wide goals, this also affords an opportunity to celebrate these teachers publicly, over PA announcements, on social media, or in newsletters.

Another idea is to establish a recurring section in the student newspaper for students to write about their favorite teacher and what makes their classroom so exciting and engaging. The options here are limited only by imagination. What matters is to know that you can creatively systematize efforts to collect and analyze qualitative student data.

Lastly, we all know learning is more fun when we believe we are learners. Revisit the indicator about the student growth mindset and always do whatever you can to make sure all students in your school *know* they are born learners.

Final Thoughts

Congratulations—you are now a coach *redefined*. You have and know where to go to get all the resources, knowledge, and tools you need to grow into the best coach you can be. You are equipped with the processes and steps to *redefine* what coaching can be and what it can achieve in your school. As such, you've joined a movement to dramatically change and improve how we work and learn together to deliver rigorous, relevant, and engaging instruction to *all* students.

Perhaps, for the purposes of your own growth, most important—you are now a leader. One fully capable of leading those in your influence to grow into people capable of leading their own learning and, in turn, doing the same for their students. There is no stronger, more effective, and more memorable way to leave a legacy than to provide for others the gift of their own power to live from their limitless growth.

PONDER & POST

To help turn my school into a stronger learning organization, I will
_____.

#coachingredefined

Afterword

"I've learned that people will forget what you said, people will forget what you did, but people will never forget how you made them feel."

Maya Angelou

A few years ago, I was in a one-on-one meeting with a school leader I'd been coaching to help her grow into a coach *redefined*. It was one of those difficult but critical conversations that happen now and then as we coach. This particular conversation required that I respectfully and compassionately deliver to her some tough feedback. I shared that I'd observed in her a strong unwillingness to hear opinions different from her own and that it was frustrating her colleagues and contributing to stalled progress.

My words were met with great resistance, to say the least. Specifically, I got an education in how many four-letter words could be crammed into one sentence. In my attempt to calm her, I emphasized that this was not personal feedback, but a comment on a behavioral pattern. My attempt to defuse the situation failed. Without explicitly saying so, it was clear that she wanted me to leave her office.

In the days that followed, I waited for the call I was certain would come to cancel my contract. To be honest, I considered canceling it myself. After all, if this person didn't want help, how could I help her?

After reflecting on the encounter, I decided to leave the light on. Having done this work for years, I knew that if I were to serve her best, I would have to be honest with her. Having had several of these challenging conversations throughout my career, I knew the power of extending patience, grace, and forgiveness in such scenarios. After all, I am a coach *redefined*, and that's what we do.

The call to cancel my contract never did come, and my next monthly visit rolled around. I would be lying if I said I wasn't nervous returning to that campus. Nonetheless, I took a deep breath, dug deep, and made my way to the school.

The school leader was waiting for me at the entrance when I arrived. "I need to speak with you," she said. With some unease, I followed her into her office. After she closed the door and invited me to sit down, she sat down herself. And immediately broke down crying.

Her apologies were as profuse as her tears. She said she regretted the way she had spoken to me. She admitted to having built a protective wall around herself and blocking out anyone who didn't agree with her. "You were right," she said in between sobs. "I couldn't see it until you pointed it out." It occurred to her, she went on to say, that I was the first person in years who'd been truthful with her. While hearing constructive criticism was jarring, it jarred her enough to step out of her defensive shell and into the space of being honest and wanting honesty.

I was so moved and inspired by the strength she was showing and sharing with me. It is challenging to hear constructive criticism. But it is part of growing.

To this day, this school leader and I keep in touch. Anytime I have the pleasure of seeing her, we greet each other with a hug. Watching her break beyond her self-limiting behaviors and her fears to become a truly excellent instructional coach and leader is why I do this work.

As you now well know, to be a coach is to be a leader. To be a leader is to leave an imprint. That is ultimately what leadership is about—changing those you lead. We can consciously decide for that imprint to be positive and affirming, or we can forget to make a conscious decision and leave room for it to default to the negative.

Let's decide to leave a positive imprint on all those whom we lead. And let's understand that sometimes it takes moving through challenging situations and uncomfortable conversations to arrive at that positive imprint. When you do that, you have become a courageous, honest leader.

When it's all said and done, and with Maya Angelou's beautiful sentiment in mind, go into every interaction with educators thinking about how you want to make them *feel* . . . how you want them to remember you years down the line.

Make educators remember you as someone who helped them to see their boundless potential, their value and importance to children, and their power to change lives for the better.

Thank you, truly, for joining me in this co-creation. It's been an honor.

—Sherry St. Clair

APPENDICES

Appendix 1

Resources for Ongoing Learning: Business and Leadership

Referenced in chapters 2 and 11

The business and leadership world has no shortage of books, podcasts, and online resources, as business and leadership ideas necessarily change as circumstances change. This is the point of ongoing learning—to stay abreast the latest thinking. A selection of my current favorite business and leadership books, podcasts, and online resources follows. Bear in mind that it is an ever-evolving list.

Books

Made to Stick **by Chip Heath and Dan Heath**
The authors explore what makes some ideas stick while others do not. They share critical principles of winning ideas that coaches can utilize when vision casting.

Multipliers: How the Best Leaders Make Everyone Smarter **by Liz Wiseman**
A look at two types of leaders: those who drain energy, intelligence, and capacity from those they lead; and those who do the opposite by encouraging people to stretch themselves. The book can help coaches multiply instructional leaders in schools.

This Is Marketing **by Seth Godin**
According to Godin, the best marketers know how to solve problems for people. The greatest way to do this is to help others become who they want to be. Coaches can take the techniques in this book and learn to build and market ideas that help teachers become their best.

The One Thing: The Surprisingly Simple Truth Behind Extraordinary Results **by Gary Keller and Jay Papasan**
Pursuing too many goals at once often means failing to meet any of them. Instead, deep focus on the "one thing" is the path to big results. The book guides the process of identifying that one instructional thing that will see the greatest impact on teachers' growth.

Start with Why **by Simon Sinek**
Why do some leaders fail, and others inspire people for generations? This is the central question of Sinek's book, which outlines the common characteristics that inspiring leaders exhibit. In starting with why, coaches can build momentum and inspire educators to do great things together.

Drive **by Daniel Pink**
Based on four decades of scientific research, Pink examines three fundamentals of intrinsic motivation—autonomy, mastery, and purpose—and how to draw on these fundamentals to drive people to greatness. Coaches will benefit from understanding how to motivate adults as they lead school-wide improvement efforts.

Strengths Based Leadership **by Tom Rath and Barry Conchie**
Thirty years of research and 20,000 interviews with leaders yielded three keys to effective leadership: know your strengths, recruit those with the right strengths to your team, and invest in others' strengths. The book will help coaches learn to build on the strengths of the educators they lead.

Good Leaders Ask Great Questions **by John Maxwell**
Maxwell outlines the profound questions leaders should ask of themselves and their teams if they want profound results. The book will guide

coaches to a new relationship with questions and a skill for asking the ones that can help educators transform schools.

Boundaries for Leaders by Dr. Henry Cloud
Psychologist Dr. Cloud explains the role of healthy boundaries in leadership to galvanize teams around healthy cultures, strong values, and satisfying work. Coaches will find practical leadership and management advice backed by psychology and neuroscience.

Podcasts

Coaching for Leaders hosted by Dave Stachowiak
Stachowiak emphasizes action-oriented leadership advice to help leaders become more effective coaches.

Engaging Leader hosted by Jesse Lahey
Lahey focuses on topics such as communication, cultivating a team, and accountability, which help leaders engage those they lead.

EntreLeadership hosted by Ken Coleman
Through interviews with the top thinkers in business and marketing, this podcast offers practical tips and thoughtful ideas to grow business and grow into inspiring, effective leaders. A range of guests from a range of industries give insight into the skills business leaders value today.

Leaders in the Trenches hosted by Gene Hammett
Through deep discussions with various leaders and coaches, Hammett helps listeners learn the types of issues and challenges that leaders will face and how to address and persevere through them.

Online Resources

Harvard Business Review—hbr.org
This site, affiliated with Harvard Business School, has a wealth of articles, videos, and interviews that address every aspect of business and

leadership and provide expert advice and practical steps for implementation of ideas and strategies.

Lolly Daskal—www.lollydaskal.com
On her blog, Daskal discusses a comprehensive list of topics to help leaders develop their skill sets to become more effective.

Let's Grow Leaders—letsgrowleaders.com
The blog authors focus on the skills needed to encourage the growth of leaders within teams.

Appendix 2

Resources for Ongoing Learning: Valuable Educational Organizations

Referenced in chapter 2

ASCD
ASCD provides excellent resources connected to teaching and learning. Their *Educational Leadership* magazine, often with pieces from renown educators and thinkers, offers leaders and array of articles that can help lead deep professional learning conversations.

International Center for Leadership in Education
I have collaborated with ICLE for over a decade. Please know that I publish this book with them—and with their incredible support. With the Rigor/Relevance Framework® as their capstone philosophy, coaches will especially benefit from the numerous resources available connected to rigor, relevance, and learner engagement. The company routinely publishes thought-leadership pieces by some of education's most notable thinkers of the day.

Learning Forward
An organization dedicated to helping leaders grow their schools into meaningful learning organizations.

Content-Specific Organizations

Content specific organizations will help a coach develop a deep understanding of content. Some to follow include: National Science Teachers Association, National Council of Teachers of Mathematics, National Council of Teachers of English, National Council for the Social Studies, and Advance CTE.

Appendix 3

Rigor, Relevance, and Learner Engagement Rubrics (RRE)

Introduced in chapter 5 and referenced in ensuing chapters

Visit www.leadered.com/coachingredefined to download the RRE rubrics.

Rigor Rubric

Support teachers in building effective instruction based on rigorous expectations. The three indicators for rigor are: thoughtful work, high-level questioning, and academic discussion.

Thoughtful Work	1 – Beginning	2 – Emerging	3 – Developed	4 – Well Developed
Student Learning	• Students demonstrate their learning by completing recall and retell tasks. Most tasks draw on memorization and focus on answering recall-type questions.	• Students demonstrate their learning by completing tasks that require comprehension. • There are opportunities for students to demonstrate mastery through learning tasks that require them to apply knowledge and comprehend content.	• Students demonstrate their learning by completing tasks that validate their ability to analyze, synthesize, and/or evaluate new instructional content. • Tasks include the opportunity for students to respond to content through inquiry and interpretation.	• Students develop their own learning tasks that stretch their creativity, originality, design, or adaptation. • Tasks include the opportunity for students to assess their own learning and move forward to adapt their knowledge to new activities.
Instructional Design	• Learning tasks include one assigned way for students to demonstrate their thinking.	• Learning tasks include one or more assigned ways for students to demonstrate their thinking.	• Learning tasks allow students to self-select options to best represent their thinking.	• Learning tasks extend students' learning, inspiring them to pursue self-discovery.
High-Level Questioning	**1 – Beginning**	**2 – Emerging**	**3 – Developed**	**4 – Well Developed**
Student Learning	• Students respond to questions that mainly focus on basic recall and retell. • Few students ask questions, and most questions asked focus on basic recall or retelling of content.	• Students respond to questions that demonstrate a comprehension of content. • Students have opportunities to ask questions during the lesson and most questions focus on comparing and contrasting information.	• Students fully explain and justify their thinking when responding to questions that demonstrate different levels of thinking, including questions that require analysis, synthesis, and evaluation of information. • During the lesson, students generate questions about content that demonstrate rigorous independent thinking.	• Students actively engage in developing rigorous questions to challenge the thinking of their peers. • Students are able to respond to rigorous questions generated by peers with little guidance from the teacher.
Instructional Design	• Lesson mainly includes questions at the recall and retell level, and/or not all students are required to respond to each question.	• Lesson includes questions at a range of levels, but not all students are required to respond to each question.	• Lesson uses questioning to carefully support students in moving to higher levels of thinking, ensuring that all students have an opportunity to respond.	• Lesson is designed to inspire all students to engage in high-level questioning around the learning task with their teachers and peers.
Academic Discussion	**1 – Beginning**	**2 – Emerging**	**3 – Developed**	**4 – Well Developed**
Student Learning	• Student discussion is driven by the teacher and mainly remains at the retell level, mostly using everyday language, with little to no evidence of academic or domain-specific vocabulary. • Student discussion focuses on a variety of topics with each student offering his/her own thinking without using ideas from peers.	• Student discussion, structured by prompts from the teacher, includes a combination of retelling, analysis, and/or stating a claim and defending it with evidence. • Students provide explanations or evidence of their thinking and respond to their peers' comments.	• Students engage with peers in teacher-guided academic discussions focused on analysis, synthesis, and evaluation of content-driven topics, using academic language to express their thinking regarding the major concepts studied. • Students support their ideas with concrete explanations and evidence, paraphrasing as appropriate, and build on or challenge the ideas of others.	• Students primarily drive the discussion, consistently adding value to the dialogue with their peers and teacher, and respecting the opinion and thoughts of both; the lesson shifts to conversation rather than a Q&A session regarding the major concepts studied. • Students are able to stay focused on the activities of inquiry and engage in dialogue, using content-rich vocabulary with their peers.
Instructional Design	• Lesson mostly structures discussion as teacher-led, with the majority of interactions as teacher to student.	• Lesson structures discussion as a mix of teacher-led and peer-to-peer with the teacher facilitating the majority of discussions.	• Lesson mostly structures discussion as independent peer-to-peer. The teacher facilitates and redirects the discussion as needed, while evaluating the quality.	• Lesson is designed to inspire students to independently engage in dialogue and add valuable academic content around the learning tasks.

Relevance Rubric

Support teachers in building effective instruction based on relevance of experiences to learners. The three indicators for relevance are: meaningful work, authentic resources, and learning connections.

Meaningful Work	1 – Beginning	2 – Emerging	3 – Developed	4 – Well Developed
Student Learning	• Student work is procedural and structured, reflecting a basic understanding of information learned during the lesson/unit. • Student work focuses on class-specific content, with an emphasis on building skills, developing comprehension, or other foundational skills.	• Students think critically about content and apply information learned to address a specific task. Student work demonstrates originality. • Student work requires application of knowledge learned during the lesson/unit.	• Students think critically about content and apply information learned to address a range of cross-disciplinary tasks. Student work demonstrates creativity and originality. • Student work requires real-world predictable and/or unpredictable application that has a direct connection to a career in the related field of study.	• Students think and act critically to curate content and apply information learned to address a range of cross-disciplinary tasks which are both creative and original. • Student work requires the ability to select, organize, and present content through relevant products with multiple solutions.
Instructional Design	• Lesson provides students an opportunity to demonstrate foundational understanding of content.	• Lesson provides students an opportunity to complete a specific task that requires application of knowledge.	• Lesson provides students an opportunity to select from a range of real-world, relevant tasks, using critical thinking about new learning to complete the task.	• Lesson inspires students with an opportunity to think critically about new learning to create their own real-world, relevant tasks.

Authentic Resources	1 – Beginning	2 – Emerging	3 – Developed	4 – Well Developed
Student Learning	• Students mainly engage with one source of information for the lesson and/or unit. • Students use one source to complete tasks focused on making simple connections to content.	• Students engage with one primary source of information for the lesson and/or unit, and use secondary resources to support it. • Students use one or more sources to complete real-world tasks focused on making simple connections to content.	• Students engage with multiple sources of information, both primary and secondary, during a lesson/unit. • Students use multiple sources of information to complete real-world tasks involving comparisons, analysis, argument, and research.	• Students engage with multiple sources of information, both primary and secondary, during a lesson/unit, including multi-format resources. • Students select and use a variety of resources to solve predictable or unpredictable real-world scenarios.
Instructional Design	• Lesson relies on one source of information. The unit/lesson is organized around the structure of the content-specific text.	• Lesson is structured around an essential understanding/question, uses primary and secondary sources, and includes opportunities for students to connect content to a content-specific text and an additional resource.	• Lesson is structured around an essential understanding/question and relies on multiple authentic texts and resources to conduct comparisons, analysis, arguments, research, and other relevant, real-world tasks.	• Lesson is structured around an essential understanding/question and relies on students to select multiple authentic texts and resources to engage in real-world problem solving.

Learning Connections	1 – Beginning	2 – Emerging	3 – Developed	4 – Well Developed
Student Learning	• Students seldom have the opportunity to engage in content that has explicit connection to real-world application. • Some students may attempt to make connections between content learned and real-world application, but these connections are volunteered rather than included as part of the lesson.	• Students occasionally engage in content that has explicit connection to real-world application. • Some students begin to articulate the connections between content learned and real-world application.	• Students engage in content that has explicit connections to real-world applications. • Students clearly articulate the connections between content learned and real-world application.	• Students discover opportunities to apply content to their lives as well as real-world application. • Students independently make thoughtful connections between content learned and real-world unpredictable situations.
Instructional Design	• Lesson provides appropriate content, but without explicit connections to real-world application.	• Lesson provides some opportunities to connect content learned to real-world application.	• Lesson provides multiple explicit opportunities for students to connect content learned to real-world applications.	• Lesson inspires students to create their own opportunities to connect content learned to their lives, as well as real-world applications.

Learner Engagement Rubric

Support teachers in creating and implementing an effective learner environment that is engaging and aligned to learner needs. The three indicators for learner engagement are: active participation, learning environment, and formative processes and tools.

Active Participation	1 – Beginning	2 – Emerging	3 – Developed	4 – Well Developed
Student Learning	• Limited student engagement, with the exception of hand-raising. Some students are off-task or have disengaged from the lesson and are not redirected. • Lesson is teacher led and students progress through new learning with some challenges with productivity.	• Most students remain focused and on-task during the lesson. Students answer questions when asked, but not all students have the opportunity to actively respond. • Lesson is led by the teacher, and students productively progress through new learning.	• All students remain on-task, responding to frequent opportunities for active engagement throughout the lesson. • Lesson is led by both teacher and students, and students productively progress through new learning.	• All students remain on-task and proactively engaged throughout the lesson. • Students take ownership of learning new content, actively seeking ways to improve their own performance.
Instructional Design	• Lesson relies mainly on direct instruction with few opportunities for student engagement through application.	• Lesson relies on one or two strategies designed to engage students, with the lesson focused more on direct instruction than on student engagement through application.	• Lesson provides multiple strategies designed to maximize student engagement, and contribution is monitored to ensure full participation.	• Lesson achieves a focus on student-centered engagement where the students monitor and adjust their own participation.
Learning Environment	**1 – Beginning**	**2 – Emerging**	**3 – Developed**	**4 – Well Developed**
Student Learning	• Students rely on peers or teacher for answers to questions. There is a lack of evidence of students being required to persevere in responding to rigorous tasks or questions. • Students demonstrate a lack of respect for peers, teacher, and/or learning environment.	• Students exhibit some evidence that they are beginning to take risks and persevere in learning rigorous content. • Students demonstrate respect for the learning environment, but challenges exist in demonstrating respect for peers.	• Students are encouraged to take risks and persevere through productive struggle. Students are praised for demonstrating commitment to learning. • Students demonstrate respect for peers, teacher, and the learning environment.	• Students are encouraged to take risks and persevere through productive struggle. Students are provided with effective feedback to guide them in their learning. • Students demonstrate respect for peers, teacher, and the learning environment.
Instructional Design	• Classroom learning procedures and routines are inconsistently communicated and/or implemented.	• Classroom learning procedures and routines are visible, but are not consistently implemented.	• Clear classroom learning procedures and routines are visible and are consistently implemented.	• Classroom learning procedures and routines are clearly established, but remain flexible and fluid to adapt to the learning task as needed.
Formative Processes and Tools	**1 – Beginning**	**2 – Emerging**	**3 – Developed**	**4 – Well Developed**
Student Learning	• Lesson includes few instances of formative assessment to evaluate students' mastery of content. Assessment results indicate that student growth is minimal. • Students are partnered or grouped, but all students receive the same lesson content, process, and product.	• Students demonstrate mastery of content by engaging in formative assessments that allow for reciprocal feedback. Assessment results indicate that student growth is progressing. • Students are partnered or grouped and receive some opportunities for differentiated learning based on adjusting content, process, and/or product.	• Students demonstrate mastery of content through completing a variety of formative assessments that allow for reciprocal feedback. Assessment results indicate that students are meeting expectations. • Students are strategically partnered or grouped based on data. Lesson content, process, and/or product is clearly differentiated to support varying and specific student needs.	• Students demonstrate mastery of content through opportunities to self-reflect, set learning goals, and share responsibility for their learning. Assessment results indicate that students are exceeding expected outcomes.
Instructional Design	• Results from formative processes and tools are used to monitor progress.	• Results from formative processes and tools are used to plan and implement aspects of differentiated instruction and monitor progress.	• Results from formative processes and tools are used to strategically adjust instructional pacing, plan differentiated instruction, and monitor progress.	• Results from formative processes and tools, along with effective feedback, are used to immediately adjust instructional pacing, plan differentiated instruction, and monitor progress.

Appendix 4

Classroom Observation–Data Quantitative Analysis
Referenced in chapter 5

I n chapter 5, we walked through how to do an initial wave of classroom observations to ascertain the school's overall instructional levels before building the school-wide plan. The classroom observation process will leave you with raw data that needs to be analyzed. In chapter 5, we walked through the largely qualitative approach to analyzing data. Here, we will walk through the quantitative approach.

Once you've done sufficient classroom observations for your first wave, you will complete each step that follows to calculate data. As you do this, you will be looking for three things:

1. How strong or weak the school is in all nine indicators across rigor, relevance, and learner engagement.
2. How strong or weak the school is generally in each category.
3. In which of the three categories the school is strongest or weakest.

The steps correspond with a chart titled RRE Rubrics: Total Classroom Observation Data & School-Wide Instructional Calculations and Analysis, which you can find in this appendix, after the steps.

To help clarify this process, we'll return to our fictional school, PS 1, which, recall, is a medium-sized middle school where you observed 14 teachers. Reference the observation data and analysis chart that follows as needed to help you visualize each of these three steps to calculate observation data from all 14 classrooms.

Step 1:

- Add up how many growth level 1s, 2s, 3s, and 4s you recorded in each of the three rigor indicators. Let's say that for the thoughtful work indicator, you counted 3 growth level 1s, 5 level 2s, 4 level 3s, and 2 level 4s, totaling 14, as you observed 14 classrooms.
- Now calculate each growth level's number of occurrences as a percentage of the total classroom observations. So, for level 1, you would calculate what percent 3 is of 14, which is 21.43 percent. For level 2, you would calculate what percent 4 is of 14, which is 35.71 percent, and so on for levels 3 and 4. **These calculations will show you, in general, how strong or weak the school is in each rigor indicator.**

Step 2:

- Now tally the number of occurrences of each of the four growth levels observed for all three rigor indicators. For example, let's say for thoughtful work, you observed 3 level 1s; for the high-level questioning indicator, you observed 7 level 1s; and for academic discussion, you observed 2 level 1s. You will now add all level 1 occurrences, which comes to 12 (3+7+2). You will do this for levels 2, 3, and 4 as well.
- Next, you will want to determine each growth level's percentage of all total possible growth level observations. To calculate the total growth level observations in this example, we multiply 14 times 3, or the number growth level occurrences (which equals how many teachers you observed) for all three indicators. This comes to 42; put another way, you counted growth levels of rigor 42 times.
- Now divide 12 by 42 to determine the percentage of level 1 observations of overall rigor growth level observations. This comes to 28.57 percent, meaning that the teachers were level 1 in the rigor category 28.57 percent of the time. Repeat this for levels 2, 3, and 4. **Once you have, you will arrive at a general rigor average of**

all teachers, meaning generally how strong or weak the school is in the rigor category.

Step 3:

- Repeat these steps for relevance and learner engagement. Once you have done so, you can get a macro perspective and **determine in which of the three categories the school is strongest and weakest**.

Visit www.leadered.com/coachingredefined to download the editable Excel spreadsheet document, which has embedded equations that will automatically calculate your classroom observation data for RRE. You will find instructions on using this spreadsheet below the chart in the Excel file. Simply input your observation numbers and the percentages will automatically calculate.

With these steps in mind, look over the following observation data and assessment chart in full. This chart is from the Excel document I use to automatically calculate all the data from my classroom observations. Once everything is calculated, you will see where the school is strongest and weakest in each of the nine indicators, in each of the three categories, and in each category relative to the others.

Take a moment to read the individual rigor, relevance, learner engagement, and general analyses in the chart following the calculations. Reflect on how these relate to the percentages in each category and in each indicator to grasp how I arrived at each analysis. Please be aware that these analyses are also in chapter 5—just without the corresponding calculations.

RRE Rubrics: Total Classroom Observation Data & School-Wide Instructional Calculations and Analysis (Example) PS 1 Middle School

RIGOR	Level observed in classroom	1—Beginning	2—Emerging	3—Developed	4—Well Developed	Row totals
Indicator: Thoughtful Work	level # of occurrences	3	5	4	2	14
	% of indicator	21.43%	35.71%	28.57%	14.29%	100.00%
Indicator: High-Level Questioning	level # of occurrences	7	4	1	2	14
	% of indicator	50.00%	28.57%	7.14%	14.29%	100.00%
Indicator: Academic Discussion	level # of occurrences	2	4	4	4	14
	% of indicator	14.29%	28.57%	28.57%	28.57%	100.00%
General Rigor Assessment: column totals	total level # of occurrences	12	13	9	8	42
	% of all 3 indicators	28.57%	30.95%	21.43%	19.05%	100.00%

RELEVANCE	Level observed in classroom	1—Beginning	2—Emerging	3—Developed	4—Well Developed	Row totals
Indicator: Meaningful Work	level # of occurrences	4	4	4	2	14
	% of indicator	28.57%	28.57%	28.57%	14.29%	100.00%
Indicator: Authentic Resources	level # of occurrences	3	4	7	0	14
	% of indicator	21.43%	28.57%	50.00%	0.00%	100.00%
Indicator: Learning Connections	level # of occurrences	6	6	1	1	14
	% of indicator	42.86%	42.86%	7.14%	7.14%	100.00%
General Relevance Assessment: column totals	total level # of occurrences	13	14	12	3	42
	% of all 3 indicators	30.95%	33.33%	28.57%	7.14%	100.00%

LEARNER ENGAGEMENT	Level observed in classroom	1–Beginning	2–Emerging	3–Developed	4–Well Developed	Row totals
Indicator: Active Participation	level # of occurrences	0	3	4	7	14
	% of indicator	0.00%	21.43%	28.57%	50.00%	100.00%
Indicator: Learning Environment	level # of occurrences	1	1	6	6	14
	% of indicator	7.14%	7.14%	42.86%	42.86%	100.00%
Indicator: Formative Processes and Tools	level # of occurrences	3	1	8	2	14
	% of indicator	21.43%	7.14%	57.14%	14.29%	100.00%
General Learner Engagement Assessment: column totals	total level # of occurrences	4	5	18	15	42
	% of all 3 indicators	9.52%	11.90%	42.86%	35.71%	100.00%

Rigor Analysis: Generally, teachers' growth levels are pretty evenly spread in their understanding of and competence in achieving high levels of rigor in the classroom. Yet rigor is a clear opportunity for growth. Most teachers need help improving levels of rigor in their classrooms. Currently, teachers are strongest in academic discussion and weakest in high-level questioning.

Relevance Analysis: Of all three categories of the RRE rubrics, teachers demonstrate the weakest evidence of growth on relevance. As of now, they are strongest with authentic resources and weakest in learning connections.

Learner Engagement Analysis: Of all three categories, teachers showed the greatest growth with learner engagement. They are, more or less, having equal success with active participation and learning environment. The most room for improvement is with formative processes and tools.

General Analysis: In terms of the scope of improvement needs, the needs are from largest to smallest scope: relevance, rigor, and learner engagement. The school needs most help with relevance, as many teachers struggled to demonstrate an understanding of all three relevance indicators in instruction and learning. In terms of current instructional successes, the most positive starting point with the most likely quick and easy wins would be learner engagement. From there, the next most positive starting point would be in rigor, since more of the school's teachers are having some success with rigor right now. Because relevance will need the most effort and improvement gains, it will be the most challenging.

Appendix 5

Most Valuable Career Skills by 2020

Introduced in part 3 introduction and referenced in ensuing chapters

Per the annual World Economic Forum report, the most valuable career skills by 2020 will be the following 10 skills:

1. **Complex problem solving:** To solve complex problems requires being able to identify the problem, evaluate all pertinent information and factors, consider a range of possible solutions, think critically through different solution options and their potential outcomes, and then make a judgment as to which solution to select. A series of skills go into complex problem solving, including observation skills, analysis, creativity, innovative thinking, evaluation, perseverance, and resilience, to name some.

2. **Critical thinking:** To think critically is to think deeply. Critical thinking requires that you first suspend judgment to evaluate all related factors and perspectives as objectively as possible. It entails taking time to think through what you might not be considering or yet seeing. Reason, logic, and judgment are all used to analyze and evaluate information to, ultimately, probe far beyond the surface of the matter at hand.

3. **Creativity:** To be creative is to imagine something new from the information and data available. Creativity emerges from a capacity to view the world differently, connect seemingly disconnected

dots, and unearth unseen patterns to conceive something new. To be creative is to apply critical thinking and empathy to imagine experiences, ideas, and things from other perspectives.

4. **People management:** To manage people effectively is to see their strengths and weaknesses, guide them to develop their skills, help them grow, and motivate them through setting and reaching goals. Successful people management rests heavily on emotional intelligence, particularly empathy; to manage each individual effectively requires imagining her circumstances from her point of view and making decisions and recommendations accordingly.

5. **Coordinating with others:** To coordinate with others well requires strong collaboration skills. Productive coordination can only happen when you can empathize with those with whom you are coordinating to discern their needs, assess how they can and cannot contribute, and understand their values. From there, you must adapt your thinking, responses, and behaviors accordingly if coordination is to be productive.

6. **Emotional intelligence:** In most distilled terms, emotional intelligence is empathy; it is your capacity to stand in the shoes of another person and imagine her experience. The application of emotional intelligence is taking this imagined experience and using it to adjust decisions, behaviors, and actions appropriately. To be emotionally intelligent is to adapt your actions for each person based on your empathetic analysis of their perspectives and needs. Emotional intelligence also includes your ability to recognize, understand, and manage your own emotions.

7. **Judgment and decision making:** Sound decision-making skills rest first on sound judgment skills. To judge smartly is first to analyze and evaluate information or a circumstance as objectively as possible. Then you analyze and evaluate it from a perspective of emotional intelligence to consider all human components at play. Taking this full appraisal, you make the most reasonable and justifiable decision. The final factor of effective judgment and decision-making skills is knowing how to get buy-in and from whom.

8. **Service orientation:** To have a service orientation is to proactively seek ways to help others and be of value to them. It is to become

known as someone who is available to assist others, think together, and grow together. It is also to become known as someone who adjusts her contribution and deliverables based on the needs and preferences of others. However, a service orientation requires a boundary of not sacrificing one's own values and principles.

9. **Negotiation:** Strong negotiation skills require a range of skills, including creativity, to see new potential ideas and possibilities; emotional intelligence, to imagine the needs, values, and priorities of all those at play and anticipate their actions; and judgment and decision making to keep negotiations moving forward. It also takes strong communication skills and the ability to listen actively to those involved. Negotiations require emotional control and interpersonal skills so that they can remain respectful and productive. Ultimately, to negotiate is to problem solve; it is to find a way for all involved parties to be included and advantaged in a reasonable solution.

10. **Cognitive flexibility:** To show cognitive flexibility is to be able, swiftly, to switch thinking between and among multiple concepts, topics, or ideas, such that you ultimately can process all factors simultaneously. Those with strong cognitive flexibility can quickly adapt their thinking and comprehension as circumstances and information change around them.

Appendix 6

I Know, You Know
Graphic Organizer

Referenced in chapter 8

I Know, You Know

Name _____ Date _____

Text _____ Author _____

Directions: Before reading the text, record what you and your group know about the topic. After reading the text, record what your group learned from the text. Then, record any questions you still have.

What I Know	What My Classmates Know	What We Learned	Questions I Have
1			
2			
3			
4			
5			
6			

Visit www.leadered.com/coachingredefined to download the I Know, You Know graphic organizer.

The "I Know, You Know" strategy in chapter 8's "Strategies & Tools for Elevating Rigor in Instruction and Learning" allows students to think critically together about a specific text. Students record what they know before reading the text, what they know after reading the text, and what they learned as a group after academic discussion.

Appendix 7

Jigsaw Graphic Organizer
Referenced in chapter 8

Jigsaw

Name _____ Date _____ Text _____

Group Members _____

Directions: As you carefully read the text, write down important information about your topic and the page where the information was found. Once all group members are finished reading, each will share what they learned with the rest of the group.

Important Information	Page
1	
2	
3	
4	
5	

Important Information from Group Members	Page
1	
2	
3	

Summary of Article:

www.reflecttolearn.com

Reflective
LEARNING

Visit www.leadered.com/
coachingredefined to
download the Jigsaw graphic
organizer.

As referenced in the "Jigsaw" strategy in chapter 8's "Strategies & Tools for Elevating Rigor in Instruction and Learning," group members will fill out the graphic organizer as they move through the jigsaw learning task, which centers upon a text.

Appendix 8

Reciprocal Teaching Graphic Organizer

Referenced in chapters 8 and 10

Reciprocal Teaching	
Predict What do you think will happen? Why do you believe that will happen?	**Summarize** What are the most important ideas from the text?
Questions What questions can you ask to ensure the group understands the most important information?	**Clarify** What vocabulary terms are new or unclear?

Reflective
LEARNING

Visit www.leadered.com/coachingredefined to download the Reciprocal Teaching graphic organizer.

As referenced in the "Reciprocal Teaching" from chapter 8's "Strategies & Tools for Elevating Rigor in Instruction and Learning," students are assigned specific roles (e.g., predict, summarize, question, and clarify). In groups or as individuals, students fill in the sections of the graphic organizer after they read and consider a text.

Appendix 9

Student Conversation Starters

Referenced in chapter 8

Conversation Starters

Disagree

I disagree with _____ because ___

Respectfully, I disagree because ___.

I see it differently because ___.

Looking at it a different way, I think ___.

I see what you're saying, but I think ___.

Agree

I agree with _____ because ___.

The evidence ___ shared is critical because ___

I believe the same thing as ___ because ___.

As ___ pointed out, ___.

Like ___, I believe ___ because ___.

Paraphrase

I believe that you are saying ___.

Is it fair to say you believe ___?

It sounds like you think _____.

I'm hearing that ___.

In other words, ___.

Let me see if I understand you correctly. I think you're saying ___.

Summarize

Overall, I think ___.

My whole point is that ___.

It all boils down to ___.

To summarize, I think _____.

To summarize, I learned that ___.

Clarify

Can you help me understand what you mean by ___?

Can you explain what you mean by ___?

I think I hear you saying _____.

Could you say that another way?

I'm confused about _____. Can you please explain it to me a different way?

Visit www.leadered.com/ coachingredefined to download the Student Conversation Starters tool.

As referenced in the "Student Conversation Starters" from chapter 8's "Strategies & Tools for Elevating Rigor in Instruction and Learning," give students questions to support them as they learn how to engage in meaningful and rigorous discussions.

Appendix 10

Trade-a-Thought
Graphic Organizers

Referenced in chapter 8

Trade A Thought

Name: _____

My thought:

_____

_____

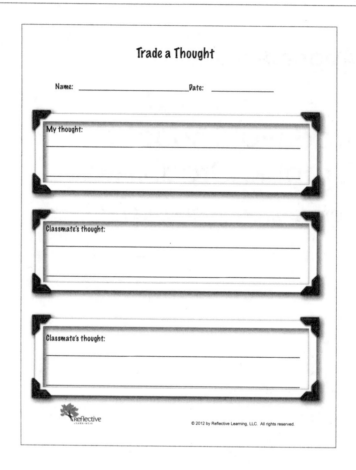

If you use the "Trade-a-Thought" strategy in the "Strategies & Tools for Elevating Rigor in Instruction and Learning" section at the end of chapter 8, please consider using this or a similar graphic organizer (slightly amended for students in grade 3 or above), or build one of your own.

Appendix 11

RAFT Worksheet
Referenced in chapter 9

RAFT

Name _____ Date_____

Text_____ Author_____

Directions: Read the text closely. Then write a response, giving special consideration to your role, audience, format and topic.

Role:	Audience:
Format:	Topic:

Writing:

www.reflecttolearn.com

reflective

Visit www.leadered.com/
coachingredefined to
download the RAFT tool.

RAFT is a literacy strategy that allows students the opportunity to demonstrate the ability to see a subject or idea from various real-world viewpoints. Students will decide all components of RAFT—their role, audience, format, or topic—or teachers will assign them. Based on the RAFT, students write about a subject or idea accordingly.

Appendix 12

You're Important to Me Tool
Referenced in chapter 9

You're Important to Me

Name:

I love that you're in my class, and I look forward to learning with you this year! Please fill in the following information so I can learn more about you.

1. What do you like about school? Is there anything you dislike about school?

2. How do you feel about using technology to learn?

3. Do you like to work in groups or do you prefer individual work?

4. What are your greatest talents?

5. If you could improve in one area, what would it be?

6. How do you feel about reading and writing? What do you like to read and write in your free time?

7. How do you feel about completing class projects as part of your learning?

8. Describe your favorite teacher, and share why they were your favorite.

9. What do you like to do in your free time?

10. Is there anything else that you would like me to know about you? Please add it to the back of this sheet.

Visit www.leadered.com/ coachingredefined to download the You're Important to Me tool.

To help teachers get to know all students such that high levels of personal relevance can be reached for each, I encourage teachers to ask all students to fill out this chart at the beginning of the school year (or at whatever point they meet and begin teaching new students).

Appendix 13

Group Guidelines Sheet
Referenced in chapter 10

Group Guidelines

1. All members of the group stay focused on the task.

2. All members of the group contribute to the conversation and the task.

3. Noise from group is kept at an appropriate level.

4. Group members respect each other.

5. Group members actively listen to each other.

Group Feedback

_____

_____

Reflective

Visit www.leadered.com/ coachingredefined to download the Group Guidelines sheet.

Before starting any group work, I suggest that teachers share a group-guidelines sheet with students to outline expectations of group work and behavior. Students will assess their abilities to abide by the guidelines as a group and then as individuals. This concept is further explained in chapter 10's "Strategies & Tools for Elevating Learner Engagement in Instruction and Learning."

Appendix 14

Group Roles and Responsibilities Tool

Referenced in chapter 10

Group Roles and Responsibilities

Date: _____   Group Members: _____

_____

Leader: The leader is responsible for leading group discussion and encouraging everyone to be a part of the group's decisions. They make sure everyone is respected. They also make sure everyone gets a chance to speak and participate. In our group, the leader is

Manager: The manager is responsible for keeping the group focused on the task. They encourage all group members to complete their portion of the task by the decided deadline. They also gather any materials the group needs to complete the task and collect the group's work at the end of each class. In our group, the manager is

Recorder: The recorder is responsible for recording who is present during group work, the group's decisions and any answers to the group's questions. In our group, the recorder is

Spokesperson: The spokesperson is responsible for investigating any questions had by the group. They will also share the group's ideas with the rest of class when necessary. In our group, the spokesperson is

Visit www.leadered.com/
coachingredefined to
download the Group Roles
and Responsibilities tool.

Group Roles and Responsibilities, included in chapter 10's "Strategies & Tools for Elevating Learner Engagement in Instruction and Learning," help bring structure to group work. They also make students feel accountable for their own learning and for that of their group members.

Appendix 15

My Goals Worksheet
Referenced in chapter 10

My Goals

Name:_____   Date: _____

My first goal is
_____
_____
_____
_____
_____
_____
_____

To reach my goal, I will
_____
_____
_____
_____
_____
_____
_____
_____

I will complete my goal by
_____

My second goal is
_____
_____
_____
_____
_____
_____
_____

To reach my goal, I will
_____
_____
_____
_____
_____
_____
_____

I will complete my goal by
_____

www.reflecttolearn.com

Visit www.leadered/coachingredefined to download the My Goals tool.

From chapter 10's "Strategies & Tools for Elevating Learner Engagement in Instruction and Learning," students use the "My Goals" goal-setting tool to record content standards and/or behavior goals and track their progress toward reaching them.

Appendix 16

My Vocabulary Progress Tool
Referenced in chapter 10

My Vocabulary Progress

Name _____   Date_____

Directions: Record the words you intend to study on the chart below. Write the definition in your own words. Then, find the word in the text and record its location. Show an example of the word with a picture, by writing a synonym or using the word in a sentence. When you feel you have mastered the meaning of the word, check the appropriate box.

Focus Word	What It Means	Location	Example	Mastered
1				
2				
3				
4				
5				
6				

www.reflecttolearn.com

reflective
LEARNING

Visit www.leadered/
coachingredefined to
download the My Vocabulary
Progress tool.

Teachers can use the My Vocabulary Progress tool to engage students in thinking deeply about and learning new vocabulary. As outlined in chapter 10's "Strategies & Tools for Elevating Learner Engagement in Instruction and Learning," students focus on specific vocabulary words and record their understanding of it on this chart.

Appendix 17

Group Norms
Referenced in chapter 11

Group Norms

1. We will be respectful of all team members.
2. We will make every possible effort to be present at all meetings, both physically and mentally.
3. We will start and end our meetings on time.
4. We will only use technology to enhance meeting topics and not to interrupt our thoughts.
5. We will share responsibility for tasks evenly among team members.
6. We will be considerate of others when we speak, avoiding side conversations.
7. We will table topics not on the agenda when time does not allow for adequate discussion.
8. When members miss a meeting we will share the responsibility of bringing them up to date.
9. We will each notify the team in advance of any absences.
10. We will leave titles at the door. All team members are equals.
11. We will address conflict by dealing with the issue not the person.
12. We will ask questions when in doubt.
13. We will complete our assigned tasks by our assigned deadlines.
14. We will bring instructional materials, technology, and data to each meeting.

Reflective
LEARNING LLC

Visit www.leadered.com/
coachingredefined to
download Group Norms.

I advise all groups of teachers who meet regularly to abide by a list of group norms, or behaviors all group members are expected to exhibit in meetings. In chapter 11, we discussed how these can be used for PL team meetings and can be vital for helping teams manage conflict and remain positively productive. I will often lead teams to establish their own group norms, in which case I will compare their list with the list I've included here, to ensure no major points were missed.

Appendix 18

Weekly Team Meeting Agenda

Referenced in chapter 11

WEEKLY TEAM MEETING AGENDA

Team: _____   Date: _____

Members Present: _____

_____

Instruction & Student Learning:

1) What do we want students to learn in the upcoming week?

2) How will we measure success?

3) What strategies will we use to help students have success?

4) How are we responding to students who are currently having difficulty?

Plans for next meeting:

Needs from coach prior to next meeting:

Date for next meeting:

Reflective
LEARNING

Visit www.leadered.com/ coachingredefined to download the Weekly Team Meeting Agenda.

The weekly team meeting agenda helps bring structure and intentional focus to teachers as they discuss instructional improvements that can better serve their students' learning and growth.

Appendix 19

Books to Foster a Growth Mindset in Students

Referenced in chapter 11

T he following books can encourage the development of a growth mindset in students. As with other resources, this is but the start of an evolving list. Add to it as you learn of more.
For K–5 students, teachers might want to read books from the grades K–5 book list aloud, followed by a learning task or academic discussion focused on the aspects of the book that promoted and showcased a growth mindset.

For grades 6–12, some K–5 books will still be appropriate for the students in grades 6–8; please research the books and use your judgment. For students in grades 6–8, books on the grades 6–12 list will offer valuable growth mindset learning opportunities. While students at this age level might be able to manage reading these books on their own or in groups, the teacher will likely need to scaffold their learning and use formative assessments as needed to check for understanding.

At the high school level, students can do book studies around any of the books on the grades 6–12 list. Or teachers can select certain chapters for an academic discussion or learning task to emphasize a specific aspect of the growth mindset.

Teachers are encouraged to include these books in their classroom libraries, and librarians are encouraged to include them in the library. Teachers should aim to provide students with opportunities to do silent readings of books that match their reading level.

Growth Mindset Books for Grades K–5

A Whistle for Willie by Ezra Jack Keats

After the Fall by Dan Santat

Beautiful Oops by Barney Saltzberg

The Book of Mistakes by Corinna Luyken

Brave Irene by William Steig

The Dot by Peter H. Reynolds

Drum Dream Girl: How One Girl's Courage Changed Music by Margarita Engle and Rafael Lopez

Emmanuel's Dream: The True Story of Emmanuel Ofosu Yeboah by Laurie Ann Thompson

Everyone Can Learn to Ride a Bicycle by Chris Raschka

Flight School by Lita Judge

The Girl Who Never Made Mistakes by Mark Pett

Hana Hashimoto, Sixth Violin by Chieri Uegaki

How to Catch a Star by Oliver Jeffers

I Can't Do That, YET by Esther Pia Cordova

Ish by Peter H. Reynolds

Jabari Jumps by Gaia Cornwall

Making a Splash: A Growth Mindset Children's Book by Carol E. Reiley

The Most Magnificent Thing by Ashley Spires

My Strong Mind by Niels Van Hove

Nadia, the Girl Who Couldn't Sit Still by Karlin Gray

The OK Book by Amy Krouse Rosenthal

Rosie Revere Engineer by Andrea Beaty

Salt in His Shoes: Michael Jordan in Pursuit of a Dream by Deloris Jordan

A Splash of Red: The Life and Art of Horace Pippin by Jen Bryant

Thanks for the Feedback, I Think by Julia Cook

What Do You Do with an Idea? by Kobi Yamada

What Do you Do with a Chance? by Kobi Yamada

What Do You Do with a Problem? by Kobi Yamada

When Sophie Thinks She Can't . . . by Molly Bang

Your Fantastic Elastic Brain: Stretch It, Shape It by JoAnn Deak, Ph.D.

Growth Mindset Books for Grades 6–12

Big Life Journal for Tweens/Teens (ages 11+) available at biglifejournal. com

Drive by Daniel Pink

Grit (7 Character Strengths of Highly Successful Students) by Ramona Siddoway

The Grit Guide for Teens: A Workbook to Help You Build Perseverance, Self-Control, and a Growth Mindset by Caren Baruch-Feldman, Ph.D.

Growth Mindset Journal for Tweens and Teens by Iona Young

Grit: The Power of Passion and Perseverance by Angela Duckworth

Appendix 20

Reflecting on the Day Worksheet

Referenced in chapter 11

Reflecting on the Day

Today I expected to learn....	What I learned. ...
What worked best for me...	**What I need or need to know now is ...**

Reflective
LEARNING LLC

Visit www.leadered.com/
coachingredefined to
download the Reflecting on
the Day graphic organizer.

In providing this graphic organizer to all teachers at the end of a professional learning session, the coach can get a sense of what teachers find most and least effective in PL. The coach can also discover what teachers want to focus on or learn next. Ultimately, this tool helps ensure that teachers are contributing to the school's PL process, which is key to building a learning organization.

References

Almarode, J. (2018). 8 Ways to Increase the Engagement in Your Classroom. Retrieved from http://corwin-connect.com/2018/02/8-ways-increase-engagement-classroom/

Bachelder, C. (2016). The CEO of Popeyes on Treating Franchisees as the Most Important Customers. *Harvard Business Review*. Retrieved from https://hbr.org/2016/10/the-ceo-of-popeyes-on-treating-franchisees-as-the-most-important-customers

Bachelder, C. (2017). #269: Dare to Serve. Podcast. Podcast retrieved from https://www.entreleadership.com/blog/podcasts/cheryl-bachelder

Byrne, J. (1998). How Jack Welch Runs Ge Part 1: A Close-up Look at How America's #1 Manager Runs GE. *Bloomberg*. Retrieved from https://www.bloomberg.com/news/articles/1998-06-07/how-jack-welch-runs-ge-part-1

CNBC Staff. (2014). The List: CNBC First 25. Number 12: Jack Welch, 20-year Chairman and CEO of GE. Retrieved from https://www.cnbc.com/2014/04/29/25-jack-welch.html

Cobb, J. (2015). What We Can Learn From Coca-Cola's Biggest Blunder. *Time Magazine*. Retrieved from time.com/3950205/new-coke-history-america/

Collins, J. & Porras, J. (1994). *Built to Last: Successful Habits of Visionary Companies*. New York: Harper Collins.

Darling-Hammond, L., Hyler, M., & Gardner, M. (2017). Effective Teacher Professional Development. Learning Policy Institute. Retrieved from https://learningpolicyinstitute.org/product/effective-teacher-professional-development-report

Edwards, P. (2015). New Coke debuted 30 years ago. Here's why it was a sugary fiasco. Retrieved from https://www.vox.com/2015/4/23/8472539/new-coke-cola-wars

Ewenstein, B, Smith, W. & Sologar, A. (2015). Changing change management. Retrieved from https://www.mckinsey.com/featured-insights/leadership/changing-change-management

Federal Reserve Bank of New York. (2019). The Labor Market for Recent College Graduates. Retrieved from https://www.newyorkfed.org/research/college-labor-market/college-labor-market_underemployment_rates.html

Gaetano, K. (2016). 5 Ways Adults Learn Differently than Children. Retrieved from https://learnkit.com/2016/01/13/adult-learning-needs/

Gallo, C. (2012). Alan Mulally, Optimism, and the Power of Vision. *Forbes*. Retrieved from https://www.forbes.com/sites/carminegallo/2012/04/25/alan-mulully-optimism-and-the-power-of-vision/#66362a1c37ab

General Electric. (nd). John F. Welch, Jr.: Chairman & CEO 1981–2001. Retrieved from https://www.ge.com/about-us/leadership/profiles/john-f-welch-jr

General Electric. (2018). General Electric. *Wikipedia*. Retrieved from https://en.wikipedia.org/wiki/General_Electric

Glossary of Education Reform. (2013). Relevance. Retrieved from https://www.edglossary.org/relevance/

Godin, S. (2008). *Tribes: We Need You to Lead Us*. New York: Penguin Group.

Gordon, J. (2017). No One Achieves Success Alone. *Jon Gordon's Weekly Newsletter*. Retrieved from http://www.jongordon.com/positivetip/success-alone.html

Grant, A. (2014). *Give and Take: Why Helping Others Drives Our Success*. New York: Penguin Books.

Gray, A. (2016). The 10 skills you need to thrive in the Fourth Industrial Revolution. *World Economic Forum*. Retrieved from https://www.weforum.org/agenda/2016/01/the-10-skills-you-need-to-thrive-in-the-fourth-industrial-revolution/

Haoues, R. (2015). 30 years ago today, Coca-Cola made its worst mistake. *CBS News*. Retrieved from https://www.cbsnews.com/news/30-years-ago-today-coca-cola-new-coke-failure/

Hastings, R. (2009). Netflix Culture Deck. Retrieved from https://www.slideshare.net/Barbaragill3/Netflix_culture_deck

Hattie, J. (2018). Feedback in schools by John Hattie. Retrieved from https://visible-learning.org/2013/10/john-hattie-article-about-feedback-in-schools/

Heath, C. & Heath, D. (2010). *Switch: How to Change Things When Change is Hard*. New York: Broadway Books.

Institute of Play. (nd). Socratic Smackdown Teaching Guide. Retrieved from https://www.instituteofplay.org/learning-games

Jensen, E. (2013). *Engaging Students with Poverty in Mind: Practical Strategies for Raising Achievement*. Alexandria, VA: ASCD.

Ladson-Billings, G. (1995). Toward a Theory of Culturally Relevant Pedagogy. *American Educational Research Journal*, Vol. 32, No. 3. (Autumn, 1995), pp. 465–491.

Lego. (2018). Friends. Retrieved from https://www.lego.com/en-us/themes/friends

Lego. (2018). The LEGO Brand. Retrieved from https://www.lego.com/en-us/aboutus/lego-group/the_lego_brand

Lego. (2018). The LEGO Group History: 1930–1939. Retrieved from https://www.lego.com/en-us/aboutus/lego-group/the_lego_history/1930

Lego. (2018). The LEGO Group History: 1940–1949. Retrieved from https://www.lego.com/en-us/aboutus/lego-group/the_lego_history/1940

Lego. (2018). The LEGO Group History: 1950–1959. Retrieved from https://www.lego.com/en-us/aboutus/lego-group/the_lego_history/1950

Maxwell, J. (2007) *The 21 Irrefutable Laws of Leadership: Follow Them and People Will Follow You*. Nashville: Thomas Nelson Publishers.

McKinsey & Company. (2013). Leading in the 21st century: An interview with Ford's Alan Mulally. Retrieved from https://www.mckinsey.com/business-functions/strategy-and-corporate-finance/our-insights/leading-in-the-21st-century-an-interview-with-fords-alan-mulally

McKinsey & Company. (2015). How to beat the transformation odds. Retrieved from https://www.mckinsey.com/business-functions/organization/our-insights/how-to-beat-the-transformation-odds#0

Mikkelson, K., & Jarche, H. (2015). The Best Leaders Are Constant Learners. *Harvard Business Review*. Retrieved from https://hbr.org/2015/10/the-best-leaders-are-constant-learners

Netflix. (2019). Netflix Culture. Retrieved from https://jobs.netflix.com/culture

New York CTE Center. (2016). Assessment. Retrieved from https://nyctecenter.org/instruction/assessment

Peak Performance Center. (nd). How Children and Adults Learn. Retrieved from http://thepeakperformancecenter.com/educational-learning/learning/principles-of-learning/adult-learning/children-adults-learn/

Pink, D. (2011). *Drive: The Surprising Truth About What Motivates Us*. New York: Riverhead Books.

Sackett, R. (1985). Thirsting for Days When the Fizz Was Familiar, Gay Mullins Crusades to Can the New Coke. *People Magazine*. Retrieved from https://people.com/archive/thirsting-for-days-when-the-fizz-was-familiar-gay-mullins-crusades-to-can-the-new-coke-vol-23-no-25/

Schwantes, M. (2017). This Popular Female CEO's Leadership Style May End the Debate on Best Leadership Style: How she turned her company around is reason alone to call this debate over. Retrieved from https://www.inc.com/marcel-schwantes/this-popular-female-ceos-leadership-style-may-end-the-debate-on-best-leadership-.html

Senge, P. (1990). *The Fifth Discipline: The Art & Practice of The Learning Organiza-tion.* New York: Currency Doubleday.

Shapiro, D., Dundar, A., Huie, F., Wakhungu, P.K., Yuan, X., Nathan, A. & Bhim-diwali, A. (2017). *Completing College: A National View of Student Completion Rates–Fall 2011 Cohort (Signature Report No. 14).* Herndon, VA: National Stu-dent Clearinghouse Research Center.

Student Loan Hero. (2019). A Look at the Shocking Student Loan Debt Statistics for 2019. Retrieved from https://studentloanhero.com/student-loan-debt-statistics/

Toren, M. (2014). Marissa Explains It All: 5 Motivating Quotes From Yahoo's CEO. Retrieved from https://www.entrepreneur.com/article/234222

Trangbaek, R.R. (2012). LEGO Group Commentary on Attracting More Girls To Construction Play. Retrieved from https://www.lego.com/en-us/aboutus/news-room/2012/january/lego-group-commentary-on-attracting-more-girls-to-construction-play

Truini, J. (2017). How to Build a Shed, Colonial-Style: A Colonial-style storage shed that anyone can build. Retrieved from https://www.popularmechanics.com/home/how-to/a170/how-to-build-a-storage-shed/

Wagner, T. (2010). *The Global Achievement Gap: Why Even Our Best Schools Don't Teach the New Survival Skills Our Children Need and What We Can Do About It.* New York: Basic Books.

Welch, J. (2000). To Our Customers, Shareholders and Employees. Retrieved from https://www.valuewalk.com/wp-content/uploads/2014/11/jack-welch-ge-annual-letters-1980-to-2000.pdf